STUDIES ON ETHNIC GROUPS IN CHINA
Stevan Harrell, Editor

Lessons in Being Chinese

Minority Education and Ethnic Identity in Southwest China

METTE HALSKOV HANSEN

UNIVERSITY OF WASHINGTON PRESS

Seattle and London

Library of Congress Cataloging-in-Publication Data
Hansen, Mette Halskov.
Lessons in being Chinese : minority education and ethnic identity
in Southwest China / Mette Halskov Hansen
p.   cm. — (Studies on ethnic groups in China)
Includes bibliographical references and index.
ISBN 0-295-97809-0 (alk. paper)
ISBN 0-295-97788-4 (pbk)
1. Minorities—Education—China, Southwest.
2. Ethnicity—China, Southwest.
I. Title.
II. Title: Minority education and ethnic identity in Southwest China.
III. Series.
LC3737.C6S687   1999   98-49028
370'.951'3 — dc21   CIP

Photographs are by Mette Halskov Hansen unless noted otherwise.

Contents

v

CONTENTS

Acknowledgments

The content of this book is to a large extent based upon fieldwork carried out in Yunnan Province in southwest China in 1994–95. My first and foremost thanks are therefore directed to the nearly two hundred teachers, students, parents, peasants, monks, and cadres in Kunming, Lijiang, and Sipsong Panna who agreed to tell me their stories and who often went far beyond my expectations in their friendliness, helpfulness, hospitality, and concern. They taught me a lot and made my fieldwork possible and enjoyable. It is impossible to name them all here, but there are some people and institutions in China who deserve special mention. During fieldwork I was accompanied by three assistants (*peitong*): Li Yunping, Mu Rongping, and Yila. All were very young and were given sometimes arduous tasks, such as arranging interviews in villages, dealing with high cadres for the first time in their life, and walking in the mud for hours to reach a village where the teacher might not even have time to talk. However, they all accepted this with good humor, and I am grateful for their help and friendship. At my host organization (*danwei*) in China, the Yunnan Institute of the Nationalities, Wang Ningsheng and his wife Wang Yunhui were extremely helpful in all matters while also providing scholarly inspiration and advice. I am grateful to the authorities of the institute and the Office of Foreign Affairs, represented by Hu Maoxiu, for accepting my way of doing fieldwork while providing their assistance. I also especially thank the local governments in Lijiang and Sipsong Panna for making possible my research in schools and temples. The conclusions I draw, based upon my own interpretations of the stories told to me in China and my experiences in schools and villages, may not be accepted by all of the people mentioned here. Nevertheless, I hope that my presentation and interpretation of data will contribute to the continued discussion in China about the education of ethnic minorities and about the minority people's own perceptions of and responses toward education.

During the process of researching, writing, and revising this book, I have been fortunate to receive excellent supervision, comments, and critiques from several people. I am especially grateful to Stig Thoegersen for his detailed comments, expert suggestions, and continued engagement in the project; to Mikael Gravers for broadening my narrow local interest in China; and to series editor Stevan Harrell, two anonymous readers for the University of Washington Press, and editor Lorri Hagman for their invaluable comments and suggestions for improvement of the manuscript. A number of other colleagues and friends in and outside China have provided me with all kinds of scholarly, personal, and practical help, encouragement, and inspiration over the years. I especially want to thank Amei (Yang Xueying), Jackie and Nagib Armijo-Hussein, Chen Suofen, Greg Kulander, Rune Svarverud, Yinangiao, Zheng Yuerong, and colleagues and friends at the Centre for Development and the Environment as well as the Department for East European and Oriental Studies at the University of Oslo. Endless (and mostly enjoyable) discussions with Koen Wellens, his well-informed criticism, and encouragement during fieldwork have been crucial for the whole research process and the final product of it. Finally, I should like to thank Sine and Nele for putting up with all the travel and making me see China with new eyes.

Financially the project was made possible by a three-year grant and generous support for fieldwork from the Danish Council for Development Research in 1992–96. Material from chapters 3 and 5 has previously been published in Kjeld Erik Broedsgaard and David Strand, eds., *Reconstructing Twentieth-Century China: Social Control, Civil Society and National Identity* (Oxford: Oxford University Press, 1998); and Gerard Postiglione and Regie Stites, eds., *Education of National Minorities in China* (New York: Garland Press, 1999). I thank the publishers for permission to use that material.

Of course all interpretations and conclusions in the book are entirely my own, as are any mistakes or shortcomings.

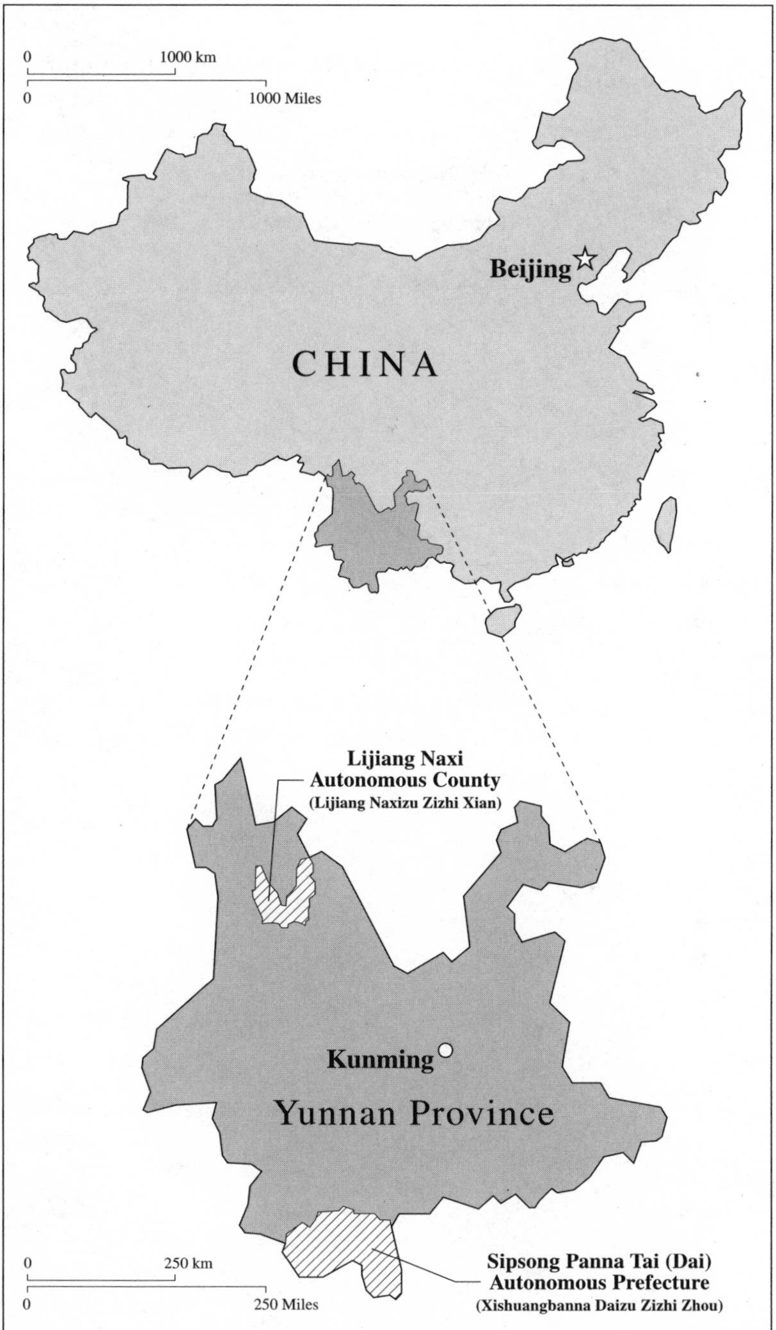
0
1000 km
0
1000 Miles
Beijing
CHINA
Lijiang Naxi
Autonomous County
(Lijiang Naxizu Zizhi Xian)
Kunming
Yunnan Province
0
250 km
0
250 Miles
Sipsong Panna Tai (Dai)
Autonomous Prefecture
(Xishuangbanna Daizu Zizhi Zhou)

MAP 1. Yunnan Province

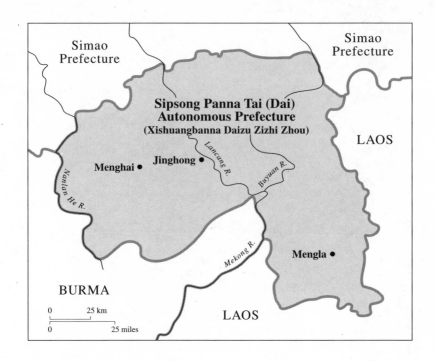

Simao
Prefecture

Simao
Prefecture

**Sipsong Panna Tai (Dai)
Autonomous Prefecture**
(Xishuangbanna Daizu Zizhi Zhou)

LAOS

Menghai ● Jinghong ●

Lancang R.

Buyuan R.

Nanlan He R.

Mekong R.

Mengla ●

BURMA

0   25 km

0   25 miles

LAOS

MAP 2. Sipsong Panna Tai (Dai) Autonomous Prefecture

Introduction

As a formal institution of socialization, education is necessarily also co-responsible for and engaged in sociocultural socialization, i.e., in socialization for ethnic membership and for ethnic consciousness. The elementary school's social studies curriculum, with its emphasis on national history, civics and geography, not to mention its rituals (salutes to the flag, patriotic assembly programs and commemorations of national holidays and great leaders), is essentially an explicit and implicit course in mainstream ethnic socialization or resocialization. Mainstream education is also an arena for the discussion and explication of values and moral issues, of national virtues and dilemmas, of national accomplishments and shortcomings, of supra-national dedication, aspiration and concern.

—Joshua A. Fishman
Language and Ethnicity in Minority Sociolinguistic Perspective

Since the Qing dynasty (1644–1911), many Chinese leaders and intellectuals have regarded institutionalized education as a means of integrating, controlling, and civilizing the various peoples who inhabit the border or peripheral regions of what was the empire, then the Republic, and now is the People's Republic of China (PRC). Especially since the reform period in the 1980s, the Chinese government has paid increasing attention to development of education among the peoples now officially classified as non-Han, the so-called minority ethnic groups (*shaoshu minzu*). In spite of government attempts to spread school education after 1949, many minority areas are still characterized by low levels of school enrollment and educational attainment. Strengthened school education among the non-Han peoples living in the vast border regions of China is now put forward as the precondition for successful modernization of their economy. No less significant is the belief that mass education is the most efficient and extensive medium for promoting, and ultimately ensuring, integration of ethnic minorities into the Chinese state. Via the state-controlled educational system, the government seeks to transmit the message of national commitment, love of the ruling Chinese Communist Party (CCP), and cultural homogeneity. Therefore, patriotic education (*aiguozhuyi jiaoyu*) is especially high on the state's agenda for non-Han peoples living in the border areas. It preaches the common history of all ethnic groups within China since the legendary Yellow Emperor, and the common political, economic, and cultural interests of all people in the PRC. Thus, it promotes the idea of one "Chinese nation" (*Zhonghua minzu*), as a common denominator for all fifty-six officially recognized *minzu* ("nationalities").[1]

Chinese state education attempts to achieve a high degree of cultural and political homogenization for several reasons: to make communication possible among different parts of the country, to ensure the integration of peripheral areas into the Chinese state, to promote patriotism and loyalty to the CCP, and, in a broader sense, to "improve the quality" of or to "civilize" the presumably more "backward" parts of the population. These include most of the minority *minzu,* whose languages, cultural practices, and economic life are often described in Chinese media and publications as obstructing the development and modernization of the areas they inhabit. *Lessons in Being Chinese* explores how Chinese education attempts to mainstream ethnic minorities with regard to language, religion, interpretation of history, and, consequently, ethnic identification. Through the educational system powerful interpretations of what it means and implies to belong to a minority *minzu* in China are transmitted as facts beyond dispute. The national school system's representations of ethnic entities and ethnicities in China are not open to discussion or alternative interpretation in the classroom. Minority students therefore must relate to, consider, or in other ways take into account these powerful representations of themselves. My main focus is on these repre-

1. Throughout the text I use the term *minzu* rather than the standard PRC translation "nationalities" in reference to China's fifty-six officially recognized ethnic groups, including the Han and the fifty-five minorities. However, the term *minzu* in China is often used to imply only the minority *minzu* (*shaoshu minzu*). In such cases I translate *minzu* as "minority" (e.g., "minority education" [*minzu jiaoyu*] and "minority school" [*minzu xuexiao*]).

sentations and on the *responses* that state education produces in terms of ethnic identification: the degree to which education succeeds in forming national sentiment and eliminating or reducing ethnicity, and *why* different people respond the way they do. I have asked, and attempt to answer, three main questions: What do minority students in China learn about themselves as members of an ethnic group during their education? Why does standardized education, aimed at achieving a high degree of cultural homogenization, produce profoundly different reactions in terms of ethnic identity among different ethnic groups? And what role does education then actually play in directing and forming ethnic and national identities? I argue that the Chinese government's and most educators' belief in the school as an institution capable of controlling the transformation of minorities' cultural values and eliminating ethnic identities is exaggerated. For most ethnic minorities in China, school education is entirely based upon Chinese language and history. It leaves no room for the transmission of cultural values that might contradict the state's interpretation of nationalism, atheism, and the common interests of multiethnic China. However, by denying the significance of the minorities' own languages, histories, religions, and cultural values, education sometimes strengthens focus on ethnic identity.

The central and provincial governments in China have suggested and implemented various methods to increase school attendance and accomplish basic compulsory education among the minority *minzu,* such as establishment of special (mostly boarding) minority schools, experiments with bilingual education, introduction of locally edited teaching materials, and easier access for non-Han students to higher education. Very often, though, government proposals and even regulations concerning special minority education are carried out only half-heartedly, either because they are rejected by local cadres or because the government fails to provide sufficient economic support. Frequently, financial difficulties dictate the educational practice in a local area, and many special programs come to serve primarily as superficial demonstrations of good-will, such as bilingual education's affirmation of minorities' principal rights to develop their own languages. Especially in areas where most educators are Han and the level of integration is low, many cadres controlling the minority education fear that extensive experiments inevitably will result in increased ethnic diversity and identities. The general attitude among these cadres and among many Han teachers and Party and government leaders is that the Chinese school has a positive civilizing effect on what is so often regarded as the culturally and economically "backward" (*luohou*) minorities.

The outcome of an education that succeeds in significantly raising the educational level of a minority group might well result in an increasing focus on ethnic identity, formulation of local political demands, and introduction of alternative forms of education. Even in the Chinese school system, where most non-Han students have to disassociate themselves from their cultural heritage in order to be successful, the influence of education on ethnic identity is to a certain extent unpredictable and depends on external factors such as the level of the group's political and cultural integration into the Chinese state, the degree to which it perceives Chinese school education to be advantageous, local educational history, religion, cross-border ethnic contacts, and economic development. Obviously, education is only one of many factors that influence ethnic identity, and it is impossible to isolate it. However, by looking into the aspects of education that are most directly related to ethnic identification and categorization, this book discusses the impact of education on the changing forms, contents, and expressions of ethnic identity among ethnic minorities in China.

When promoting the education of minority *minzu* with the combined purposes of modernizing the economy and ensuring integration and "ethnic amalgamation" (*ronghe*), the Chinese government faces the paradox that successful minority education sometimes leads to increased ethnic demands. On the other hand, failed attempts to spread education could cause an ethnic group to support local alternative education with the consequence of further alienation from the Han majority and the Chinese state. In either case, the mission of achieving cultural homogenization and "ethnic melting" through education is not accomplished. There is, however, a significant difference between the form and content of ethnicity that develops from (though not necessarily originates in) education and that which is strengthened among people who are excluded from education. The spokesmen for a revival of ethnic identity who have themselves participated in state education are better able to express and make themselves heard within the context of the state. Their ethnic identity might have been strengthened through a basically assimilative education, but, unlike those who have been excluded from state education, they have been provided with the means to strategically formulate their ethnic demands within the politically acceptable framework.

Lessons in Being Chinese is based mainly upon data collected during field-work in two autonomous areas in Yunnan Province and among two ethnic minorities: the Tai (Dai) in Sipsong Panna (Xishuangbanna) Tai (Dai) Auton-omous Prefecture and the Naxi in Lijiang Naxi Nationality Autonomous County. These two groups have different histories and experiences of Chinese education and equally distinct reactions to and perceptions of this education. Also included in the discussion are the Akha (officially classified as part of the Hani *minzu*) and Jinuo of Sipsong Panna, who were previously under the rule of the Tai king and government. In education and response to edu-cation, these two groups have much in common because of their historical relationship to the Tai in the Sipsong Panna area. The Akha and Jinuo pro-vide an example of a third way of responding to Chinese minority education.

The Chinese government and its civilizing envoys have not been able to spread and popularize Chinese education efficiently among the Tai in Sipsong Panna. One important reason is that most Tai fail to see any significant eco-nomic or social advantage in spending money on school education. Another reason is that the content and form of state education is in direct opposition to the traditional Tai Buddhist education of monks and to Tai values in gen-eral. The Tai in Sipsong Panna historically made up a nation separate from the Chinese empire (Hsieh 1995), and it was only in the 1920s that the area effectively became an integrated part of China. The Chinese system of edu-cation was introduced in 1911, and Chinese schools became widespread in the area only after 1949. In many respects Chinese education in Sipsong Panna resembles the education established by colonial powers for indigenous peo-ples in other parts of the world. The few Tai who pass through the school sy-stem need to alienate themselves from their cultural heritage (their religion, language, and history, in particular) in order to be successful. In this respect education has an assimilative effect, but only on the few. For most Tai, Chinese education has little direct bearing on their ethnic identity and cultural prac-tices simply because they do not participate in it. This also means that they are deprived of the possibility of gaining influence in a political system that is based entirely upon Chinese language and on cultural values different from their own. If the government wanted to reverse this tendency, it would have to make education directly relevant to and clearly advantageous for the Tai, in which case most local educators would feel that they were supporting the already-strong Tai ethnicity rather than promoting ethnic amalgamation and unity. Neither the government nor local educators are prepared to run this risk. As a result, an increasing number of Tai seek instead to extend their own traditional temple education and their cultural and economic contacts with other Tai in Thailand. These contacts support them in their religious belief and prove to them that their language and script are useful in a modernizing society, even though they are apparently worthless in the present-day Chinese state.

The Akha make up the third-largest ethnic group (after the Tai and the Han) in Sipsong Panna. They were historically regarded as inferior by the Tai, and today the two groups rarely intermarry or have close social relations. The same applies to the Jinuo, who, like the Akha, live higher up in the mountains. These groups do not have their own script, and Chinese education has developed slowly in their villages. However, whereas many Tai tend to reject Chinese education because it forces them to assimilate to mainstream cultural practices and reject their own language, religion, and history without offering economic or social advantages, these much poorer minorities from the mountains may find in Chinese education a way to escape hard labor in the villages, to occupy more important and influential positions in society, and thereby also to reject their historical subordination to the Tai. This partly explains why the Akha and Jinuo students appear, at least for the time being, to more easily accept that they learn only Chinese in school and not their own language, and to accept the school's representation of them as members of a backward group. Participation in Chinese education is thus in some respects a way of combating traditionally low status in the local ethnic hierarchy.

The situation for the Naxi is strikingly different. Except in the poorest villages, education among the Naxi in Lijiang has been successful in that most Naxi nowadays complete primary school (*xiaoxue*), and many continue on to junior secondary school (*chuzhong*). The number of students in senior secondary school (*gaozhong*) and college is as high as the average of the Han and higher than that of most other minorities. Many high cadres and influential researchers and teachers today are Naxi, even at the provincial level. Han and Naxi researchers alike agree that the early establishment of Confucian education and the long history of Han influence in Lijiang has facilitated this development. Unlike Sipsong Panna, Lijiang has for a very long time been an integrated, though peripheral, part of the Chinese empire and in recent history has not constituted a separate nation. The content of education in Lijiang today—with its focus on Han history and language, nationalism, and Communist political training—does not deviate from the standard of the rest of China, and Naxi parents' complaints about their high educational expenses and the lack of technical or agricultural training for their children are similar to those in many rural Han areas. Generally, the state-controlled education in Lijiang is perceived by the Naxi as "their own," not as a foreign institution imposed to civilize or change them. Success in Chinese education—whether Confucian, Nationalist, or Communist—in fact constitutes an important part of many Naxis' ethnic self-perception today. In the last five years especially, the Naxi have shown a remarkable talent for expressing their own increased concern for preserving and reviving ethnic characteristics while utilizing a common Naxi identity to extend their own local political influence in areas such as education. This tendency is perhaps best illustrated by the well-trained Naxi Party cadres who are now not only calling for extended research on Naxi history and culture, but are themselves playing a central role in reviving previously vilified religious rituals. This was certainly not the Chinese state's intent in spreading education among non-Han peoples. The main point here is that successful education of the Naxi has unintentionally and unexpectedly supported their ability to develop a stronger common Naxi identity and to formulate their ethnic demands within the context of the state. Paradoxically, an education denying the value of Naxi traditions, religion, language, and history, and aimed at facilitating the disappearance of ethnic entities, has provided the Naxi with a voice and a means to express themselves as an ethnic minority in the People's Republic of China without threatening the political system.

RESEARCH

> If there is no such thing as a perfect translation or interpretation, there are still better, worse and idiotic ones.
>
> —Mark Hobart
> "Summer's Days and Salad Days"

The focus on local practices and perceptions of education and on the relationship between state education and processes of ethnic identity has to a

large extent determined my primary research methods: interviews, participation in local events, sitting in on classes, and preparatory documentary work.
Fieldwork was carried out between 1994 and 1996 in Sipsong Panna, Lijiang,
and Kunming. During the main part of the fieldwork, between July 1994 and
September 1995, I conducted 173 formal interviews, sat in on twenty-two classes
in two middle schools (*zhongxue*), talked informally to many other people,
and participated in local events such as weddings, festivals, family celebrations, competitions in schools, and other school activities.

Formal interviews constituted a significant part of the fieldwork, and analysis of them has been crucial to the interpretations presented here. The interviews were formal in the sense that the interviewees were specifically told that
they were participating in an interview and the purpose of the interview. Usually
only the interviewee, my assistant *peitong* (an officially approved and oblig-
atory assistant provided by my host organization), and I were present. When
interviewees spoke Chinese, interviews were conducted in Chinese. Otherwise
they were conducted in Tai or Naxi through the assistants' interpretation.
Sometimes villagers would gather to listen, or students who shared the dormitory of an interviewee would be present. Sometimes I interviewed two or
three students or teachers together. Occasionally the interview developed into
an interesting discussion between students, sometimes of different ethnic
groups, or between villagers. Whereas some interviewees were deliberately
selected (headmasters, representatives of education commissions, researchers
who had written about education or ethnicity among Naxi and Tai, etc.), most
were randomly chosen according to the focus of the research: I wanted to
interview schoolteachers, present and former students, parents of students,
people who had never participated in education, and people (for instance
monks) who were part of a learning institution outside the state-controlled
schools. I also wanted to interview people from different age groups, preferably equally balanced between male and female, and from villages as well as
from county capitals. In spite of my intention to avoid gender bias, I ended
up interviewing more female than male students, parents, and peasants. Male
students were often rather timid talking to me, and even more so with my
local female assistants of approximately their age. The interviews with female
students more often developed into discussions or gossiping among several
students or into dialogues. However, almost all interviewed government and
Party cadres and heads of schools were male, since very few women occu-

pied these powerful positions. I also interviewed a number of old people to get an impression of life in the schools before the Communist period began in 1949. The historical chapters in this volume are to a large extent informed by the presentations of these interviewees, many of whom had experienced education in recent years as well as in earlier periods.

The purpose of the interviews with representatives of government departments was to get information about local government policy and attitudes toward the education of minorities. When interviewing school headmasters I tried to get basic information about schools (ethnicity of students and teachers, differences among *minzu* in terms of enrollment and achievement, and specific measures for educating minorities) and to let them tell about their own experiences in education and their own attitudes toward minority education. In interviews with all—students, teachers, parents, peasants, old, and young—I first asked a set of "closed" questions (e.g., age, parents' occupations, level of education, participation in specific religious activities, knowledge of spoken and written languages, ethnicity of best friends) and then a number of "open" questions that prompted the interviewee to tell about school experiences, attitude toward family, cultural practices at home, religious belief, relationships with other *minzu,* hopes for the future, and so on. Each interview lasted between one and a half and two and a half hours, and many of the interviewees were interviewed several times.

During my fieldwork I sat in on twenty-two classroom hours of politics and history, as well as some geography and Tai-language training. Teachers very rarely deviated from what was written in the textbooks, which I could read for myself. However, it was very informative to observe which topics and contents the teacher emphasized and which sentences she asked the class to learn by heart and read out loud. Even after I stopped sitting in on classes, I continued to participate in special events at the schools, such as speech competitions with the subject of patriotism and various celebrations for which students wore minority costumes to dance and perform. All of these activities were important parts of the school as an institution concerned with establishing the nation as a common denominator and point of identification for all citizens of the People's Republic of China.

The task of processing interviews is of course always deeply influenced by the researcher's own experiences, analytic abilities, involvement in the project, and attitude toward the subject. My goal in interpreting what I was told during the interviews, what I saw and heard during my time in the field, and what I read in the textbooks was to draw a picture of how state education directs or influences ethnic identity. Obviously, the interviewees decided which story to tell in each situation and which things to omit. My role as an officially approved researcher with an assistant sometimes made people feel relaxed in the interview situation because they felt sure that what I was doing and asking was officially approved. But it also sometimes prevented people from telling me in detail about politically sensitive aspects of religious and ethnic identity. I consciously chose interviewing, rather than relying on participant observation alone, because I was particularly interested in the ways people would choose to tell about their educational experiences (or sometimes lack of same), the things they had learned about themselves in school, and their memories of the content of education related to the constructions of the Han, minority *minzu,* and the Chinese nation and the relations among them. My own attempt to understand more about, and account for, the relationship between the powerful Chinese discourse of *minzu* and local processes of ethnic identity is based on my interpretation of these stories. As Mark Hobart writes, "Sharing language, in the sense of using the same words (or 'tokens'), does not entail people extracting the same meanings from them—if indeed they extract meaning at all—any more than they represent things in the same way" (Hobart 1987: 36). This insight does not rule out the possibility of providing interpretations based on thorough data. It merely opens them up to conflicting views and alternative translations—an acknowledgment of the fact that no descriptions are exclusively true since one can hope only to tell how *a* world is, not how *the* world is (Goodman 1972: 31).

TRANSCRIPTIONS OF FOREIGN TERMS

Most Chinese terms are transcribed in the standard pinyin form, and their corresponding characters are listed in the Glossary. Some names of places, people, and ethnic groups are transcribed in their most widely accepted Anglicized form (e.g., Tibet, Manchu, Mongol, Sun Yat-sen). Other ethnic groups are transcribed in ways that best reflect their self-appellation (e.g., "Premi" instead of the pinyin form "Pumi"). The most commonly used romanized transcription for the Tai people is "Tai" which is pronounced in the same way as the Chinese pinyin transcription "Dai." As with all Tai terms, I prefer the transcriptions that are modified on the basis of Standard Thai transcription (and are commonly used in publications such as the *Thai-Yunnan Project Newsletter*), and therefore the area in which the Tai discussed in this book live is called "Sipsong Panna" rather than the Chinese form "Xishuangbanna." Other Tai terms are transcribed in accordance with those commonly used by scholars with a profound knowledge of Tai languages. Concerning Naxi terms, I use the Chinese term *dongba* for the name of the Naxi ritual specialists rather than the Naxi romanized transcription *dobbaq*. The reason for this is that Naxi intellectuals, as well as Chinese and foreign researchers, tend to prefer this form, especially in the phrase "*dongba* culture" (*dongba wenhua*).

Lessons in Being Chinese

1 / Education and Chinese Minority Policy

EDUCATION, CIVILIZATION, AND
ETHNIC IDENTIFICATION

Traditional Chinese Confucian ideology was based upon literary and moral education, and the imperial elite consisted of the scholars most well versed in literature and Confucian moral doctrines. Chinese people around this cultural and polical center were rendered capable of being civilized through proper education thanks to family organization, religion, language, and customs that were close to those of the rulers. The further the cultural distance from the central Confucian-trained elite, the more difficult it was (though still not impossible) to achieve civilization based on Confucian values. This has been referred to as a Chinese "civilizing project" in which a center, claiming to be on a superior level of civilization, interacts with its peripheral peoples and attempts to raise their levels of civilization (Harrell 1995a: 4). The ideology of inequality is legitimized by the conviction that the dominance of the center is truly *helping* the culturally inferior peoples. Confronting Confucian ideology, the Chinese Communist Party (CCP) denied that any cultural group was superior to others. The Communists granted legal equality to "peripheral peoples" who became classified and countable ethnic minorities (*shaoshu minzu*) among an overwhelming majority of Han, in a modern nation-state with fixed borders. The Communist government's classification project of the 1950s divided all people within the borders of the People's Republic of China (PRC) into five major stages of modes of production (primitive, slave, feudal, capitalist, and socialist), and, as Stevan Harrell points out, it just happened that the Han were higher on this objective scale than most of the other *minzu* (ethnic groups or "nationalities") (Harrell 1995a: 26). Since culture was regarded as a direct reflection of the mode of production, it was scientifically proven that, economically as well as culturally, the non-Han peoples were more backward than the Han. In this way the people described as peripheral

3

by Harrell are, in another sense and at the same time, central in the Chinese Communist ideology because it is only through the construction of a less developed minority group that a contrasting, more developed, or civilized majority group such as the Han can be constructed (Gladney 1994).

The importance of this objectified scale of development of Chinese *minzu* is reflected in its integration into national education, the main arena for reproducing the ideology of cultural inequality. As has been argued by Richard Jenkins, for instance, ethnic identity, like other social identities, is as much a product of external processes of definition and categorization as it is an ongoing process of internal definition and group identification (Jenkins 1994). The external and the internal processes are mutually interdependent, and in the relationship between state education and ethnicity among ethnic minorities in China, the external process of identifying ethnic groups—giving them a name and defining the content of this name—plays a significant role. The external ethnic definitions transmitted through the education of minorities influence the people's own internal processes of formulating and negotiating ethnic identity. While ethnic identities, as well as other social identities, are fluid, overlapping, and multifaceted,[1] the Chinese government's version of ethnic categorization, as transmitted in the state school system, is categorical and definite. Thus, the study of minority education and ethnicity is also a study of power relations and the authority to define and categorize ethnic groups.

One of the striking contradictions in the Chinese education system is the fact that it preaches the constitutional equality of *minzu* while impressing on minority students immense feelings of cultural inferiority. Education is praised by the government, educators, many intellectuals, and researchers in China as a means of "improving backward habits" or civilizing the "backward," and therefore it is maybe not so surprising that the form and content of this education often contradicts the outspoken message of national equality. This perception of education as a civilizing institution is closely connected to the idea of cultural deficiency, which dominates much of the Chinese theoretical debate on minority education. In many Western, industrialized countries as well, theories of cultural deficiencies are commonly used to explain low school achievement among minorities (Churchill 1985). In China, due

---

1. See, e.g., Eriksen 1993; Ong 1987; De Lauretis 1986; Williams 1989.

to the powerful and manifest belief in minority education as a civilizing institution, this is done very explicitly. It is, for instance, not uncommon to explain unsuccessful Chinese education of the Tai in Sipsong Panna by pointing to the damaging influence of religion, the habit of marrying early, and the Tai's unfortunate preoccupation with maintaining their own language and culture.[2] This way of explaining low participation in education with deficiencies related to culture has also been adopted by researchers outside of China. One article argues, for instance, that "there are problems related to cultural tradition. Some national minority groups still believe in magic and superstition" (Postiglione 1992: 324–25). In China the so-called cultural and linguistic deficiencies of non-Han peoples in education are mostly regarded and presented as objective facts, or they are implicitly understood through the very positive evaluations of cases of cultural change in the direction of the Han. One example of an objectified statement of unequal cultural relations between Han and non-Han is: "Since the Chinese are in the majority, spread out widely throughout the country, because they are most highly developed in science and culture, and finally, because Chinese characters have the longest tradition and are used in the widest area, every ethnic group has close ties with the Chinese" (Zhou Yaowen 1992: 38).[3] The argument that the Han have the most highly developed culture is directly transferred into the discussion of language, and consequently a commonly heard argument against the spread of a minority language is that it is "too backward," it belongs to a lower stage of evolution, and therefore its vocabulary is unfit for a modernizing society.

Much of the Chinese debate about minority education has been dominated by discussion of bilingual education (*shuangyu jiaoyu*). The majority of researchers in China concerned with minority education seem to agree that developing bilingual education is necessary in many areas. The argument is that it facilitates the learning of standard Chinese (*putonghua*, "Mandarin"), which in Yunnan and most other provinces is the only language of instruction, at least at the level of junior middle school and above.[4] Therefore, bilin-

2. See, e.g., Feng Chunlin 1989; Wang Xihong et al., eds., 1990; Sun Ruoqiong et al., eds., 1990.

3. The author has written this text in English and obviously translates "Han" as "Chinese."

4. Among Western sociologists debating the education of linguistic and cultural minorities as well, there has been an inclination toward emphasizing language as the prime marker

gual education among minorities in China generally is a variant of so-called transitional bilingualism, which promotes study of the mother tongue with the purpose of hastening proficiency in the majority language (Churchill 1985: 54–56). Chinese minorities whose language lacks a script are normally excluded from the discussion of bilingual education. "They do not have a script, so how could we carry out bilingual education?" was an argument I often heard from local educators and cadres. When ethnic groups with different languages are classified in the same *minzu*, it is impossible to use bilingual teaching material in only one of those languages for all the members of the *minzu*. For instance, the people classified as Hani in Sipsong Panna do not use the romanized script created for their *minzu*, because it is based on the Luchun dialect of Hani living mainly in Luchun, Honghe, Yuanyang, and Jinping. Consequently, there is no bilingual teaching for the people classified as Hani (mainly Akha, Akhe, and Phusa) in Sipsong Panna, although many publications mention the Hani as one *minzu* that has bilingual education. The development of bilingual education is legitimized in the PRC Constitution, which supports the study of minority languages in autonomous regions. However, very often local educators and government officials reject political decisions or proposals about bilingual education because they disagree with the argument that bilingual education is necessary and useful or because they lack financial support and qualified teachers.

"REGULAR EDUCATION"
AND "MINORITY EDUCATION" IN CHINA

In the last four decades there has been a growing concern about the education of immigrants and indigenous peoples all over the world; educational

---

of an ethnic minority group and as a principal symbol of ethnic identity. Partly for this reason, much research on minority education has logically focused on language. See, e.g., Megarry et al., eds., 1981; Churchill 1985; Fishman 1989; Skutnabb-Kangas 1981.

Junior secondary school is three years of study (7th–9th grades). Normally students are between thirteen and fifteen years old, but ages vary in some areas due to starting school late. Some primary schools in Sipsong Panna had students in the first or second grade who were between nine and thirteen years old, but most of these students do not manage to continue on to secondary school. Senior secondary school is three years (10th–12th grades), with students being between sixteen and eighteen years old.

reports from various countries describe and discuss the aims and results of local education of so-called linguistic and cultural minorities.[5] Most researchers of minority education have focused on form of education, goals, bilingual education, and (in cases where the focus has been on effects) academic achievement. Fewer studies have used local research to examine how the content and form of state education influences members of different minority groups' ways of conceiving of their status as minorities, their ethnic identification, and expressions of ethnicity. This is especially so in China, where foreign educational researchers have until now largely ignored the specific problems of education among non-Han peoples.[6]

The Chinese term "nationalities education" (*minzu jiaoyu*) is in fact best translated as "minority education" because it is normally conceived of in two ways in China: either as all forms of education directed toward and practiced among the officially recognized minority *minzu*, or, more specifically, as the special educational measures adopted among some of the minority *minzu* (such as bilingual education and special curriculum). One of the broadest definitions of minority education was given by a cadre in the Bureau of Education in Lijiang County, who said, "All education here is minority education because the majority of people living here belong to minority *minzu*." However, the term commonly covers the specific educational policies for developing and expanding state education among the minorities. Thus, minority education has played an important role in government policy toward the non-Han population in the PRC and has become a specialized area of research in China. Most Chinese studies of minority education in China focus on enrollment, retention and graduation rates of minorities, practices of bilingual education, and comparisons between different minority *minzu* (because they

5. See, e.g., Carnoy 1974; Smith 1992; Gosth and Abdulaziz 1992; Jaespert and Kroon 1991; Cummins and Skutnabb-Kangas, eds., 1988; Ogbu 1978.

6. Exceptions are Wurlig Borchiged's article about Mongolian education (Borchiged 1995), Chae-Jin Lee's study of education among the Koreans (Lee 1986), Alexander Woodside's and William Rowe's articles about Chen Hongmou's education of minorities during the Qing dynasty (Woodside 1983; Rowe 1994), and several papers in an anthology about minority education (Postiglione and Stites, eds., 1999). Other studies have focused on more general aspects of minority education policy, e.g., Kwong 1989; Postiglione 1992; Zhou Yaowen 1992; Xie Qihuang et al., eds., 1991; Feng Chunlin 1989; Chen Hongtao et al., eds., 1989; Wang Xihong et al., eds., 1990; Sun Ruoqiong et al., eds., 1990.

concentrate the research on the officially recognized minorities, not on ethnic minorities as such). They often offer suggestions for improved policies
directed at increasing these rates. Thus, there is a very close connection between
the ways in which the government has formulated minority education as a
specific part of its minority policy in general, and the ways in which Chinese
researchers tend to approach the issue. The topic of minority education by
definition includes all of the highly diversified one hundred million people
who happen to be officially classified as minorities. The agenda for research
on these peoples is mostly directed at providing evidence of their lack of proper
education and suggesting measures that will enhance their chance of eventually being able to participate in the kind of *regular* education that already
exists among most Han and which, by definition, is superior. The special considerations taken by the government toward defining and practicing a specific
"minority education" thus constitute a real chance for improving and adapting education to local needs, while at the same time the government supports a structural inequality between the constructed categories of the
"majority Han" as opposed to the "minority *minzu*."

Chinese governments prior to 1949 also, in different ways, saw education
as a means of integrating or civilizing peoples living on the geographic periphery of the state. Especially during the Qing dynasty, the Chinese empire
expanded significantly in size and population, and the spread of Confucian
education was part of an ambitious program to unify the empire through
moral and cultural transformation of the non-Han population. The spread
of Confucian education to the periphery of the empire was far from being a
purely idealistic civilizing mission. It was also a means to facilitate imperial
control in areas where agrarian and mineral resources were still not fully
exploited.[7] Whereas Confucian learning among non-Han peoples in the southwest prior to the eighteenth century was confined to sons of local hereditary
chiefs (*tusi*), Qing educators such as the zealous Chen Hongmou (1696–1771)
attempted to extend education to the commoners. Chen initiated seven hundred charitable schools in Yunnan alone between 1733 and 1737 (*YMJFG* 1992:
46). During the Qing many Confucian scholars believed that not only could
Confucian learning eventually provide "barbarian" peoples with proper
knowledge and conduct of behavior, but disregard of education could cause

7. See Woodside and Elman, eds., 1994; Woodside 1983; Rowe 1994.

8

Han people to become uncivilized. This was clearly expressed by a scholar who stated in 1738 that "if savages cherish learning, they may advance to become Han; if Han people neglect learning, they may degenerate into savages" (quoted in Rowe 1994: 423).

Education in the frontier regions of the empire became sharply focused as the late-Qing government tried to strengthen its control in response to threats such as the British expansion into Yunnan and Tibet through Burma and India, and the Muslim ruler Yakūb Beg's secession of Xinjiang. In 1909 the Qing government founded a Mongolian and Tibetan school in Beijing to train local officials in the modern subjects of political science and finance in addition to language, geography, history, and so forth (Dreyer 1976: 12). In Yunnan, where at least one-third of the population was estimated to be non-Han, the Bureau of Education in Border Regions (Yanbian Xuewu Ju), the first such administrative unit, was set up in 1909 (Liu Guangzhi 1993: 68). One of the purposes of this bureau was to promote new schools in the border regions of Yunnan in order to facilitate the integration of these areas into the empire. By the end of the Qing the bureau had started 128 free "native simple literacy schools" (*tumin jianyi shizi xueshu*) with a total of 3,974 students in the province (*YMJFG* 1992: 48). These schools taught basic knowledge of Chinese characters to non-Han peoples such as the Jinghpaw, Lisu, A'chang, Akha, and Tai. One Chinese publication estimates that 10 to 20 percent of the students in these schools acquired such knowledge, but we have no information as to how this figure was reached (*YMJFG* 1992: 7).[8] Generally, the late and weakening Qing empire left the task of promoting education in non-Han areas such as Yunnan to local administrators and educators. Therefore local development of Chinese education depended very much upon the existence of a local elite prepared to create Chinese schools other than traditional Confucian ones.

The Republican government after 1911 wanted to transmit nationalist commitment via mass education in the hope that it would help to prevent ethnic conflicts from destabilizing the state. Therefore, shortly after the founding of the Republic of China, the new Ministry of Education decided to expand education of Mongols, Tibetans, and Moslems. The government considered

---

8. Between 1912 and 1915 the government changed the "native simple literacy schools" into normal lower elementary schools.

these groups to be part of China's "five races" (which also included the Han and Manchus), and they were now supposed to be given the education they had been denied under the Qing (Bailey 1990: 142–43). At the same time Sun Yat-sen strongly emphasized the common features of the Han people (Hanren), the absolute majority in China:

> The Chinese nation totals four hundred million people. Of mixed races there are only a few million Mongolians, about a million Manchus, a few million Tibetans, and over a million Mohammedan Turks. These foreign races do not exceed ten million people. So we can say that the greater part of the four hundred million Chinese [Zhongguoren] are Han people [Hanren] with common descent, common language, common religion, and common customs—one single race. (Sun Yat-sen 1926: first lecture on nationalism, 4)

Sun Yat-sen argued that due to the assimilative power and highly developed civilization of the Han, it would be in the interest of the other races along the periphery of China to be part of the Chinese state, to join the Han against the imperialists and ultimately assimilate with them.[9] Following the severance of Tibet and Outer Mongolia from Chinese control in 1911, the government established schools in 1913 in Beijing offering instruction in Mongolian and Tibetan. Apart from these few exceptions, the promotion of modern schools among non-Han groups was exclusively based on the standard Chinese language (or Mandarin; *guoyu*), and no specific considerations were given to the content of education for the numerous non-Han peoples in Yunnan or elsewhere. In 1931 the Yunnan government made public its first decrees concerning special education of non-Han peoples in border and mountain areas, including the establishment of special primary schools. Although this marked the beginning of a period of increasing political concern for the development of education in border regions, the practical implications of the various decrees were limited by factors such as political and economic instability, difficult or nonexistent communications, weak central government, the Japanese invasion, and fighting between Communists and Nationalists.

The government in Nanjing, led by Chiang Kai-shek after his defeat of

9. See also, e.g., Dreyer 1976: 15–43; Duara 1993; Wang Tianxi 1988: 80–87.

the northern warlords in 1928, adopted a highly politicized educational program in which inclusion of the Nationalist Party's (Guomindang) doctrine was to be mandatory (Cleverley 1991: 59–60). The Nationalist government regarded the spread of education among non-Han peoples as a means to ease assimilation with the Han and ensure their loyalty to the state. Education was in principle entirely based upon the language, culture, and history of the Han. However, for a variety of reasons the assimilative education policy did not come up to expectations. Central control was constantly disrupted, and the financing of education depended mostly on the lower administrative levels. Local teachers were to a large degree left free to teach as they pleased, and therefore many teachers in lower primary schools employed their local language for instruction rather than Chinese. Education still reached a relatively small part of the population, and women were still socialized mainly in the family and the village. In spite of the introduction of vocational schools in the early twentieth century, by far the most common way of transmitting vocational skills remained the master-apprentice relationship (Thoegersen 1997: 15).

During the 1930s and 1940s the war against Japan and the civil war between the Nationalists and the Communists resulted in serious disruption of education in many areas. Cleverley regards it as likely that by 1949 about 85 percent of the total population were illiterate, with an even larger percentage among women and the rural population (Cleverley 1991: 69). Among the non-Han population there was great diversity in the degree of literacy and the number of students in Chinese schools. Some areas resembled rural Han areas, some had no functioning Chinese schools at all, and some ethnic groups had a relatively high degree of literacy in their own language due to factors such as religiously based teaching.

With peace reestablished in the new People's Republic of China after 1949, promotion of education became a priority of the new Communist government. The CCP wanted to establish a homogenized, socialist-oriented national education system reaching all corners of China. The most important curricular change was that history was rewritten and adapted to Marxist views of the government. Courses in Nationalist Party doctrine and Sun Yat-sen's Three Principles of the People (Sanminzhuyi) for the salvation of the nation were displaced by political lessons teaching communist ideology. Concerning policy toward ethnic minorities and the establishment of state education among them, it was important for the new government to encourage support from the minorities by emphasizing their right to develop their own languages and incorporate them into education. Because the government wanted to eradicate so-called Han chauvinism (*da Hanzuzhuyi*) while promoting "a unified multiethnic country" (*tongyi de duo minzu guojia*), it maintained that non-Han populations had the right to preserve their own languages, customs, and religions over a long period of time until all *minzu* would ultimately (and naturally) "melt together" (*ronghe*). Meanwhile, the non-Han peoples should be "assisted" in developing their "backward" customs, economy, and political awareness in order to achieve, in unity with the Han, a developed socialist society. For all these purposes the new government advocated intensified education of ethnic minorities with an initial focus on the education of minority cadres (*minzu ganbu*). Furthermore the government wanted to strengthen primary education among minorities, promote literacy among adults, and train minority teachers, of whom there was a shortage.

But first the government needed to identify non-Han peoples. Therefore, shortly after the founding of the PRC, it organized a large-scale program of team fieldwork in which linguists, ethnographers, and historians were sent to minority regions to identify all *minzu* within the territory of China.[10] The teams were to define all *minzu* and identify their present stage of social development. In principle this was done on the basis of presumed objective criteria for definitions of ethnic groups formulated by Stalin in 1913 — common territory, language, economy, and psychological makeup manifested in a common culture (Hutchinson and Smith 1994: 20).[11] In order to decide how to implement land reforms, the government also wanted descriptions of the *minzu*'s economic and social stages of development based on Engels's and Morgan's theories of evolution. Thus many *minzu* were described as having fully or partly developed a "feudal landlord economy." These included the Han, some of the Naxi, and all or most of the Zhuang, Hui, Uygurs, Man-

---

10. In 1992 the total Chinese population constituted 1,130,510,638 people, with more than 91 million minority *minzu* representing 8.08 percent (*Zhongguo minzu tongji* 1992: 53–54).

11. Concerning the classification work, see, e.g., Fei Xiaotong 1981; Lin Yaohua 1987; Diamond 1995; McKhann 1995; and Wellens 1998.

chus, and others. Groups on the next broad level of evolution, for instance the majority of Tibetans and those classified as Dai (Tai) and Hani, were described as having a "feudal serf system." Lower on the evolutionary scale were societies that were believed to practice a "slave system," represented mainly by the Nuosu (classified as Yi) from Daliangshan. Finally, a number of ethnic groups in the border regions of Yunnan (e.g., Dulong, Nu, and Wa) were considered to be living in "primitive society."

In order to facilitate the integration of the minority *minzu,* the government adopted, in the early period of the People's Republic, the highly significant policy of a "united front" that implied cooperation with the bourgeois, upper strata of the minority *minzu*. Theoretically, this move was legitimized by the special economic and cultural backwardness of the minority *minzu,* which manifested itself in low class-consciousness (Dreyer 1976: 94–95). Through the education of locally accepted religious, ethnic, and political elites, the government hoped to be able to pass on ideas of patriotism, national unity, and socialism. Therefore, an important feature of early minority education was the establishment of special minority institutes (*minzu xueyuan*),[12] which trained minority cadres to work in minority regions as representatives of the CCP and government. Through these minority cadres, and through the vast number of Han who were sent as teachers, soldiers, and government workers to minority areas, the government gradually spread the message of its nonassimilationist policy, the new objectified classification of *minzu,* and the determination of stages of economic and cultural evolution. Thus, for the first time in China, the government managed gradually to consolidate an official version of the relationship between a Han majority and a group of minority *minzu* through a widespread, popular educational system. Ethnic groups all over China learned that they were minority *minzu* and younger brothers of the Han, and had equal rights with the Han, but that most, alas, were less developed than the Han.

By 1950 the government had established forty-five special minority primary schools and eight provincial minority secondary schools. In principle

12. Although the term is usually translated as "nationalities institute," the primary purpose of these institutes is to educate members of minority *minzu*. Therefore, they are also often called "minority institutes."

the minority students in these schools were guaranteed free education, books, and school supplies and were subsidized for food and, eventually, housing at the school. The First National Conference on Minority Education (convened and led by Zhou Enlai), in 1951, concluded that minority education was to further develop in line with the national plan, taking into consideration the special conditions and demands in the different areas inhabited by minorities.[13] The conference also emphasized that political and patriotic education (*aioguozhuyi jiaoyu*) should be promoted in minority areas. The language policy adopted in minority regions was one of the special features of so-called minority education. During the 1951 conference it was made clear that the content of education and the language of instruction should be adapted to special needs in minority regions. In Yunnan, for instance, the Bureau of Culture and Education issued a plan in 1951 for developing education among minorities. In line with national policy on minority education, the aim was to make private schools public, start new schools in remote areas, and grant special financial support to minority students. With regard to the content of education and language of instruction, the bureau idealistically stated,

> In accordance with the spirit of the minority policy, [we will] assist each *minzu* in popularizing its language and imbue it with the ideas of our policy. Where conditions exist we shall use teaching material that combines the scripts of our brother *minzu* [*xiongdi minzu wenzi*], Chinese characters, drawings, and pinyin. As for the *minzu* without a script, we should use pinyin based on their language and, to the best of our abilities, create new scripts. In addition to common knowledge, the teaching material should especially give consideration to *minzu* history, local customs, and strengthening of the unity of the *minzu* [*minzu tuanjie*]. (Yunnan Province Bureau of Culture and Education, "Primary School Education of Yunnan's Minority Brothers in 1951," reprinted in *YMJFG* 1992: 282–84)

With the purpose of promoting literacy among ethnic minorities by supporting education in their own language, in 1951 the Chinese government set up a national committee that was to suggest guidelines for the development of written languages for minorities. Thirty-two minority languages were

13. Ma Xulun 1952.

considered, and after years of extensive research, a plan was put forward in 1958 to create eighteen new scripts for twelve minorities.[14] In practice most local areas were not able to live up to the standard proposed in the quoted statement by the Yunnan Bureau of Culture and Education, and rapid policy changes during the 1950s and 1960s often put a stop to the creation of special teaching material for minorities.

During the early years of the People's Republic, when the total number of students and graduates increased significantly, the proportion of minorities in schools also increased. According to the official statistics, 1.4 percent of college and university students in 1951 belonged to minorities; the figure was 6.9 percent in 1991. In primary schools 2.2 percent were minorities in 1951, compared to 8.1 percent in 1991 (*Zhongguo minzu tongji* 1992: 241).

Development of higher education had a relatively high priority during the time of the Soviet influence in the early years of the PRC, and therefore the highest increase in students was in higher education and middle schools. In connection with the political conflict between China and the Soviet Union in the latter part of the 1950s, CCP chairman Mao Zedong (and later, teachers and students) started to criticize the Chinese tendency to copy from the Soviet educational system. Agricultural production in the PRC had so far been disappointing, and Mao's solution was to heighten production through mass mobilization and reorganization of agriculture. He launched the disastrous Great Leap Forward in 1958, and agriculture was collectivized in People's Communes all over China. Mao wanted basic education for the majority — education that was directly relevant to, and combined with, productive work. Based on the ideology of "education as revolution" and "revolution as education," educational change was focused on combining study with agricultural or industrial work, strengthening political awareness of students, achieving comprehensive mass education, and intensifying collectivization (Chan Hoiman 1992). The government sought to decentralize schools and establish lower primary education in all villages, higher primary education in the production teams (*dadui*), and agricultural secondary schools in the communes (*gongshe*). The goal was to be "red and expert," and often peas-

14. Finally ten *minzu* scripts were created for the Zhuang, Buyi, Miao, Dong, Yi, Hani, Lisu, Wa, Li, and Naxi. Other *minzu,* such as the Dai, had their script simplified, just as Chinese characters were simplified.

ants, workers, cadres, and soldiers acted as teachers. An increased number of young people were sent to the countryside to learn from the peasants and transmit their middle-school knowledge to the rural population. Many young middle-school graduates became teachers in minority areas, and some of them came to have a lasting influence on education there.

In the summer of 1957 a forum on *"minzu* work" (*minzu gongzuo*) decided to organize the struggle against "local nationalism" (*difang minzuzhuyi*), which was synonymous with antisocialism (Dreyer 1976: 151). In minority areas the so-called Three Statements (San Lun) — special conditions in border regions, backwardness of minorities, and special treatment of minorities — came under fierce attack. Many minority cadres were criticized for promoting "local nationalism" and harming the "unity of the *minzu."* The use of minority languages in schools also was attacked. In general, the Great Leap Forward, the Rectification Campaign (1957–59), and the struggle against "local nationalism" focused on spreading the Chinese language rather than minority languages.

Facing the economic fiasco of the Great Leap Forward, officials and teachers criticized education for emphasizing quantitative expansion, physical labor, and politics at the expense of technical knowledge and for lowering the general standards of education. Regulation and central control of education was again accepted by the government, and beginning in 1960, new elite schools, keypoint schools (*zhongdian xuexiao*), experimental schools, and boarding schools were started with the purpose of providing superior facilities for the best students and for children of senior cadres. Minority education policy again became more open toward the use of minority languages. Although Chinese language had to be strengthened, teachers were told not to ignore local minority languages and scripts. For a short time it again became acceptable to translate teaching material into local languages. On the other hand, the government's call for standardization (*zhengguihua*) of education in 1962 closed down many local "people-run" (so-called *minban*) schools, which had been started without adequately educated teachers, mostly in the poorest minority villages. Hardly any new standardized schools were opened to compensate for the closed ones, and consequently many rural children lost access to basic education.

The Cultural Revolution (1966–76) put a stop to the government's attempts to develop minority languages, experiment with bilingual education, cooperate closely with local elites, and tolerate cultural differences.

Chairman Mao declared that all ethnic conflict was the result of class conflict, and the perception of minority *minzu* as backward peoples who needed special consideration and treatment was now severely attacked. One of the slogans of the time was that "the small classroom" should be destroyed in favor of "the big classroom of society." Mobilization and participation of the masses was the core of the revolution, and education now had to be in the hands of the masses, rather than the elite, and adapt to their needs. This implied a great deal of change within the educational system, and new entrance criteria for higher education favored children with "correct" class background, such as peasants and workers. Studying was again to a larger degree combined with productive labor; the length of courses was cut; schools were placed under the administration of revolutionary teachers, students, workers, and peasants; and curriculum was directed toward study of texts by Mao Zedong. Moreover, whereas many secondary schools and colleges closed down, for months or years, many new primary schools and attached secondary schools (*fushe zhongxue*) were started.

Mao had declared that it was essential that the educated youths (*zhishi qingnian*) go to the countryside and receive their second education from the poor and lower-secondary peasants, and, according to Thomas P. Bernstein, an estimated twelve million educated youths did go "up to the mountains or down to the countryside" (*shangshan xiaxiang*) between 1968 and 1975 (Bernstein 1977: 24–25). Many of them went to minority regions that were among the poorest in the nation and in which "remnants of feudal society" were easily detected. Some became teachers in the new primary and secondary schools. The dominant ideology of the time maintained that minority *minzu* were equal to the Han and therefore should be treated equally. This legitimized a brutal suppression of all expressions of ethnic identity—of religious activities, local festivals, and use of local-language teaching material. Whereas minority students had previously learned through their education that minorities in the Chinese state had their own cultural and economic characteristics, which would eventually fade away with the helpful assistance of the Han and the CCP, they now learned that the time had come to quickly eradicate the backward customs that separated them from the forefront of the revolution.

In the years following Mao's death and the fall of the Gang of Four (Jiang Qing, Wang Hongwen, Yao Wenyuan, and Zhang Chunqiao) in 1976, China's new policy of the Four Modernizations (in agriculture, industry, defense, and science and technology) profoundly influenced the development of education, and a number of measures have since been taken to promote education of minorities. Since state-sponsored education is regarded as a basic means to achieve economic development while ensuring loyalty to the state through teaching of patriotism, promotion of schools in minority regions has been, and still is, high on the political agenda. In 1977 the competitive examination system was reinstated, and since then institutionalized education has again been emphasized as crucial for achieving a technically and economically developed nation. Keypoint schools providing selected students with the best possible education were established at all levels. Selection was based on an examination system using curriculum-based content that favored knowledge of standard Chinese language, history of the Chinese nation, and the policy of the CCP, in addition to technical subjects. Proficiency in a minority language or substantial knowledge of a field such as local history was irrelevant. In 1980 the Ministry of Education and the Commission on Nationalities Affairs evaluated the state of education in minority areas and made suggestions for future work. They concluded that most of the minority *minzu* were "extremely backward" as to level of education, that schools were in a very bad state, that the percentage of minority students in higher education was actually dropping, and that the scope of illiteracy was worrisome.[15]

The government decided that in order to achieve modernization in the minority regions, it again had to allow for special measures within education. Therefore, central and local governments created special primary and secondary minority schools (*minzu xiaoxue* and *minzu zhongxue*), where students were subsidized, and earmarked funds for minority education. Minorities were to be given additional points in examinations to give them easier access to higher education. Furthermore, governments at different levels tried to strengthen the training of local teachers and reestablish bilingual education, particularly among Tibetans, Mongols, and Uygurs. Koreans in Yanbian have themselves established bilingual education even at the college level (Lee 1986). The Ministry of Education issued several statements saying that while the study of Chinese would greatly benefit the cultural and tech-

15. A document called "Suggestions Concerning the Strengthening of Educational Work among National Minorities" was approved by the Central Committee of the CCP and the State Council. It is reprinted in *Minzu gongzuo wenxuan* 1986: 274–80.

nical level of the minorities, those who had their own language and lived in areas where it was widely used should also be able to learn it in school (e.g., *YMJFG* 1992: 202–3). All governments of autonomous regions had to establish departments specifically dealing with minority education. The right of these governments to organize minority education in accordance with local demands and special conditions was confirmed in a 1984 law on local autonomy in minority regions. The autonomous governments of minority *minzu* were allowed to decide (based upon general national laws on education) which kinds of schools they would establish, the length of schooling, whether special curriculum was needed, which languages to teach in addition to Chinese, and how to recruit students. In poor areas, pastoral areas, or areas where minorities lived widely scattered, the governments were to establish boarding and semiboarding primary and secondary schools (Sun Ruoqiong et al., eds, 1990: 77).[16] To ensure that poor and underdeveloped rural minority areas would benefit from minority higher education, it was decided in 1978 that minority students studying in cities should be allocated jobs in their home counties after graduation.

MINORITY EDUCATION
IN YUNNAN PROVINCE SINCE 1980

Since the beginning of the reform period, the central government has granted financial support to Yunnan as a border province with an underdeveloped economy, and a part of these funds is still earmarked for minority education. According to statistics from 1990, 103 out of 127 counties and cities in Yunnan depended on state financial support.[17] Of forty-one special "poor counties," 75.6 percent were "minority counties" (*YMJFG* 1992: 109). Although minorities account for only one-third of the provincial population, they represent two-thirds of the twelve million people officially declared poor.

Official Chinese statistics concerning illiteracy and level of education of minorities in Yunnan also point to a generally lower level of education as com-

16. At a semiboarding school, pupils eat at school during the lunch hour and return home when school finishes in the afternoon.

17. See also *Yunnan jiaoyu bao,* 2 Sept. 1995: 7, for a list of educational expenditures in Yunnan in 1993.

pared to the Han and to the Chinese national standard. In 1982, for instance, 45.09 percent of Han in Yunnan above the age of twelve were illiterate or semiliterate, whereas the figure was 58.53 percent for minorities and as high as 74.04 percent for minority women. Among Yao and Miao, more than 90 percent of women above the age of twelve were illiterate or semiliterate (*Yunnan jiaoyu sishi nian, 1949–1989*: 120). Of the Han, 13.53 percent had a junior secondary school education, as compared to 4.68 percent for minorities (Li Ping 1989: 74). According to the same statistics, Yunnan Province had the lowest percentage of university students and the second-lowest percentage of people educated beyond primary school (Liu Baoming 1993: 44). Statistics from eight years later, in 1990, show a remarkable drop in the number of illiterates or semiliterates, which fell to 25.44 percent of the population above the age of fifteen (*Yunnan tongji nianjian* 1991: 821). The city of Kunming had the lowest number, but Lijiang County was lower than the provincial average, with only 19.5 percent illiterates or semiliterates, whereas many other minority counties still had between 30 and 40 percent. In 1990 statistics showed that as many as 91.5 percent of all minority children in Yunnan had started school.

The official statistics concerning illiteracy and school enrollment among minorities must be read with caution. When reporting on the number of children in primary schools, schools and local governments sometimes count only the pupils who start, not those who drop out. People who have once participated in a short-term literacy course are often counted as literate, whereas those who have never been to school but have learned to read the local language in a monastery may be registered as illiterates. On the other hand, literacy in the Chinese language is not always the only measure of literacy: between 1984 and 1990, literacy campaigns in Lijiang County reportedly taught 10,946 people to read. Only 1,744 of these became literate in Chinese; a majority of 6,062 learned Lisu script (created in the 1950s) and a minority learned Naxi or Yi scipts (CLNAC 1995: 41). The illiteracy rate of the Tai (classified as the Dai *minzu*) was only 39.38 percent in Yunnan in 1982. This is relatively low because many who learned the Tai script in monasteries were counted as literate. Another more important reason for the lower rate compared to other *minzu* in Yunnan is that Chinese education is much more developed among the Tai Na in Dehong than among the Tai Lue in Sipsong Panna. All are officially classified as members of the Dai *minzu* and therefore are included in the same statistics. Thus, in Sipsong Panna the people classified as part of the Dai nationality had a 49 percent illiteracy and semiliteracy rate for people above the age of twelve. In Mengla County alone the figure was 56.8 percent.[18]

Official statistics clearly indicate that fewer minority pupils graduate from primary school and, most important, fewer continue beyond primary school compared to the Han. Official figures from the 1990 census suggest that Koreans in China have the highest percentage of graduates at all levels beyond primary school, and that Koreans, Mongols, and Manchus are the only minorities with more graduates at all levels beyond primary school than the Han (*Zhongguo tongji nianjian* 1993: 91).

In 1980 the Yunnan provincial government made plans for the further education of the numerous poorly qualified *minban* teachers who were still working in many of the primary schools, especially in minority areas, and it emphasized the need for local governments to establish technical and agricultural vocational education. Special courses were started in all prefectures to educate *minban* teachers, and each year a quota would decide how many of those who passed the examination would become regular teachers. In 1994–95 all *minban* teachers I talked to hoped to become regular teachers through this kind of course, both because their wages would almost triple and because they felt that they had been looked down upon as irregular teachers.

The provincial government also decided to financially support the establishment of forty minority primary and secondary boarding schools. For several reasons, the boarding-school system in minority areas is still regarded very positively by the government and most local teachers and educators: the boarding school has more control over students, who cannot easily leave; students spend more time studying because they live at school; their parents have no influence on what they do in their spare time; they cannot participate in time-consuming religious activities; and they use the Chinese language more than they would at home. All minority secondary boarding schools are situated in county or prefectural capitals, where students from various minority ethnic groups and villages are gathered and subjected to a standardized education and exposed to cultural values that are often incongru-

18. See *Yunnan jiaoyu sishi nian, 1949–1989* 1990: 120; and *Yunnan Sheng Xishuangbanna Zhou Jinghong Xian di san ci renkou pucha shougong huizong ciliao huibian:* 27.

ent with those learned in the family and the village. Because boarding-school pupils' scores in examinations are generally higher than those of minority students in regular schools, educators and governments praise boarding schools for their practicality and academic success. Equally important, however, is the structure of the boarding school, which facilitates transmission of certain values and social practices to students who live far away from home for years and creates a sense of commonality and shared experience among students from various ethnic backgrounds.

The responsibility for developing and administering schools in Yunnan, as elsewhere in China, is shared in a hierarchical structure in which townships and administrative villages are responsible for their own local schools at the elementary levels, and county and prefectural governments administer the highest-level local educational institutions. Teachers in villages are paid by the county, apart from *minban* teachers, who are paid partly by the local community, which also finances school buildings and equipment. In Yunnan minority regions, villages (*ziran cun*) typically have a lower primary school (two or four years), administrative villages (*xingzheng cun*) have a full primary school (six years), townships (*xiang*) have a junior secondary school (*chuzhong;* three years), and county capitals have at least one senior secondary school (*gaozhong;* three years). Since 1993, when the central government emphasized that the national goal was to achieve nine years of compulsory education throughout China as announced in 1985, Yunnan has developed a strategy in the minority regions to gradually attain this goal. According to this plan, all minority areas must establish six years of compulsory education by the year 2000, while 70 percent must establish nine years.

At the provincial level there have been special minority classes at Yunnan University and the Teachers College, but today only one college in Kunming is specially designed to educate members of minority *minzu*, namely the Yunnan Institute of the Nationalities (the institute's own translation; YIN). In 1951 YIN started enrolling students recruited from among Yunnan's minorities. The main purpose for the establishment of YIN was to train local minority cadres who could implement government policy in minority areas and future autonomous regions. Curriculum emphasized socialism, patriotism, unity of the *minzu,* CCP minority policy, and Chinese language. Students were recruited from among local religious leaders, the local aristocracy, and secondary schools. Later in the 1950s and early 1960s, "culture classes" (*wenhua ban*) were started to educate "cultural workers," who were supposed to improve the cultural level of the presumably backward minorities and to function as minority teachers and translators. Classes to teach selected minority languages were also started. After a period of severe criticism, periodical disruptions of education, and one-sided emphasis on political education during the Cultural Revolution, all classes and departments were restarted in 1976. Since 1977 examination results have determined enrollment. In 1979 enrollment was integrated into the national university entrance examination,[19] and education responded to the demands of the new modernization policy, so that common university subjects became relatively more important than short cadre-training courses.

In addition to teaching common university subjects, YIN offers, through the Department of Minority Languages and Literature (Minzu Yuwen Xi), classes for teachers and translators in Sipsong Panna Tai, Dehong Tai, Jingpo, Lisu, Lahu, Yi, and Wa languages. The history and anthropology departments include the history of minority regions in their curricula, and there is a special minority research department. However students (and many teachers as well) tend to regard the technical departments as the strong ones, while the department teaching minority languages is not highly valued. Many students in this department fail to enter YIN on the basis of their examination results, but are chosen and sponsored (*baosong*) by a senior secondary school or a special or technical school (*zhongzhuan*) to which they were expected to return after graduation.

Since the institute began enrolling students based on examination results, special measures have been taken to ensure that all minority groups are represented. A maximum of 5 percent Han students from poor border areas are accepted. In higher education in China a member of a minority *minzu* is preferred when scores equal those of a Han. In 1994 approximately 95 percent of the students and 33 percent of the staff at YIN were minorities. Compared to their total number in Yunnan, the Hui, Bai, and Naxi were best repre-

19. After the Cultural Revolution's abandonment of the examination system, the government announced in 1977 that university entrance again had to be based primarily on examination results. In 1978 tests were standardized, and students participating in the national exam received the same questions in each subject on the same day (see also Cleverley 1985: 223–25). In the minority institutes, additional criteria for admission remained to ensure that all minorities would be represented at the schools in spite of low examination results.

sented at the school. In spite of the special policy of allocating extra points to selected minority members, the ratio of Tai students has fallen significantly since the introduction of the examination system.[20]

The system of job assignment (*fenpei zhidu*) for graduates is an important tool in realizing the political purpose of the institution. The idea behind establishment of special education for minority people was that graduates should return to their local areas as transmitters of official government policy, as competent Communist cadres capable of acting as the indispensable link between the central government and the local minority population. Therefore the guiding principle is still "Where they come from, they should return to" (*Na lai na qu*), and the majority of graduates are still—with or without their own approval—sent back to their native places. Because this has generated growing dissatisfaction among students, the Yunnan government decided to release graduates from their obligation to be sent back if they pay a fee.[21]

Pu Linlin estimates that as many as 92 percent of students at the Central Institute of the Nationalities[22] in Beijing in 1991 wished to stay in the capital after graduation, and about one-third of the students at YIN wanted to stay in Kunming (Pu Linlin 1994: 64). This tendency is obviously of concern to many teachers and political authorities in Yunnan who need the minority graduates as a link between local minority populations and the central levels of government and to assist in modernization programs in minority areas. Consequently, students are often criticized for being more concerned about their own individual aspirations than about the common good. Clearly, the problem for political authorities and educators alike is how to teach minority students to dissociate themselves from their parents' and grandparents' worldview, religion, and customs while convincing them to return as civilizers to presumably backward areas.

20. See Li Li et al., eds., 1991: 129 for a complete scheme of all *minzu* at YIN from 1952 to 1990.

21. In 1994 students who did not want to be sent to a certain job officially had to pay between three thousand and four thousand yuan. However, even though some graduates manage to pay this fee, it is sometimes impossible for them to get household registration in the city, so that they have to return to their home county anyway. In 1994 only a very small number of YIN graduates had managed to find a job themselves.

22. Now the Nationalities University (Minzu Daxue).

2 / History of Chinese Education among the Naxi in Lijiang

The Naxi and Mosuo people (all normally called Mosuo in Chinese literature before 1950 and all classified as Naxi since 1954) are descendants of the nomadic proto-Qiang people. During the Han dynasty (206 B.C.E.–C.E. 221) they migrated southward to northwestern Yunnan from what is now the border region of Sichuan, Gansu, and Qinghai and probably reached the Lijiang plain later during the Tang dynasty (618–907) (McKhan 1995:54). After Qubilai Khan and his army defeated the kingdom of Dali (the successor of the Nanzhao kingdom, which in 835 had broken all connections with the Chinese empire) in 1253, the different Mosuo chiefdoms also came under central Mongol authority. During the Mongol Yuan dynasty the system of granting official status to local hereditary chiefs (known as *tusi*) was established. Later, during the Ming dynasty, the *tusi* family in Lijiang was given the Chinese name Mu, and, to further distinguish themselves from the commoners, the royal Mu family decided that commoners should adopt the family name He. Today the family names Mu and He are still common in Lijiang.

Until the 1950s, when a new road bypassed Lijiang, the town was located on the important trade route between south China and Tibet. Thriving trade — combined with the ruling Naxi Mu lineage's openness toward Tibetan and especially Chinese craftsmen, artisans, monks, and scholars — helps to explain the Tibetan and Chinese Confucian influence in the area. In the early eighteenth century the Manchus sent armies to Tibet to fight Mongols who were trying to get a foothold in this buffer state between India and China. Lijiang's strategic situation on the road between China and Tibet was probably one of the reasons why the Qing government in 1723 decided to transfer direct power from the native Mu *tusi* in Lijiang to its own representatives. This policy of replacing local hereditary chiefs with imperial bureaucrats (known as the system of *gaitu guiliu*) was part of the Qing policy to expand the empire and fully incorporate frontier regions into the Chinese state. Most Chinese publications on Naxi history and educational history regard the early implementation of *gaitu guiliu* in 1723 in Lijiang as a major historical reason for the relatively high level of education and so-called "cultural development" of the Naxi today.

The officially classified Naxi *minzu* (Naxizu) currently consists of 277,750 people.[1] This includes the people living in the area of Lugu Lake and the Yongning basin who are called Mosuo or Yongning Naxi in Chinese, and Hli-khin or Na(re) in their own language, and who prefer to distinguish themselves from the Naxi.[2] The majority of Naxi live to the west and south of the Jinsha River in the counties of Lijiang, Zhongdian, and Weixi. They call themselves Naxi, also transcribed "Na-khi" by Joseph Rock[3] and "Naqxi" in the Naxi Latin script created in the 1950s. My investigation of education and ethnicity among the Naxi is based upon research conducted in Lijiang Naxi Autonomous County (Lijiang Naxizu Zizhi Xian) and through interviews with Naxi living in Kunming, the provincial capital. The Mosuo people of Yongning are *not* included here, nor do I consider education or ethnicity among Naxi in other counties. The majority of Naxi (192,448 in 1994) live

---

1. *Zhongguo minzu tongji* 1992.

2. For recent studies of the Mosuo, see Knödel 1995 and Shih Chuankang 1993. Another brand-new publication is Cai Hua 1997.

3. The most well-known and comprehensive Western study of the Naxi people is published in the works of the famous Austrian botanist Joseph F. Rock, who lived on and off for twenty-five years in Lijiang between 1922 and 1949. He studied historical Chinese gazetteers; wrote about Naxi (Na-khi) history, society, and religion; and collected and translated Naxi manuscripts written by ritual specialists, *dongba*. Rock's works are widely acknowledged as pioneering. Recently one of his major sources for the study of Lijiang history, *Lijiang Fu zhi lüe* (1743) was reprinted and published by Lijiang County. Rock's studies have inspired Western researchers such as Anthony Jackson (1979) and Gernot Prunner (1969) to further explore the history and the manuscripts of the Naxi. Silvia Sutton has written an entertaining biography about his life (Sutton 1974). In contrast to Rock's style, Peter Goullart, who also left Lijiang in 1949 after living there for almost nine years, wrote a very personal and romantic book about his life there, *Forgotten Kingdom* (1955), which has recently been translated into Chinese and is popular among many Naxi in Lijiang. None of these books is concerned with education in Lijiang, but they contribute to the understanding of the culture and history of the Naxi before 1949.

in Lijiang Naxi Autonomous County, which was established in 1961. Today Lijiang County, together with the counties of Ninglang, Yongsheng, and Huaping make up Lijiang Prefecture (Lijiang Diqu). In 1994, 329,160 people lived in Lijiang County. The Naxi make up 58.4 percent of this population, the Han 17.7 percent, the Bai 11.4 percent, the Lisu 7.7 percent, and the Yi 2 percent. More than half of the population in the county (and prefectural) capital of Lijiang Town (or Dayan Zhen) are Naxi. The development of tourism (Chinese, Asian, and Western) in recent years has encouraged locals (not to mention the many incoming people, especially Bai and Han) to establish small businesses. There is very little industry in Lijiang, and the majority of the population is engaged in agriculture (or pastoralism) involving a range of crops grown at different altitudes. People in the highlands above three thousand meters—mostly Nuosu, Lisu, Miao, and Premi (officially classified as Pumi)—often produce only potatoes and turnips, and they are among the poorest inhabitants in Lijiang County.

The language of the Naxi is a Tibeto-Burman language that belongs to the Yi group of the Burman-Yi branch, and Chinese linguists normally distinguish between the Western and the Eastern dialects spoken by Naxi and Mosuo respectively. The Naxi have three written scripts: the most famous is the pictographic *dongba* script developed and used by Naxi ritual specialists (*dongba*) for recording rituals and legends. The *dongba* script has more than six thousand characters, most of which are pictographic symbols.[4] The other Naxi script, usually called *geba* script, is a syllabic phonetic script that was never widely used. Both scripts were used exclusively among *dongba,* and neither was standardized. The third script is the Naxi Latin script, which Chinese linguists developed in the 1950s in cooperation with Naxi intellectuals. Because ordinary Naxi had never used the *dongba* script, they were chosen as one of the ten ethnic groups to be given a new script, but the Latin script never gained widespread use.

4. Especially since James Bacot's 1913 publication about the Mosuo, the pictographic *dongba* script has caught the interest of many Western researchers, and many manuscripts in *dongba* script belong to Western collections and museums. Since 1980 researchers in China, many of them Naxi, have published articles and books containing new translations of *dongba* texts, discussions of the script, and descriptions of *dongba* rituals. There is a massive interest in *dongba* culture as a research subject and as a focus for tourism in Lijiang.

In Chinese descriptions the Naxi are commonly praised for their supposedly pragmatic attitude toward religion, which allows the coexistence of Daoism (Taoism), Chinese and Tibetan forms of Buddhism, and shamanistic and *dongba* rituals. The Naxi *dongba* were not organized in temples or monasteries, and usually they transmitted their ritual knowledge from father to son. Most *dongba* were farmers who practiced as ritual specialists in connection with events such as death and marriage and who made ritual sacrifices to heaven. The influence of the *dongba* rituals had already declined considerably in the 1940s, when Joseph Rock had difficulty finding practicing *dongba*. After 1949 the rituals were banned, and today only a few practicing *dongba* remain. About four hundred years after the Ming rulers complimented the Naxi Mu family for adapting to Confucian values, a publication based on the Chinese government's large-scale fieldwork in the 1950s also concluded that the Naxi were an especially open-minded *minzu* interested in learning from "more advanced" groups:

> It is characteristic that the Naxi of Lijiang County do not close themselves off to outsiders, do not blindly oppose everything foreign, and do not stick to their old ways. They actively try to make progress and are good at studying. Although the Lijiang Naxi have their own traditional culture, they are extremely eager to learn from other *minzu*'s advanced cultures. They are especially energetic in studying the Han people's culture. (*LNZG:* 33)

Until the 1950s Chinese school education existed simultaneously with different forms of religious education among the Naxi in Lijiang. The *dongba* transmitted their knowledge of rituals through their own script (usually to one son), but never as formalized or institutionalized education. We still lack thorough knowledge of the influence of Tibetan culture and education in Lijiang.[5] What kind of education took place in Buddhist monasteries in different periods? How widespread, or limited, was knowledge of Tibetan script and texts (of which the Mu lineage possessed a large collection)? These subjects lie outside the scope of this book, which concerns only institutionalized Chinese school education.

5. Apart from He Shaoying 1995, few publications have focused on the impact of Tibetan culture in Lijiang.

CONFUCIAN SCHOOLS

Chinese publications about education among the Naxi often accentuate the early establishment of Confucian education in Lijiang as a decisive explanation of the relatively high number of educated Naxi today.[6] It is hardly possible to determine exactly how relevant and important the history of Confucian education in the eighteenth and nineteenth centuries in Lijiang is to the educational situation today. Certainly Han influence on the Lijiang plain increased during the Qing dynasty, and in addition to the sons of the Mu family, an increasing number of Naxi received education in charitable schools (*yixue*) or private Confucian schools (*sishu*). Only a few Naxi in the Lijiang area were educated in the three academies for classical learning (*shuyuan*).

According to historical records from Yunnan, private Confucian schools were already established in Lijiang Prefecture during the Yuan (1271–1368) and Ming (1368–1644) dynasties.[7] During the Ming, the local Naxi Mu chiefs expanded their contacts with imperial China and established Confucian private schools that were exclusively used for teaching male members of the Mu lineage. The Mu *tusi* owned a library containing Confucian classics and a large number of Tibetan books, and the Mu lineage invited Han scholars from China's cultural center to come to Lijiang as teachers, painters, medical workers, and mining experts. Their private Confucian education was organized in family schools (*zuxue*), where a clan or lineage hired a teacher to tutor a very small class of boys from the same clan. These schools received no economic support or recognition from the government and had no regulations to follow concerning the content and form of education.[8]

Yang Qichang regards the early establishment by the Mu family of private Confucian education as the beginning of a long tradition of Han "advanced" (*xianjin*) influence on the Naxi and, more importantly, as a

---

6. E.g., Yang Qichang 1987; *YMJFG* 1992; Zhang Daqun 1988b.

7. See, e.g., Yang Qichang 1987 and *LNZG*. The amount of published material concerning education among the Naxi is limited compared to that concerning the Tai. This partly reflects the fact that Naxi are not considered to have specific problems regarding education. The Naxi in Lijiang have a long history of Han influence, established Chinese education, and a good record of educational attainment. Therefore most of the published material about education of the Naxi in Lijiang deals with historical development.

8. See also Borthwick 1983: 1–38 for a description of the different kinds of premodern schools in China.

demonstration of how willing the Naxi have always been to learn from "more advanced cultures" (Yang Qichang 1987: 29). This view is very common among both Han and Naxi scholars in China writing Naxi history. It expresses a deep-rooted belief in the civilizing effect of Confucian education while establishing "Han culture" (*Hanzu de wenhua*) as the most developed and civilized form of culture in China. As early as the Ming dynasty, the members of the Mu lineage were praised in a chronicle for their ability to study and absorb Confucian ethics: "Of all hereditary chiefs in Yunnan, those from the Lijiang Mu lineage are the foremost in knowledge of *The Book of Odes* [Shi jing] and *The Canon of History* [Shi shu] and in observation of rites and ceremonies" (quoted in Zhang Daqun 1988c: 78). During the Ming it also became common practice for each *tusi* family in Yunnan to send one son to the Imperial Academy (Guozijian). In 1404 there were twenty-eight sons of Yunnan *tusi* studying and living in Beijing, the imperial capital (*YMJFG* 1992: 43).

In the year 1700 a Han scholar from Shandong (who claimed to be one of Confucius's descendants) was sent to Lijiang Prefecture as a vice-magistrate. He started Lijiang Prefectural School (Lijiang Fuxue) while forcing the Mu *tusi* to "voluntarily" pay for the establishment of a charitable school (Yang Qichang 1987:29). Yang Qichang emphasizes this event as the first break in the Mu monopoly on Confucian education. According to all Chinese sources, it was, however, the introduction of the system of *gaitu guiliu* in Lijiang in 1723 that increased the number of Confucian schools and facilitated the spread (although still very limited) of knowledge of the Confucian classics and Chinese characters. More generally, the local hereditary chiefs' loss of official power to Qing bureaucrats is believed to have had a positive effect on the development of education and the cultural level (*wenhua shuiping*) of the Naxi. *Gaitu guiliu* is praised for having contributed directly to the modern project of creating a Chinese state encompassing territories along the periphery of the empire and for facilitating successful "unification of the nationalities."[9]

The newly appointed Qing officials gradually took measures to establish charitable schools and promote the training of teachers for them. Dismissal of local hereditary chiefs was commonly followed by establishment of a pre-

9. See, e.g., Yang Qichang 1987; *LNZG* 1986; and Zhang Daqun 1988b.

fectural school where natives could participate in Confucian education together with Han students.[10] Guan Xuexuan, an official and scholar from Jiangxi, was especially influential in expanding Confucian education in Lijiang. During the first years of the Qianlong period (1736–95) he established education of teachers for charitable schools in Lijiang Prefecture's three academies (in Xueshan, Yuhe, and Tianji) and secured economic support for teachers' salaries. Within a few years he had initiated seventeen charitable schools in Lijiang. Furthermore, he issued a decree warning officials that they would be punished if they did not send their sons to Chinese schools and see to it that commoners did the same (Yang Qichang 1987: 29).

Due to the shortage of schools and lack of central political control, this kind of edict was hardly possible to enforce, as Yang points out (Yang Qichang 1987: 29–30). After the hereditary chiefs lost their monopoly on political control, participation in Confucian education and local exams became increasingly relevant for upward social mobility at the local level, and the respect for Confucian education that was common among the Han (even when it did not lead to higher positions in society) seems to have been gradually taken over by the local Naxi elite. The Mu family, who were already familiar with Confucian learning and who dressed, married, and buried their dead in accordance with Han custom, became increasingly concerned with their male offspring's level of Confucian education. Most sent their sons to private Confucian schools, which remained the most important centers for elementary Confucian learning in Lijiang until the twentieth century.

The new charitable schools constituted the first attempt to include commoners in Lijiang in the world of Confucian learning, but, as in the rest of empire at the time, participation was most likely extremely low. There were still very few schools, and it would have been difficult for the educators to reach the majority of Naxi peasants in the eighteenth century and convince them that their sons needed knowledge of Chinese characters and Confucian ethics. Furthermore, local bureaucrats and officials were not necessarily very enthusiastic or dedicated in their attempts to spread education to commoners. Between the time of *gaitu guiliu* in 1723 and the end of the Qing dynasty in 1911, seven people from Lijiang passed the highest imperial examination, the *jinshi;* more than sixty took the degree of *juren* by pass-

10. See, e.g., Liu Guangzhi 1993: 36.

ing the provincial examination; and more than 140 passed the preliminary examinations.[11]

One of the most well-known Qing advocates of charitable schools was Chen Hongmou, who initiated seven hundred in Yunnan alone between 1733 and 1737 in order to provide education in rural and peripheral areas (*YMJFG* 1992: 46). In Lijiang Prefecture there were twenty-two charitable schools in 1736 and thirty-one in 1895 (CLNAC 1995: 5). They were funded by renting out land owned by the schools, and although the schools in principle were free, students provided economic support for the teachers. The basic aim of the education itself was, in William Rowe's words, to "bring about the understanding of moral principles through familiarization with Chinese characters" (Rowe 1994: 435). Literacy was promoted first of all for its presumed capacity to transform culture rather than for its practical values. The basic primer in the curriculum designed by Chen Hongmou himself for charitable schools was *Elementary Learning* (Xiao xue) by the Song Neo-Confucianist Zhu Xi. However, in Lijiang the charitable-school students apparently studied the same primers as students in the private Confucian schools, namely *The Trimetrical Classic* (Sanzijing), *The Hundred Family Names* (Baijiaxing), and *The Thousand Character Text* (Qianziwen) for beginners. These were the most common primers in elementary education all over China from the thirteenth to the twentieth century; for their basic education, children were expected to memorize the approximately two thousand characters in these primers (Woodside and Elman 1994: 553).[12]

The most common form of basic Confucian education in Lijiang was conducted in private Confucian schools, most of which were found among the Naxi in the town of Lijiang and the surrounding villages. I have not heard of private Confucian schools among other ethnic groups in Lijiang, and to my knowledge all *sishu* teachers in Lijiang were Naxi. These schools were normally started by a prestigious, and often poor, learned local in his own home or in a local temple. Although private Confucian education generally was weakened during the Republican period (1911–49), at least four or five *sishu* in

---

11. Only the *jinshi* examination, which was taken in Beijing, made one eligible for a higher office in the imperial administration. See, e.g., Zhu Weizheng 1992 on the imperial examination system.

12. See also Rawski 1979.

Lijiang Town continued into the early 1950s. In the town of Lijiang only one former *sishu* teacher (a Naxi) is still alive. He is now ninety years old and recalled,

> I started as a teacher when I was twenty-four [in 1929]. I started a *sishu* in our own house, where my father had also taught. I had many students, perhaps eighty, but after six years the headmaster of the public primary school in Lijiang asked me to become a teacher there instead. Then I closed down my *sishu* and the students went elsewhere to study. It was easier to be a teacher in a public school. I had to teach fewer hours and taught fewer students in a day.

In Teacher Yang's *sishu*, students were boys between the ages of ten and twenty, and he usually had between fifty and seventy students at a time. They learned the reading primers by heart and recited them in class. Some studied for less than a year, whereas others continued as long as ten years. According to my interviews, all *sishu* teachers were local Naxi scholars who used Naxi language when explaining things to their students, and recited texts in the local Chinese dialect (mostly called "Hanhua" by interviewees). There were no courses in mathematics or other nonliterary subjects. However, Teacher Yang recalls how he, on his own initiative, started to teach texts written in the modern vernacular written language (*baihua*) in addition to the common primers and classics. During the Republican period, with the increase in public schools, it became harder to make a living as a *sishu* teacher. Teacher Yang had the advantage of having learned classical Chinese as well as vernacular in a public school, and therefore his school became very popular.

A sixty-nine-year-old Naxi retired teacher, who was a student in two different *sishu* in the 1930s, recalled,

> After two years [in 1935], my parents moved me to Teacher Yang's *sishu* because Teacher Yang taught the "new learning" [*xin xue*]. They thought it was useful. There were between fifty and sixty students, and we learned vernacular as well as classical Chinese [*guwen*]. On the top floor those at the highest level studied classical Chinese. Downstairs we studied the new books: "Man, a man, a man sings. . . . " All students were boys, and the wages for the teacher came from fixed presents we had to give at festivals.

33

When we gave the presents we had to bow [*koutou*] to the teacher and his wife. Afterwards we always got something to eat. For the Dragon Boat Festival [Duanwujie] we had to give two silver yuan. It was really a lot of money—just imagine, you could buy four chickens for that kind of money.

Even though we lack exact information about the number of schools functioning in different periods during Qing, as well as the number of students and teachers, there is no doubt that Confucian education was well represented in Lijiang compared to most other non-Han areas of Yunnan (the Bai region of Dali, bordering Lijiang Prefecture, being one exception). However, Alexander Woodside reminds us that the number of schools, as reported in local gazetteers, is not necessarily a useful parameter for measuring the influence of Confucian education: most charitable schools existed only for a short time, they often lacked funds, and, although they often were free, most parents had no incentive to send their children there. In addition, many Qing officials were against the spread of education to lower strata of society, fearing that literacy might produce local status ambitions and shake the legitimacy of the bureaucratic class (Woodside 1992: 30). Local support for the schools was in no way comparable, for example, to that for Islamic or Buddhist schools in surroundings where they were part of a local, traditional, religious pattern. The education of boys in the Buddhist monasteries of Sipsong Panna is one example of religiously founded education with great popular support.

Through my interviews in Lijiang, I tried to obtain an impression of how widespread Confucian education was before 1949 and, in particular, what status Confucian education had among the Naxi. Not surprisingly, the differences between the town of Lijiang and the rest of Lijiang County were immense. In the countryside, peasants were not very motivated to send their children to school. Still, the Naxi peasants living on the Lijiang plain had several *yixue* and *sishu,* unlike other minorities such as Lisu, Nuosu, Tuo'en, Miao, and Premi, who lived higher up in the mountains. According to interviews with older Naxi from the town of Lijiang and the countryside, Chinese Confucian education had a high status among the Naxi. Although most people did not send their children to school, either because it was too expensive or because they simply preferred that their sons work at home, the families who *did* have a son attending a Confucian school were highly esteemed by the other villagers. Of course, this was especially so in the town of Lijiang, where the influence of Han language and Confucian culture was most pervasive. One retired Naxi headmaster, who had himself been to public middle school while attending a *sishu* in the evenings and on holidays, told about the status of Confucian education among the Naxi in the town of Lijiang:

> Oh, it was really a burden for a family to have a son in school. But the Naxi wanted at least one son to go to school, even if the family was poor. When a Naxi couple got a boy, the mother would carry him on her back when he was one month old, to go to the market square [in Lijiang Town] to buy him a book, a pen, and some ink. This was kept until the child was old enough to start in school. It was an expression of the parents' hope that their son would study.

Almost all of my Naxi interviewees above the age of sixty-five agreed that when they were young, it was prestigious to participate in Confucian education. Many recalled their parents' and grandparents' respect for local Confucian scholars. At the same time, since most of them came from families with a tradition of sending at least one son to school, it is possible that they exaggerated the commoners' respect for Confucian schools and students — an exaggeration that might have been further reinforced by the tendency of Naxi today to present "love of learning" (*ai xuexi*) as a significant Naxi characteristic.

The relatively few Naxi who underwent Confucian education were familiarized with Confucian family virtues, which were based upon strictly hierarchic patriarchal power, and they received instruction in rituals concerning burial, weddings, ancestor worship, and so forth. Their instructors were teachers who were themselves scholarly trained Naxi enjoying prestige among the formerly royal Mu family and who were respected by the Han imperial representatives in Lijiang. It is impossible today to determine the precise influence that Confucian education in the eighteenth and nineteenth centuries had on the Naxi and on their relationship to the Han. Even though such education probably played an important role in spreading Confucian values concerning burial, filial piety, and ancestor worship, it is clear that the Naxi also continued to worship their own spirits, speak their own language, and support their *dongba*. However, to the Naxi in the town of Lijiang in particular, and to a much lesser degree in the remoter parts of Lijiang, Confucian education gradually became synonymous with prestigious learning, even when it did not (as in most cases) provide any political or economic power.

THE FIRST MODERN SCHOOLS

Education in the frontier regions of the Qing empire came into focus in the early twentieth century when the government tried to strengthen its control in response to various uprisings and to British attempts to expand into Yunnan and Tibet through Burma and India. In Yunnan, where at least one third of the population was estimated to be non-Han, the Bureau of Education in Border Regions, the first such administrative unit ever, was set up in 1909 (Liu Guangzhi 1993: 68). One of the purposes of this department was to promote new schools in the border regions of Yunnan in order to facilitate integration of these areas into the empire, and therefore 128 new, free "native simple literacy schools" were established there by the end of the Qing dynasty.

Lijiang Prefecture had no such schools, probably because they were considered unnecessary: first, Lijiang did not border the most politically sensitive areas of British Burma, and second, Chinese education was already relatively well-developed in Lijiang.[13] After the founding of the Republic, between 1912 and 1915, the government quickly changed the "native simple literacy schools" into normal lower elementary schools. Generally, the late and weakening Qing empire left the task of promoting education on the periphery of Yunnan to local administrators and educators. Therefore local development of Chinese education depended upon local elites to create non-Confucian Chinese schools. In Lijiang such an elite existed, and the course of educational development, including the problems during the late Qing, resembled to a large extent the situation in many Han areas.

All Chinese sources agree that the real break with traditional Confucian education in Lijiang followed the reforms of 1903 and the abolition of the imperial examination system in 1905. At this time the three former academies in Lijiang Prefecture were changed into primary and higher primary

---

13. Schools were started in Yongchang (today's Baoshan), Dehong, Yongde, Lianma, Puer, and Lancang Districts. Sipsong Panna was still on the extreme periphery of the empire and beyond the Qing administration's practical control. The government started only a few literacy schools there.

schools (*xiaoxuetang*), and many charitable schools became lower primary schools. However, only more thorough research will reveal to what degree these transformations were of content and form as well as name. We know that the former Xueshan Academy changed in 1905 into Xueshan Primary School. The teachers stayed, and by 1907 the school had eighty-six boy students and six teachers who had received additional training in modern subjects such as history, geography, and drawing (CLNAC 1995: 6). In 1907 the local government also started the first two lower primary schools for girls (*nüzi chu xiaoxuetang*) and twenty village primary schools offering five years of study. Some of the schools were started in Buddhist lamaseries (Fuguo, Zhiyun, and Wenfeng temples) with the lamas as students.

From 1905 the government decided that each prefecture should set up a middle school, but due to problems of finance this was impossible in many poor minority areas. However, in Lijiang Town the prefecture's first middle school, Lijiang Prefecture Middle School (Lijiang Fu Zhongxuetang) was started in 1905 under the Han magistrate Peng Jizhi from Hunan, in cooperation with He Gengji, a Naxi who had passed a high imperial civil service examination and became the first head of the school. Money for opening the new school came from fines, mainly imposed on the lamas from Dongzhulin Lamasery (near Weixi) after they had instigated a riot in 1903 against a nearby Catholic missionary station.[14] Tax revenues from a new annual horse and mule market provided the income for continuing expenses of the school. The size of the middle school at this time was small compared to the vast area it covered. In the beginning the school had two classes: a middle school class for male students recruited from counties throughout the prefecture[15] (five years of study) and a class for primary school teachers (four years of study). Most of the students were sons of Han officials, leading merchant families, and officials from the Naxi royal Mu family. The objective of the

---

14. According to Chinese historical sources, the lamas had accused the local Christians and officials of oppressing Buddhism and supporting foreign religion. This caused a popular uprising by the local population, and the government responded by sending armed forces to suppress the rebels. Finally, the magistrate of Lijiang Prefecture, Peng Jizhi, investigated the case and concluded that the government had handled it improperly. He ordered a withdrawal of government forces but nevertheless fined the lamas (see Li Shizong 1988: 65).

15. At this time Lijiang Prefecture comprised Heqing, Jianchuan, Zhongdian, Weixi, and Lijiang Counties.

school was to provide a regular secondary education based on Chinese and Western knowledge—an education that would enable the most qualified to continue studies in higher education and the rest to fill jobs as teachers, local administrators, and so forth (Li Shizong 1988: 65). Curriculum was arranged according to national regulations, including a vocational course in mining technique and courses in psychology and education for the primary school teachers. There were no special courses on the Chinese classics, or on composition of the traditional eight-part essays so crucial in the former civil-service examinations. Thus, the curriculum was profoundly different from that of the Confucian academies. Teachers and administrators connected to the school actively promoted modern and national ideas. In 1907 some of them started the first newspaper in Yunnan published in the vernacular language, which reformers promoted as essential for the emergence of a population with modern scientific knowledge. The new *Lijiang Vernacular Newspaper* (Lijiang baihua bao) contained articles about reform, science, and national policy.

In conjunction with Lijiang's first middle school, the government also started Lijiang Prefecture Higher Primary School (Lijiang Fu Gaodeng Xiaoxuetang). According to He Rugong, only a few "enlightened" (*kaiming*) parents from the township of Lijiang sent their sons to this school voluntarily. He Rugong recalls the period after the school was started, when the government required that rural districts send a few boys to the school according to the number of families. The local population strongly resisted this regulation, fearing that children at the school would be "pulled away by the Han" (He Rugong 1988: 97). Furthermore, many Naxi regarded it as most improper and indecent that children in the school would sit while the teacher was standing. To make the school more attractive, the administration decided to provide pupils with three free meals a day and a set of clothes for each season.

The local Naxi's reactions to the modern schools were similar to those of many Han in rural areas, who also were not easily convinced of the utility of modern learning and continued to prefer the well-established *sishu*.[16] Still, it is somewhat surprising that Naxi in Lijiang expressed fear that their sons would

16. See, e.g., Thoegersen 1994: 38–40.

be absorbed by the Han in the higher primary school when they were already used to education based on Chinese language, Chinese classics, and Confucian ethics. One major reason for the objection may have been that villagers for the first time were compelled to send boys to the school. Furthermore, the Confucian schools at this time were apparently to a large degree considered to be "the Naxi people's own schools," where high-status knowledge was transmitted by highly respected local Naxi teachers who instructed in Naxi and recited primers and Chinese classics in the local Chinese dialect. In the newly established modern-style schools, many teachers were Han from outside, all lessons were taught in Chinese, and some of the subjects taught were incomprehensible to most of the population.

While modern schools slowly gained ground in Lijiang, *sishu* education continued to play a role until the 1950s, as in many Han areas. While gradually (especially since the Republic) more and more pupils began attending public schools, many (especially those of learned families) continued to attend a *sishu* in the evenings and on holidays. One former student from a *sishu* recalled being moved by his parents to a public school because his uncle was a teacher there: "The other pupils stayed in the *sishu*. Many people still thought that the only real scholarship [*xuewei*] was classical studies. The 'new learning' was not really considered worth anything." Before the Republican period, institutionalized education still reached only a small part of the multiethnic population of Lijiang Prefecture. In spite of the decrees ordering that charitable schools be replaced by modern-style elementary schools, many schools were unable to modernize; teachers were not trained and funds were scarce. The local population was either not motivated to release sons from duties at home (there was no question of girls attending school) or preferred the familiar and highly valued schools for classical learning. Since statistics concerning population and school enrollment in this period are uncertain, it is impossible to determine the percentage of school-aged boys who attended school. A rough estimate, based upon population statistics from 1911 and the recorded number of pupils in primary schools, is that approximately one-third of school-aged boys attended school. Considering that the majority of pupils were in Lijiang Town and only a small minority in the surrounding rural areas, this figure is rather high. I conclude that by the end of the Qing dynasty, Lijiang already resembled many Han areas with respect to the number of schools and students. However, since many boys attended school for only a short period of time, this does not necessarily indicate a high level of literacy.[17]

Christian missionary schools have been described as the first modern schools in China (e.g., Cleverley 1991). There were quite a few of these in Yunnan, but they were never very important among the Naxi in Lijiang (or among the Tai in Sipsong Panna).[18] Missionaries had stations in Lijiang Prefecture, but according to Peter Goullart, they did not play a major role among the Naxi. Goullart met a missionary couple in the early 1930s who considered the Naxi (and Tibetans) to be a hindrance to their missionary efforts. Most of their converts were Lisu, but in Lijiang Town they were mostly Han from Sichuan (Goullart 1955: 81). There was a missionary primary school (run primarily by Dutch missionaries) in Lijiang Town during the 1930s and 1940s. I met only one Naxi who had attended this school as a child. He remembered how all students (mainly Bai and Naxi) were taught exclusively in English according to *The Goldfinch Story Book* and that several of the pupils studied in the local *sishu* during holidays.

REPUBLICAN EDUCATION: THE NATIONAL MESSAGE AND THE CONCERN FOR EDUCATION IN BORDER REGIONS

By the twentieth century the Naxi had adopted Confucian education as part of their own culture and daily life. Educational change in Lijiang had largely followed the changes in the more central parts of the Chinese empire and, later, the Republic, and locally was the result of interventions by Naxi (rather than Han) intellectuals, scholars, and bureaucrats. Confucian schools became the focus of attention for parents who wanted (and could afford) an education for one or several sons. Thus, the Naxi accepted to a large extent that education was equivalent to the study of Confucian texts in Chinese and train-

17. Evelyn Rawski (1979) has made the most comprehensive study of popular literacy in China during the Qing dynasty. She refers to significant variations in literacy not only between rural and urban areas, but also among rural areas. See also Thoegersen 1994 on school attendance during the Qing and the Republic in the Han Zouping County.

18. See, e.g., Enwall 1994 and Diamond 1996 on the importance of missionary education among the Miao.

ing in Confucian morality, behavior, and rituals. This may explain why it was relatively easy for the Naxi to later accept the dominance of new forms of education based on Chinese language, history, and culture.

Primary and Secondary Schools in Lijiang

The keypoint secondary school in Lijiang today, Lijiang Prefecture Secondary School (Lijiang Diqu Zhongxue), traces its history back to 1905, when it was started as the first secondary school in Lijiang Prefecture.[19] This school underwent tumultuous changes, especially during the Republic, and was at times divided into several schools. Although changes of administration, funding, and name occurred, these did not necessarily influence curriculum. A new teacher education program, initially financed by the provincial government, was started in Lijiang in 1913 to train primary school teachers for all counties formerly under Lijiang Prefecture. The program taught two classes of students: one for five years (as recommended in the 1912 education plan) and one for six years.[20] As Li Shizong points out, graduates from this school could hardly fill all of the teaching positions in the primary schools within the immense area of the former Lijiang Prefecture. Consequently, despite this central teacher education, teaching in many countryside primary schools continued to be based on memorizing Confucian texts (Li Shizong 1988: 65). Therefore, the government added a special one-year teachers training course, to which all the counties were expected to send graduates from higher primary schools. Since the provincial government financed the new teachers school, county governments decided to use their surplus revenues for new primary schools in the major townships in Lijiang and for a new boarding school: the Cooperative Secondary School of the Six Counties Lijiang, Heqing, Jianchuan, Zhongdian, Weixi, and Lanping (Liu Xian Lianhe Zhongxue), which replaced Lijiang Prefecture Secondary School. As the name suggests, the secondary school covered a huge area, and although for a time it coexisted with teacher education, short-lived vocational

19. Today Lijiang Prefecture includes Lijiang, Ninglang, Huaping, and Yongsheng Counties, from all of which the school accepts students.
20. I have not been able to trace the reason for this difference in length of schooling. It is possible that it lies in variations in the students' level of primary school education.

education, and another secondary school established in 1917, education beyond primary school level was still rare in Lijiang during the Republican period.

In its beginning, the Cooperative Secondary School was connected to the teachers school in Lijiang, and, resources being scarce, the school offered only one four-year class in secondary school education. The head of the school was educated in Japan, and the curriculum followed the national plan emphasizing military exercise. All students paid a school fee, and most in the secondary school still were from relatively wealthy merchant or government families. The age of the students was quite high, between fifteen and twenty-six, comparable to that of some of the teachers (Yang Shangzhi 1988: 80; Liang Jiaji 1988: 83).

He Rugong was one of the few Naxi who attended the Cooperative Secondary School. From his descriptions we learn that students and parents primarily regarded the secondary school as a step (an expensive one) toward a prestigious—but, for most, unattainable—university degree: "[Students] thought that it was more difficult to attend a higher school than to reach the sky, and if you could not go to a university, what would then be the use of learning English, mathematics, physics, and chemistry?" (He Rugong 1988: 100). Regulations of school life and behavior at the Cooperative Secondary School were to a large degree modeled on Japanese and European conventions. This was a result of the education and experiences of the people involved in developing education in Lijiang rather than of any firm control by the central government.[21] Reflecting the Japanese educational system, all students participated in military exercises, each with a rusty rifle (most of which were defective, as He dryly remarks). He Rugong recalls that the school had fixed rules about how and where to place everything: blankets had to be folded "like pieces of *doufu* [bean curd]," dormitories were inspected every day, traditional long fingernails were not allowed, and students were not to leave

21. Contacts between the central government and Yunnan were very weak when Yunnan was ruled by Tang Zhiyao between 1911 and 1928, and central interference into Yunnan's political, military, and economic affairs increased only gradually (with resistance from the provincial government under Long Yun) after 1939 (see Solinger 1977; and Dreyer 1976: 29–30).

the school (He Rugong 1988: 99). In his matter-of-fact style, He also describes how all students were obliged to speak Chinese and were fined for each sentence spoken in Naxi or Bai.[22]

The Cooperative Secondary School functioned until 1925, when administrative changes put a stop to the funding of the school by revenues from the local mule and horse market. Fighting between warlords in Yunnan also resulted in increased military expenditures, causing many schools to close down. The last class of the Cooperative Secondary School managed to graduate on private funds before the school finally closed in 1926 and transferred all of its equipment to the Third Secondary School of Yunnan Province (Yunnan Sheng Li Di San Zhongxue).[23] In the beginning, the Third Secondary School enrolled one new class a year in a four-year course. A national education conference held in Kunming in 1922 decided to change the four-year secondary school system to three years of junior and three years of senior secondary school, and in 1931 the school added senior secondary school education (Li Shizong 1988: 70).

Funding of secondary school education in Lijiang was unstable due to tumultuous political and military conditions. After a complete stop of provincial financial support for the school in 1928, mainly due to the fighting among warlords, the provincial education department decided in 1929 to spend revenues from tobacco tax on education. Between 1931 and 1940 the government ensured a separate and fixed budget for education relying on the tobacco tax revenues (*YMJFG* 1992: 8). The Third Secondary School in Lijiang benefited from this, as did other provincial schools, when general investment in education rose. This situation changed again when tobacco tax revenues were transferred to the budget of the central government. From that time on, Yunnan relied on support from the central government for education. Several provincial secondary and primary schools were closed or transferred to the county level, and special economic support for students from border areas

22. This kind of direct suppression of minority languages in schools was also common all over Europe, in the United States, and in the various colonies where nondominant ethnic groups (often majorities in their own areas) were involved in education. For example, in Taiwan, Mandarin, or Standard Chinese, was the only accepted language in schools until 1988, and in Turkey teaching Kurdish is still prohibited.

23. This name was changed in 1934 to Yunnan Provincial Lijiang Secondary School

was canceled (*YMJFG* 1992: 13). Furthermore, runaway inflation, bombing in the Yunnan-Vietnam and Yunnan-Burma border areas after the Japanese occupation of Vietnam in 1940, and the invasion of Yunnan in 1942 caused most schools in these areas to close down.[24]

Before that happened, the central government had established three state-run teachers schools (*guo li shifan xuexiao*) in Yunnan—in Zhaotong in 1939, Dali in 1941, and Lijiang in 1942. These schools recruited mainly minority students, and graduates were distributed as teachers in Yunnan, Sichuan, (the former province of) Xikang, and Guizhou border areas. A new County Secondary School (Xian Li Zhongxue) had been started in Lijiang in the late 1930s, as well as special adult classes and higher primary classes in several districts. Moreover, the central government financed elementary schools in the lower administrative units of *bao* (Yang Qichang 1987: 31).

During the 1920s the ideas of the May Fourth Movement on modern science and democracy increasingly influenced the secondary school in Lijiang. Though Lijiang was quite isolated from central China, several newly recruited teachers were Naxi who had studied in Beijing and participated in the May Fourth Movement.[25] These young teachers advocated exclusive use of the vernacular in school, introduced students to modern Chinese writers, and encouraged some of them to start a study group on modern literature, the New Lijiang Study Society (Xin Lijiang Dushu Hui).[26] The Society explicitly aimed at spreading modern literature and science in the border regions of Yunnan, and the young members (mostly Naxi) painted, wrote, and gave theatre performances in the schools in Lijiang Town (Li Shizong 1988: 69).

After the news of the Japanese invasion of northeast China reached Lijiang in 1931, military exercise and patriotic education of students were given even higher priority: teachers supported students who wished to go to the

---

(Yunnan Sheng Li Lijiang Zhongxue), seemingly without administrative consequences.

24. This included the teachers schools in Jinghong (Cheli) and Menghai (Fohai) in Sipsong Panna, which closed in 1943.

25. These Naxi teachers included Fang Guoyu and the He brothers, He Zhijian and He Zhijun, both of whom later became heads of the school.

26. The name was later changed to the Border Bell Study Society (Bian Duo Dushu Hui). The bell (*duo*) was a kind used in ancient times for official proclamations and in modern times in other May 4 contexts (e.g., the journal *Women's Bell*).

front, military training was intensified, traditional Naxi and Bai songs were rewritten into anti-Japanese songs, and students were organized to perform anti-Japanese plays in villages and at the mule and horse market (Li Shizong 1988: 71). According to Li Shizong, this period was the zenith in the early history of the secondary school, partly due to the teachers' and students' common interest in uniting against an intruding enemy. Li also points to the high educational level of the staff, which included several Han scholars invited from other provinces. Considering its geographic siting in a non-Han area, the school had a high number of qualified graduates when in 1941 twenty students out of thirty managed to pass the examination for higher education, with two even allowed into a preparatory class for students going abroad (Li Shizong 1988: 73). Li gives special credit to the strict discipline of the school for its scholarly success. His comments, together with a few former students' accounts and memories of the school, illustrate how discipline was enforced: every evening the names of all the students were called out so that instructors could comment on each student's performance, and corporal punishment in the form of thrashing or whipping was liberally inflicted. In 1936 the school had introduced a new uniform fit not only for studying but for working in the fields or raising pigs as well. The short jacket and trousers reflected the ideology of an education significantly different from the traditional Confucian one—an education that ideally would produce citizens capable of transferring their scholarly knowledge into a productive society.

During the Republic the number of schools and students in Lijiang increased steadily. Although written sources tell us very little about how primary schools in Lijiang changed during this period, many older Naxi have memories of their time in the "citizen schools" (*guomin xuexiao*).[27] At the end of the Qing dynasty in 1911, the county reported thirty-seven primary schools in Lijiang with more than a thousand students. In 1937 this figure had increased to 230 schools (CLNAC 1995: 6 and 10). Most of these were lower

27. In 1923, in accordance with national policy, citizen schools were changed into lower primary schools (*chuji xiaoxue*) and higher primary schools (*gaoji xiaoxue*). The length of study was supposed to be four plus two years, but in Lijiang until 1938 the higher primary school offered three years of study. This first extra year of higher primary was meant to prepare students for the real higher primary study. Beginning in 1940 full primary schools in townships were called *zhongxin xuexiao* and lower primary schools in villages were *baoguomin xuexiao*.

primary schools spread throughout the villages on the plateaus, and there were few schools and students among the peoples living in the mountains. As mentioned before, figures suggest that school enrollment at the beginning of the Republic was at least as high as in many Han counties. Very few girls attended school in Lijiang at this time. In 1923 the government once again emphasized that four years of primary school education should be compulsory. However, there was no basis in Lijiang for accomplishing this, and all older interviewees (and written sources) agreed that primary school attendance was still limited, not the least because extremely few girls ever started school. When male interviewees were asked about school enrollment in their village at the time when they themselves went to school, most replied that almost all children attended school for a few years. However, when asked if this included girls, the answer was always that no or very few girls went to school. It seems that the only reason for a couple to send a daughter to school was a lack of sons: "Almost all children went to school . . . except the girls, of course. There were two in my class. Parents considered the boys most important, and they sent the girls out to marry quite early. Only a family without sons would consider sending a daughter to school" (Naxi man, about sixty years old). The national education plan of 1912 had for the first time permitted coeducation of boys and girls in lower primary schools, while requiring the establishment of middle, vocational, and teachers schools for girls.[28] In 1913 the Lijiang government started the first elementary schools for girls, together with a special girls' class at the teachers school. Still, very few girls had the chance to attend these classes. Education among my female interviewees in Lijiang above the age of fifty-five was limited to a few who had attended short courses for eradicating illiteracy during the Republic or after 1949.

Most public primary schools possessed land that provided an income for the normal annual expenses, and in the countryside most parents gave presents to the teacher in lieu of wages. It was an economic burden to have a son at school, because parents had to pay while losing manpower in the fields. Moreover, because few pupils could continue on to higher primary school, not to mention secondary school, many parents considered education a waste

28. See also Borthwick 1983: 114–18 on education of girls in China before 1912, and Hayhoe 1992 for comments on female participation in education during the Republic.

of money. From 1914 onward the government outlined the curriculum in primary schools in Lijiang, and by 1931 standardized teaching materials had been published.[29] However, since most people in Lijiang were poor, students could often not afford books. The economic burden was one reason why private schools continued to exist in Lijiang as well as in Han areas all over China: they were more flexible with regard to length and time of study, and they offered a possibility of continued studies for those who had not passed the public examination. The *sishu* also offered supplementary education since public school teachers seldom taught the classical Chinese texts, although they had received some classical training (CLNAC 1995: 19).

In 1930, following the regulations laid down by the provincial government, the Lijiang Bureau of Education again tried to promote four years of compulsory education and order all primary schools to start a "common people's school" (*minzhong xuexiao*) for adult illiterates (CLNAC 1995: 40). All illiterates between sixteen and forty years of age were obliged to study from half an hour to two hours a day for at least six months. The most important subjects, apart from Chinese language, were mathematics and the study of Sun Yat-sen's Three Principles of the People for the salvation and unity of the Chinese nation: nationalism, democracy, and livelihood. Many people apparently participated in the literacy classes, but how much they actually learned (and remembered) is uncertain. In one Naxi village twelve kilometers from Lijiang Town, in 1934 the people started a common people's evening school where adults learned to read and write Chinese; some older villagers today proudly claim that their village has had no illiterates ever since. However, many older Naxi, particularly women, told me that although they had attended evening schools, they had quickly forgotten to read and write, simply because they never used these skills in daily life.

Generally speaking, school education in Lijiang was not very stable during the Republic. Many schools temporarily closed down or existed for only a short period. During the war of resistance against Japan, the government had less money to spend on education, and, due to the lack of grain, schools were no longer free to rent out land. After the defeat of Japan in 1945, the government suggested a new three-year plan for developing border area edu-

29. More details on curriculum are found in CLNAC 1995: 14. See also Rawski 1979: 173–80 on the general curriculum.

cation, and a short-lived attempt was made to restart former provincial schools in border areas. However, some estimated 1945 statistics, based on Yunnan archives, indicate the continued limitation of Republican Chinese education in these areas. Lijiang's estimated school attendance of 73 percent was higher than the provincial average (*YMJFG* 1992: 52), as compared to 1940, with 60 percent attendance in Lijiang (CLNAC 1995: 11). Both figures seem exaggerated, especially considering the low school participation of girls and the fact that school attendance for children in all of China in 1949 has been estimated at 25 percent (Cleverley 1991: 69). As for the number of Naxi students and literates, Peter Goullart reported that during the 1940s, although most Naxi in Lijiang Town spoke a bit of Chinese, he and his staff had problems finding assistants who could write Chinese. Goullart was puzzled that some teachers who were highly esteemed in the secondary school, as well as many local government officials and secretaries, could write only reports and letters "hardly worthy of comparison with a Chinese schoolboy's essays" (Goullart 1955: 23). According to a 1931 census from Lijiang, 3.6 percent of the male population and 0.2 percent of the female population in Lijiang County were literate (Rock 1947: 173).

Nationalist/Assimilationist Education

In 1913, following the Central Education Conference in 1912, the Lijiang government instructed teachers to teach *exclusively* in the "national language" (Mandarin; *guoyu*) and to try to reform and change the use of local languages. However, interviews show that this policy was often circumvented. Most interviewees who had been students in primary schools during the Republic recalled that teachers taught mostly in Naxi or at least used Naxi for explanations. Thanks to the education of local primary school teachers since the late Qing and the fact that many local teachers in Confucian schools had received extra training before their transfer into modern schools, most teachers in lower primary schools in the Republican period were Naxi.

Most interviewees remembered teachers instructing in Naxi during at least the first four years of primary school. However, the few Naxi who continued into higher primary school recalled being fined for speaking Naxi in class. In 1922 Lijiang's three first full primary schools were started, one of them in the village of Baisha. By the mid-1940s this school had grown to seventeen teachers and more than three hundred pupils. Students came from twelve nearby villages to the higher primary school. A former student estimated that about one-third of the graduates from his village school continued on to this higher primary school. Although all of the pupils and teachers were Naxi, only the Chinese language was allowed in school: "From fifth grade on we were taught only in the national language. We called Chinese [Hanyu] the 'national language' [*guoyu*] at that time. The teachers asked questions in Chinese, and if you answered in Naxi, or if the teacher just *heard* you speaking Naxi in the school, he would fine you. You would have to pay five fen." Former students from Yunnan Provincial Lijiang Secondary School during the 1930s and 1940s also recalled how all personal conversation among students (as well as in class) had to be conducted in Chinese. Yang Shangzhi remembered a sign hanging in the dormitory when he started as a fifteen-year-old student in 1930 saying, "Native language forbidden" (*Jinzhi tuyu*) (Yang Shangzhi 1988: 80). Zhao Lu, one of the few Bai students in Lijiang Secondary School, also recalled how students were punished for speaking Naxi. In principle the Bai were not allowed to speak their own language either, but since there were so few of them, two students were permitted to speak Bai together (Zhao Lu 1988: 90). Other rules clearly displayed the intention of erasing cultural and linguistic differences among the students while forcing assimilation with the Han. Li Ruoyu reported that in his own time as a student, the various ethnic groups at the school were instructed to dismantle previous prejudices against one another and live harmoniously together (Li Ruoyu 1988). Apart from insisting that students speak the language of the Han, the rule of the "three sames" (*san tong*) demanded that students "eat the same, live in the same way, and study the same." What to eat, how to live, and what to study were taken for granted in a context where modern education and way of life were seen as the property of a civilizing center represented by the Han race. By means of a proper education, the Han would ultimately improve the customs of the non-Han peoples, assimilate, and thereby civilize them. In this sense, early modern Chinese education continued the traditional Confucian belief in the modeling/civilizing effects of education, even though it broke with the traditional teaching of Confucian ethics.

Different decrees issued by the provincial government of Yunnan during the 1930s supported the national educational strategies of nationalism and assimilation. Each area still governed by a local hereditary chief was obliged to send two of his relatives to study at the expense of the government in Kunming. Increased efforts were to be made to recruit "barbarian" (*yi*)[30] children and adults for elementary schools through short courses, and specific quotas were set for the admission of non-Han students into schools in minority regions. In principle, the government granted financial aid to parents who agreed to send their children to school, but in most cases the money never reached peasant families. Teaching of the Han language was crucial, and the decree emphasized that local language was allowed in schools only when absolutely indispensable to helping children understand lessons in the first year of schooling.[31]

A decree from the provincial government in 1931 advocated the establishment of special primary schools for non-Han peoples in border regions, basic local teachers schools, and short-term vocational training. Four counties, one of them Lijiang, established two-year teacher-training courses, and between 1931 and 1940 these institutions educated some two hundred teachers (most non-Han) for primary schools in border and mountain areas (*YMJFG* 1992: 8).[32] Unlike other students, the future border teachers in Lijiang were completely subsidized by the government. Their curriculum was slightly moderated so that, for instance, they had no English lessons but instead a few lessons in the Tibetan script that would be more useful when, after graduation, they started new schools in border and mountain villages (Li Shizong 1988: 70). The central government in Nanjing, led by Chiang Kai-shek, adopted a highly politicized educational program with the purpose of strengthening border regions and incorporating them into the Republic of China. From 1942 primary schools strongly emphasized military training, and all former students during the Republic whom I interviewed remembered military training and the civics class (*gongmin ke*), focusing on Sun Yat-sen's Three Principles of the People as important parts of the curriculum.

30. In this decree the term *yi* was used to describe all peoples living in the border areas of Yunnan who were not Han.

31. Documents reprinted in *YMFG* 1992: 259–76.

32. The other counties that established special schools were Zhaotong, Puer, and Yongchang.

EDUCATION AFTER 1949

The Chinese Communist Party was active in Lijiang beginning in the mid-1940s. Based in Lijiang Secondary School, it provided students with weapons and started a Communist study group (Li Shizong 1988: 76). Li Shizong, an active Communist recruited at the school, recalled a mass meeting in Lijiang on 1 May 1949 of more than fifteen thousand people. Afterward all classes stopped, and about one hundred students from the secondary school were organized to participate in armed conflict against Nationalists who had fled into border areas, including Lijiang and Weixi. The CCP also prepared peasants for armed struggle and created several peasant literacy classes on basic Chinese and propagating Communist policy in villages (LNZG 1986: 21). When the Communists took charge in Lijiang in 1949, the new government wanted to restart primary and secondary schools. In August the two secondary schools and the teachers school were combined into one secondary school: Lijiang People's Secondary School (Lijiang Renmin Zhongxue), with about seven hundred students from all counties in former Lijiang Prefecture, and eighty employees. The school was renamed Lijiang Secondary School (Lijiang Zhongxue) in 1950 and remained the only full regular secondary school in Lijiang until 1970. It was reported in 1949 that Lijiang County had 39 full primary schools and 294 lower primary schools. There were 440 teachers and more than 13,800 students, virtually all from the Lijiang plain and almost none from villages in the mountains (Yang Qichang 1987: 31; and CLNAC 1995: 16).

In connection with the project of creating new scripts for scriptless minority *minzu* (promoted since the First National Conference on Minority Education in 1951), the Naxi were selected to receive a romanized script, since Naxi commoners did not use the *dongba* script (which had never been used for recording spoken Naxi). After a research team created a new script, some simple teaching material was compiled for eradicating illiteracy among adult Naxi. The script never gained widespread popularity, and today it is difficult to find any Naxi who know it.[33] It was taught only in Naxi villages considered very backward in terms of education and therefore not in Lijiang Town. Furthermore, Chinese culture and language had high status among many Naxi,

---

33. The majority of the Naxi I interviewed below the age of twenty-five did not even know this script existed.

and Naxi parents who wanted their children to get an education knew that upward social mobility was bound strictly to learning Chinese. Today another reason for the lack of interest in the romanized Naxi script is the revival of the *dongba* script and culture since the 1980s.

Thus, despite the creation of the new Naxi script, most schools in Lijiang in the 1950s continued to use Naxi spoken language only in the lower classes, Chinese in the higher classes, and Chinese script as the only written language. Many Naxi emphasized in interviews that although it was not official policy during the early 1950s, the teachers beyond lower primary school level continued to prohibit the use of the Naxi language in class. The main change of curriculum was that civics classes and military training were replaced with political lessons on Communist policy. Like the Nationalists, the new government was determined to use education to propagate nationalism, and in 1955 the Yunnan Bureau of Culture and Education issued a report that stressed the special need for "patriotic education" in Yunnan. The report pointed out that, living in border regions, many minority children lacked a "sense of the motherland" (*zuguo guannian*) and did not even know that they were Chinese (Zhongguoren).[34] Later, in 1963, the Ministry of Education informed the leaders of Yunnan, Guizhou, and Sichuan Education Bureaus of the urgent need to stress patriotic minority education, especially along the Burmese border, where "American spies wearing religious garments are operating secretly."[35]

During the 1950s a number of Naxi had been selected to receive short-term cadre training, preparing them for working in the new Communist local administration in what was later (in 1961) to become Lijiang Naxi Autonomous County. Mr. Zhang had graduated from the lower secondary school in Lijiang Town in 1942, and as a soldier in the People's Liberation Army, he was recruited for further minority cadre training in Sichuan:

We learned mostly about the development of society, about Engels's and Morgan's theories of human evolution. This was useful, because we had to prepare and participate in land reform work in minority regions. I was

---

34. "Report about Minority Education Work in the Coming Five Years in Yunnan," reprinted in *YMFG* 1992: 288–307.

35. Letter to heads of the Bureaus of Education of Yunnan, Guizhou, and Sichuan from the Ministry of Education, 13 April 1963, reprinted in *YMFG* 1992: 307–10.

the only Mosuo at the school . . . they did not call us Naxi at that time . . . and almost all of the other students were Han. They used to really look down upon us, so I was a bit embarrassed to be Mosuo. But I quickly realized that the cultural level of many Han was even lower than mine. Some of them would say in great surprise, "Oh, a minority [*shaoshu minzu*] who already knows this or that."

In 1953 Lijiang County established a special "literacy office" in Lijiang Town offering short-term (often only two-week) Chinese courses for local township cadres. Many local teachers in Lijiang also received brief training in CCP policy in order to adapt school education to the needs and ideology of the new government and to qualify them to participate in land reform and "improve the thoughts" (*sixiang gaizao*) of the people. Several teachers were sent to the new minority institutes and Kunming Teachers College during the 1950s and 1960s to be trained as local cadres. The minority cadres were the first (though definitely not the last) in Lijiang to learn about scientifically demonstrated ethnic differences; names of groups were consolidated in the practically irreversible naming of *minzu*, among which the Han were the clear majority, with more than 90 percent of the population. Moreover, students learned about Engels's and Morgan's theories of evolution applied to the *minzu* of China. The newly trained minority cadres returned as teachers, educators, and administrators all over Lijiang to spread this message of cultural and economic differences among *minzu* in combination with propagation of the national policy of uniting *minzu* and granting them equal rights in the new society. The differences among them were perceived as scientifically explainable, historically determined facts and not based on prejudice. Communists and Han Chinese were obliged and supposedly prepared to help the minorities eradicate these differences.

In 1957, just before the launching of the Great Leap Forward, Lijiang County reported a total of 285 primary schools.[36] Non-Han students made up 92.6 percent, of which 76 percent were Naxi, whereas 79.8 percent of teachers were non-Han, of which 68.5 percent were Naxi (Zhang Daqun 1988a: 61). Because education was relatively well established in Lijiang before 1949,

36. Of the 285, 240 were lower primary schools and forty higher; six classes for junior secondary education and twenty for senior.

the government was able to train and send out local, especially Naxi, teachers and secondary school graduates to start new schools in mountain areas. Although the number of Naxi attending secondary school was very low—only 0.51 percent between 1953 and 1956—this was second only to the Hui among minority groups (*YMJFG* 1992: 162). One of the few students who went to the secondary school in this period recalled that of the fifty students in his class, only two were girls.

Graduates from Han areas were continuously sent to Lijiang—and to other non-Han regions—to start schools, participate in setting up the government, and represent the CCP. Most of these were Han who regarded themselves as the vanguard of a civilizing movement and who for a variety of personal or political reasons wanted to work in a poor minority area. Some of those who stayed in Lijiang have now advanced to become headmasters, government officials, and Party leaders. One of them was Mr. Yang:[37]

When Mr. Yang Came to Lijiang

When I arrived here in 1958, this place [Lijiang Town] was very poor. There were no roads. There was electricity but no lights in the school or the houses. We teachers made fires ourselves and lived two or three together in a very small room. Still, compared to other minority areas, this place was quite good. I was a graduate of a teachers college, and not many minority areas had teachers with such an education. When we started here, we were twelve teachers—two or three locals, but most of us Han from the outside. The students were peasant children from this village [the outskirts of Lijiang Town] or children of county and prefectural cadres.

I came here with twenty others, and only three are still here. At that time it was most glorious to go to the poorest areas. You gained status by doing so. I wanted to go to Ludian, which was poorer than Lijiang, but they did not let me. Of course, we also had another way of thinking: "If there is no lion in the mountains, the monkey is the emperor"! And the more bitterness you ate, the higher the position you would get as a cadre or leader. Most of the people who came in the 1950s became teachers or higher cadres in the county or prefectural government. Now we have fos-

37. This is a pseudonym, as are the names of other interviewees.

tered so many minority cadres and teachers here that very few need to come from the outside.

During the first and the second year here, the local teachers often had to explain in Naxi. I taught in the higher grades and never spoke Naxi. [After thirty-seven years in Lijiang, Mr. Yang still is not able to speak or understand Naxi.] As a rule, we spoke as much Chinese as possible. If you do not teach in Chinese, it is no good. After about 1962 teachers never spoke Naxi. By then school education here was more developed, so it was no longer necessary. More and more Han people came to Lijiang, so more and more Naxi spoke Chinese. They do not have a script, so we could not offer bilingual education anyway. We always had two ways of thinking about this question and sometimes one was stronger than the other. The first is that in school, children should basically learn Chinese. The other is that we have to maintain the minority languages and scripts, but since the Naxi do not have a script this question is not so important here. Of course we also have to maintain minority traditions and festivals, but learning Chinese is still number one—otherwise no communication is possible. If the Tai learn only Tai, how can they communicate? If you leave Lijiang, or Yunnan, you have to learn Chinese—otherwise, what will you do? Language is a tool and if you do not know how to use this tool, you have no means of communication.

Mr. Yang arrived in Lijiang during the Great Leap Forward, when education was regarded not as an autonomous social sector, but as an integral part of the continuing revolution. At this time the government aimed at decentralizing schools and advocated the establishment of lower primary education in all villages. Though many villages in Lijiang were unable to establish primary schools, the number of small, local, *minban* (people-run) schools (often with only one teacher) increased.

After 1949 primary school education consisted of six years, divided into four years of lower and two years of higher primary school. Between 1953 and 1954, and again between 1961 and 1963, some primary schools in Lijiang were five-year schools. After 1969 all primary school education in Lijiang was five-year, and in 1979 the six-year system (four plus two) returned (CLNAC 1995: 14). In 1956 primary school education was divided into four years of lower and two years of higher primary school, following guidelines from the

Ministry of Education in 1955. To my knowledge, all *minban* schools in Lijiang at that time were lower primary schools. Due to the shortage of educated teachers, most new teachers in the villages were *minban* teachers—that is, they had no proper teacher education and most were graduates of lower secondary schools, though some had attended higher secondary school and others only higher primary school. The teachers in the twenty-two new agricultural secondary schools, which were started in the countryside of Lijiang in 1958, were mainly primary school teachers who had received a few months of extra training. Agricultural work occupied approximately half of the time in school, and political studies were prominent. Following the Great Leap's demand for industrial development, the government also started a vocational lower secondary school in Lijiang Town. Here students worked in factories half of the day (for which they received a small amount of subsistence money) and studied the other half.

As in the rest of China, most of Lijiang's peasants were organized into communes, and by September 1958 the 235 cooperatives had been combined into twenty-five People's Communes (*LNZG* 1986: 75). Interviewees from some of the poorest Nuosu, Lisu, Miao, and Tuo'en villages recalled that this did not have much bearing on their lives, because they were extremely poor. Even when schools were established in these villages, teachers had almost no students and had to work full-time in the fields to support themselves. According to reports, the number of lower primary classes had increased from 371 in 1951 to 630 in 1959. The number of higher primary school classes had increased from 42 to 179 during the same period. However, the total number of primary schools had increased only from 354 to 366. The officially reported number of students in primary schools had increased from 16,198 in 1951 to 26,156 in 1959 (CLNAC 1995: 16). According to interviews, the vast majority of pupils were still boys, though more girls were attending school for at least a few years.

Ideologically, the period of the Great Leap Forward and related campaigns did not leave much room for expressions of or tolerance of ethnic diversity. Chae-jin Lee has shown how the Rectification Campaign, focusing on "national unity and political centralization" rather than on "social diversity and ethnic autonomy," was carried out among Koreans in Yanbian. Textbooks in Korean were criticized and abolished for spreading local nationalism, and many Korean intellectuals and cadres were reproached for being chauvinist toward the Han (Lee 1986). The campaign against "local nationalism" was launched in 1957 and reached Lijiang by the end of 1959, when several minority cadres were severely reproached for promoting "local nationalism" and harming the "unity of the *minzu.*" Local teachers were criticized for promoting "local nationalism" via excessive use of local languages in education. Furthermore, many Naxi recalled how local festivals such as the important celebration of Sanduo (the Naxi guardian spirit) and other religious activities in the local temples were abolished. Others, such as a *dongba* from a small village in Lijiang County, recalled that "superstitious activities" such as *dongba* rituals already had been forbidden by work teams immediately after the Communist takeover. During the early 1960s, when the government faced the aftermath of the Great Leap Forward, policies concerning the education of minorities again became more open toward the use of minority languages. At the same time, the government called for a renewed standardization of education. In Lijiang, as in many other places, this resulted in the closing down of many *minban* schools, most of which were located in the poorest minority villages.

Education for Assimilation during the Cultural Revolution

In 1966 a new Cultural Revolution Work Team (Wenge Gongzuo Dui) in Lijiang gathered employees of secondary schools to carry out the Cultural Revolution. Many local students actively participated in this early phase of the Cultural Revolution, whereas others returned to their villages to participate in labor. A few months later, after the CCP's Tenth Plenum had outlined goals for the Cultural Revolution in sixteen points, several hundred students in Lijiang organized themselves as Red Guards. Most went to Beijing to see Chairman Mao, and when they returned, they divided into factions. Together with Red Guards who had come to Lijiang from other places in China, they struggled against teachers, school and government cadres, and, eventually, against one another.

At a mass meeting in Beijing in 1966, Lin Biao had launched a mass movement to attack the "four old" elements in Chinese society: old ideas, culture, customs, and habits. In Lijiang, as elsewhere, this triggered the Red Guards' destruction of temples, burning of *dongba* scriptures, smashing of old wall paintings and traditional instruments, and attacks on monks, *dongba,* and everybody else engaged in "feudal superstitious activities." Due to the gov-

ernment's relatively open attitude toward the minorities' cultural characteristics and practices in the early period after 1949, these now became obvious
targets. In many minority areas, such as Sipsong Panna, people regarded the
assaults on their cultural practices as crude expressions of Han suppression.
In Lijiang, which was well integrated into the state, some people clearly shared
this view, whereas many others believed that excessive left-wing policy in general, not Han chauvinism as such, was responsible for the misery. As one Naxi
woman remarked, "So many of the youngsters who came here to smash my
wooden carvings were Naxi. It would have been easier to bear if they had all
been Han from outside Lijiang."

In the high tide of the Cultural Revolution between 1966 and 1969, secondary schools in Lijiang hardly functioned. No new students were recruited,
and remaining students were busy participating in the revolution. Most teachers were sent to the countryside to work in the fields, or to Lijiang Town to
work in the few factories. However, in 1970 primary and secondary schools
entered a boom period all over Lijiang, and the Lijiang Normal School (Lijiang
Shifan Xuexiao) as well as the regular secondary school started to enroll new
students. The former dual system of regular and vocational/agricultural secondary schools had been criticized, so the majority of new secondary schools
were junior secondary classes "attached" to primary schools in production
brigades. Each commune also started classes for senior secondary education,
which recruited students recommended by the brigades.[38] The thirty-six secondary school classes (in three schools) reported in 1968 had increased to 121
classes (in twenty-five schools) by 1973, and the number of students in secondary schools in the communes was up by more than 100 percent.[39] The
number of primary schools in Lijiang increased by almost 40 percent in four
years, from 467 schools in 1969 (a figure similar to that of 1965) to 669 in
1973, and the number of students increased by 22 percent. This sudden increase
in the number of schools required many new teachers, and since there were
not nearly enough educated teachers, the number of *minban* teachers almost

38. Although every production team was supposed to establish a primary school during this time, 2,081 production teams within twenty-seven border counties in Yunnan did
not do so (*YMFG* 1992: 73). Interviews suggest that the reasons were that the villages in these
production teams were too poor, lacked teachers, and were so isolated that they were less
touched by the policies of the Cultural Revolution.

39. All figures here are from CLNAC 1995: 17.

tripled in this period. The majority of *minban* teachers in Lijiang today were recruited during this period. Many of them were happy to become teachers during the Cultural Revolution, because they did not have to work as hard as the peasants in the fields to achieve the same amount of work points.[40]

Most interviewees with experiences from the Cultural Revolution remembered that primary school attendance became much more common because most pupils did not have to walk far to attend school (because it was in the production brigade), schooling was completely free, and, above all, children did not earn work points (each family received a fixed amount of grain per child), so parents had nothing to lose economically by sending their children to school. When directly asked about their own educational experiences during the Great Leap Forward and the Cultural Revolution, most interviewees paraphrased the present official judgment of these periods as a time when education was "excessively left-wing," "too focused on quantity," and "wasting time on physical labor." Yet some put forward a comparison with present-day schooling, arguing that at that time it was at least free and easily accessible.

As for curriculum during the Cultural Revolution, primary schools and junior secondary schools taught mainly "Chairman Mao thought," mathematics, basic agriculture, revolutionary art, and military training. Normally, "poor and middle peasants" administered the schools, and it was common for an old and poor peasant or sometimes a soldier to come weekly to tell the pupils about the harsh times before Liberation in 1949. In the climate of disregard for minority languages, Chinese language was promoted for its ability to transmit the thoughts of Mao and, thus, promote socialist development in minority areas. Nevertheless, many interviewed Naxi teachers said that their method of teaching was to first read a text aloud in Chinese and then translate it into Naxi.

In senior secondary school, students all over the country were supposed to study the same theoretical essays by Mao: "On Practice," "On Contradiction," "On the Correct Handling of Contradictions among the People," "Where Do Correct Ideas Come From?" and "Speech at the National Conference of the Communist Party on Propaganda." One student who

40. Regular teachers during the Cultural Revolution were normally paid by the government and were not dependent on work points.

attended junior secondary school from 1969 to 1971 remembered that one of the textbooks was edited in Yunnan and concerned Yunnan geography and basic agricultural knowledge based specifically on conditions in Yunnan. Agricultural work was an integrated part of education, and most graduates from junior and senior classes in the communes and brigades returned to work in the fields or to work and teach in the primary and junior secondary schools. To spread agricultural education and promote the slogan "Everybody should be able to go to college," Lijiang opened an agricultural college (Nongye Daxue) in 1976. The school had 150 students who studied for two years. They were chosen from among senior secondary school students in the communes, to which all were expected to return after graduation. After only four years, the school was closed down in 1980, when the Cultural Revolution had come to an end.

3 / Education and Ethnic Identity
in Lijiang since 1980

In Lijiang, as in other minority areas of China, the end of the Cultural Revolution brought a renewed political emphasis on the development of minority education, including special minority schools, the expansion of teaching in minority languages, and the creation of new textbooks for minorities. In light of the social problems that the Cultural Revolution's suppression of ethnic expressions had created, the government also emphasized that patriotic education was an important part of education, not the least in minority areas. Thus, the development of minority education had the dual purpose of raising the educational level of minorities (thereby bringing about economic modernization) and ensuring minorities' loyalty to the state, the CCP, one another, and the majority Han.

MINORITY SCHOOLS

To meet the government's goal of securing, standardizing, and expanding education of minority *minzu,* the boarding-school system has been promoted as the most practical and efficient form of education. All autonomous minority counties and prefectures in Yunnan have now established at least one "minority boarding school," usually a junior secondary school that recruits students from the poorest and most remote areas. In 1981 Lijiang's first (and only) minority boarding school, Lijiang County Minority Secondary School (Lijiang Xian Minzu Zhongxue), was started initially with two classes of higher primary school. In 1986 the provincial government decided to transfer money to counties for the establishment of semiboarding primary schools in the poorest minority areas. At the same time, the Lijiang County government turned the minority school in Lijiang into a minority junior secondary school, which, since 1987, has recruited students for three years of junior secondary school education.

The school enrolls one hundred graduates of primary schools a year. It is much more difficult to get into this school than into a regular junior secondary school, though special consideration is given to approximately twenty-five students each year from townships where very few primary-school graduates are able to continue on to junior secondary school. Naxi, Han, and Bai students do not receive extra points. Generally, students for this *minzu* school need about 142 points to get in, as compared to 90 points for regular junior secondary schools. The school is very popular because students get twenty-three yuan (in 1995) in support every month from the government, it has strict regulations concerning the students' spare-time activities, and students do not have to cook for themselves. Most importantly, it has a relatively high percentage of graduates continuing on to senior or specialized secondary school, and therefore each year a number of parents attempt to enroll children through the "back door."[1] For the poorest parents it is a heavy economic burden to have a child in the school, because a boarding-school student needs a minimum of one hundred yuan per month for living expenses, and, as in other schools, they have to pay for books. Each class has a small piece of land that it may cultivate to support poorer students. The Naxi constitute the largest group of students, with almost 60 percent, and twenty of the twenty-three teachers are Naxi. Boys make up the vast majority of students, an average of 74.5 percent between 1985 and 1991. This probably reflects the preference of most villagers of all ethnic groups in Lijiang that sons (rather than daughters) receive an education, not the least so when they can afford only one student in the family.

Two other secondary schools arrange special minority classes (*minzu ban*). These classes in one of these secondary schools are exceptional in China because they are reserved for the students with the *highest* examination scores, not for students from poor areas, as is common practice in minority schools and classes. Normally, students (including the Han) need 160 points to enroll in this kind of junior minority class (compared to 90 points in a regular junior secondary class) and 470 for the senior minority class (compared to 430 points

---

1. In 1991, 45 percent of graduates continued on to higher or specialized secondary education; in 1994, 76 percent did so.

in a regular senior secondary class). In fact, students admitted to these minority classes have scored higher than is needed for specialized secondary schools, which are generally the most prestigious secondary schools apart from provincial keypoint schools. (Except for highly educated parents, the majority want their children to attend a specialized senior secondary school because they will be guaranteed work after three years of study.) All students in a special minority class live at the school, and minority students receive financial support from the local government (seven yuan per month in the lower minority class and fifteen yuan in the higher one in 1995). The purpose of this class is to educate what the administration calls "especially clever minority students," so students get the best teachers and the most extracurricular support. According to the administration, approximately 80 percent manage to continue on to higher education. This is an extremely high rate. Because it is very prestigious to be admitted to the minority class, students from the regular secondary school classes have given it the nickname "aristocratic class" (*guizu ban*). Most students in the class are Naxi, especially from Lijiang Town or Shigu, where the influence of Chinese language is strongest due to the many Han living there and where students have some of the best educational possibilities.

The keypoint secondary school also arranges special minority classes, but these recruit minority students from the poorest and least developed townships of the four counties in Lijiang Prefecture. Lisu and Yi get extra points for admission to this senior secondary school class, and although the Mosuo are officially part of the Naxi *minzu,* they, too are considered as a separate group when extra points are granted. Many of the graduates from this class return as cadres to their own townships, because only 15 to 20 percent of them pass the university entrance examination. This figure is low compared to the other regular classes in this key point school, from which approximately 50 percent continue on to higher education.[2]

Most students at the minority secondary school are between thirteen and sixteen years old, and although the Naxi make up the majority of students, all of the other *minzu* in Lijiang are represented, too. All teaching here, as well as in other secondary schools in Lijiang, is in Chinese, and only rarely do teachers explain in Naxi if students do not understand them. Many teach-

---

2. I did not obtain this school's official statistics. It is possible that these figures, which were revealed to me in an interview, are exaggerated.

ers regard poor proficiency in Chinese as one of the main problems in the school. Most students speak Chinese only as their second language, and many of their parents are illiterate. Some teachers found that students from the countryside were also in need of cultural training:

> Students here belong to different minorities and we teachers have to learn about their customs and habits from home in order to understand them. Still, they were the best students in their local primary schools, so they are quite good at learning. . . . It is also relatively easy to teach them, because they are grateful that they have come to this school. Most students are in Dayan [the town of Lijiang] for the first time. It is difficult in the beginning for them to get used to life here. They are not used to studying, to paying attention to hygiene, to following certain rules. Some have long hair when they come, are very dirty, and wear old rags. (Naxi teacher)

Teachers (most of whom are Naxi) tended to believe that most academic and social problems in the school concerned the *minzu* from the mountains, such as Yi, Lisu, Miao, and Pumi. Students also mentioned conflicts between ethnic groups from the mountains and the Naxi. Outside of class the Naxi speak Naxi with one another, and there was a tendency among many of them to look down upon the other ethnic groups as more backward.

Official rhetoric, and many individual teachers, deny that the backwardness of others justifies one's own feeling of superiority, but in fact the content and form of education support the Naxi students' feeling that the other local minorities are more "backward" and "primitive" than themselves. The Naxi are generally best in Chinese due to their long contact with the Han and to their geographical setting with good infrastructure, as compared to the poorer minorities in the mountains. During their education, students are constantly confronted with the fact that knowledge of Chinese is a strength, whereas outside their own village a minority language as a mother tongue is a cultural deficiency. Due to their large number in the minority school, the Naxi students find a forum of common cultural reference where they can speak their own language and celebrate Naxi festivals. Some Naxi students who come from poor areas that are generally considered to be rather backward experience an unexpected interest in and even respect for their local *dongba* rituals. Although the minority school itself does not teach the culture or history of specific *minzu,* rural Naxi students arrive (often for the first time) in a town where tourists, local entrepreneurs, museums, and intellectuals express interest in the *dongba* ritual specialists who remain in only a few Naxi areas today. Furthermore, because most teachers at the school (and in Lijiang in general) are Naxi, Naxi students have an opportunity to talk and ask questions in Naxi outside of class. Perhaps more important, students realize that many Naxi are able to succeed within the educational system. The students from the smaller minorities, on the other hand, experience a stronger break with home because at school they live in surroundings where all classes are in Chinese, all teachers speak Chinese, and most students speak Naxi or Chinese. They can no longer participate in local festivals or religious and family celebrations, since only the common Naxi, Han, or Communist festivals are celebrated as holidays at the school, and to a large degree they have to dissociate themselves from their village background in order to succeed in the educational system.

Naxi at the boarding school, who come to the city from remote rural areas, tend to strengthen their ethnic identity through contact with other Naxi and especially through encountering public expressions of modern Naxi identity in the town of Lijiang. While being away from home to receive an education based on Chinese language, history, and nationalism, they also experience that teachers are Naxi, the local government is Naxi, and "*dongba* culture" is an aspect of being Naxi that one can feel proud of. Yet some of them also told me that because they knew that they looked poor, and everybody would guess from their dialect that they were from a remote rural area, they were embarrassed to walk around in the town. Despite such concerns, they discovered, through their boarding-school experience, a hitherto unknown dimension of being Naxi, and, unlike many of the other ethnic minorities at the school, they tended to emphasize the positive aspects of Naxi culture rather than negative notions of "backward culture" or "backward economy."

RURAL SCHOOLS

There are considerable differences between schools in the county and prefectural capital of Lijiang, and the rural schools elsewhere in the county.

Generally speaking, the poorest areas also have the poorest schools, the least educated teachers, and the biggest problems concerning attendance, dropout rate, and matriculation. There are still more than two hundred *minban* teachers in Lijiang, and all of them teach in rural primary schools. Many are single teachers in lower primary schools (two to four years of study), their wages are often only one-third of those of a regular teacher, and they depend upon (often unstable) local financial support. Teachers in mountain villages among the Lisu, Miao, Nuosu, and Tuo'en (the last two both classified as Yi), especially, complain that parents cannot afford to buy books for their children and therefore prefer to let them work in the fields rather than send them to school.[3] In most schools in the countryside girls are in the minority, often because parents prefer to support the education of a son rather than a daughter. Some parents complain that when they have to pay up to thirty yuan per semester for tuition and more for books, they consider this a proper investment only if their children will be able to continue on to a specialized secondary school that will at least guarantee them work outside the village after graduation. On the other hand, all parents I talked to know about the compulsory education law. Because children must start primary school at age seven, most parents agree to let their children attend for at least the first four years.

Many of the problems in rural education in Lijiang are related to middle school education, where few students start and even fewer graduate. For example, in one rural junior secondary school in a township near Lijiang Town, about 20 percent of students drop out each year. Almost all students in this school are Naxi (more than 60 percent are boys), and many walk five to six hours home for the weekends. When they return to school, they carry food for the whole week, and at school they have to find firewood for the cooking, which they do themselves. This is also common practice in some of the primary schools in the same township, where pupils between the ages of eleven and thirteen sometimes have to walk several hours to school on Sunday, carrying food for the whole week, and then walk back home on Friday. The government supports these schools only as semiboarding schools, giving seven yuan per student, while in fact they function as full boarding schools and

---

3. According to the Bureau of Education, the Lisu township of Liming is among those with the most severe problems. Approximately 75 percent of children start school, but more than 20 percent drop out.

should receive at least three times more. Thus insufficient financial support and student hardship are the common reasons for dropout. Another is the parents' focus on specialized secondary school education, which causes them to consider junior secondary school a waste of time and money unless they feel certain that their child can go on to the School of Finance (Caizheng Xuexiao), School of Hygiene (Weisheng Xuexiao), or Normal School (Shifan Xuexiao) after graduation and secure a job later.

Many village children in Lijiang also face language barriers, but in this respect Naxi children are privileged compared to those from ethnic groups such as the Tuo'en, Lisu, Miao, and Premi. Most rural teachers are themselves Naxi, and although bilingual education is not explicitly promoted among the Naxi (as it is among some of the Lisu), I often heard teachers explaining in Naxi when I attended classes in rural schools. The majority of rural Naxi secondary school students I interviewed recalled teachers speaking Naxi during the first years of education. Moreover, because many Naxi villages have had schools at least since the 1920s, education is not regarded as foreign or as a Han imposition from the outside, but rather as an integrated part of local village life. To the degree that parents care about which language the teacher speaks to their children in class, most rural parents seem to consider Chinese the only proper language, either because it will increase students' chances of upward social mobility or because minorities are simply accustomed to the fact that education is Chinese by definition. Most parents agree with teachers that the only reason for teaching in Naxi the first year is to facilitate the learning of Chinese.

Education obviously has less direct influence on ethnic identity among Naxi in the countryside than in Lijiang Town, where most children complete nine years of education and the intellectual Naxi actively attempt to spread their ideas of Naxi identity. However, especially in recent years, the strong interest in the *dongba* script and rituals and traditional Naxi music and dances, which had been centered in the town of Lijiang, has started to spread into rural Naxi areas. Since these are the places where *dongba* rituals are sometimes still practiced, where Naxi festivals are still celebrated in the old way, and where people play and sing Naxi music and songs, Naxi intellectuals and foreign researchers are seeking out these areas to collect material. The influence of local Naxi teachers on local Naxi identity is also considerable. Today most teachers have been educated at the Normal School in the town of Lijiang, and they have been confronted with the extensive local and international interest in the *dongba* script. Many of these teachers express regret that they never learned about Naxi culture in school, and they take the initiative to tell their pupils traditional Naxi stories that they have read in Naxi publications such as the local magazine *Yulong Mountain* or that they were told by their grandparents. Thus, modern expressions of Naxi identity are also influencing the rural Naxi to an increasing degree and are closely related to the content and scope of education.

TEACHING ETHNIC CATEGORIES AND SOCIAL EVOLUTION

In Lijiang County minority *minzu* make up 82 percent of the population, of which the Naxi constitute more than 58 percent. Therefore, many educators say that in Lijiang "all education is minority education." The minority secondary school is not reserved for non-Han, but for *minzu* from the poorest, most remote areas with the fewest secondary school graduates. However, the content of education in primary and secondary schools in Lijiang, including the minority school, follows the national standardized teaching material, with a short course in Yunnan history in junior secondary school as the only supplement.[4] Also Lijiang Normal School, which educates teachers for primary schools all over Lijiang Prefecture, has one course in Yunnan history as the only addition to the national standardized teaching material. The two brief Yunnan history volumes (*Yunnan lishi* for regular secondary schools and *Yunnan difang shi* for normal schools) were edited by the provincial Bureau of Education in 1990 after the 1989 student protests in Beijing, which caused the central government to demand strengthened focus on nationalism in education.[5] The government's basic idea behind the support of more local teaching material is that love of one's native area should be explicitly put into perspective with broader nationalist feelings. With the ultimate goal of promoting "love of the country and the Party," the government encourages stu-

---

4. A few Lisu schools teach Lisu script, whereas experiments teaching Naxi romanized script in a few villages have now stopped.

5. To my knowledge, all secondary school students in Lijiang receive eight to ten hours of teaching in Yunnan history in junior secondary school, and it is normally part of their history examination.

dents to "love their native place" as an inseparable part of the Chinese state represented by the Communist Party. Therefore, the Lijiang government is currently preparing a collection of articles about Lijiang history, cultural relics, nature, the Red Army in Lijiang, and famous local people. Within the next few years this volume probably will become supplemental teaching material in primary and secondary schools in Lijiang County. It is likely to be well received among the Naxi teachers who complain that even though they would like to teach their students about Naxi history and culture, they themselves do not know much about it.

One of the important purposes of teaching Yunnan history is to transmit the message that Yunnan, with all its inhabitants, has been an inseparable part of the Chinese empire for two thousand years. Thereby, the government hopes to create among minority students a strong sense of belonging to the modern Chinese Communist state and being a historical part of the Chinese nation. The introduction to one of the history books, quoted here in full, clearly illustrates this intention:

> Yunnan is an inseparable part of China. Yunnan local history is an organic part of China's history. Yunnan is a place where humans originated. On this piece of land, people have lived and labored since ancient times, opened up land, created civilization, and made history with their own hands.
>
> Since Qin founded the fully unified centralized state power, Yunnan has been an administrative unit in this unified multiethnic country. For more than two thousand years, Yunnan has been called an administrative unit. First it was called a county, then a prefecture, and then the Yuan dynasty established Yunnan Province. The political connections between Yunnan and China in dynastic history have changed, so that sometimes Yunnan was directly ruled by the empire, while at other times rule was indirect. However, in spite of different kinds of rule, Yunnan has always been an inseparable part of China.
>
> The great People's Republic is a unified multiethnic country. Today all minority *minzu* within the borders of China are members of the Chinese nation [*Zhonghua minzu*]. Yunnan is the province in our country that is inhabited by most nationalities. It is a miniature of our multiethnic fatherland. Almost all forefathers of each *minzu* can be traced back to the times before Qin. They all have a very long history.

The purpose of studying Yunnan history is to deepen knowledge of Yunnan; to receive patriotic teaching and education in revolutionary tradition; and to foster feelings of love of one's local area, love of the people, love of the fatherland, and love of the Chinese Communist Party. Furthermore, the purpose is to protect the unity of the fatherland, strengthen the unity of the *minzu,* and actively participate in building socialism in Yunnan. (*Yunnan difang shi* 1992: "Introduction")

Yunnan history is studied in most secondary schools and normal schools throughout the province and is part of the "patriotic education" that the central government emphasizes as essential for ensuring integration of minorities. The textbooks present a general survey of events in Yunnan's history profoundly influenced by Morgan's and Engels's theories of social evolution, which still dominate much of China's social sciences. Apart from the focus on Yunnan's historical incorporation into the Chinese empire, a dominant theme is the close relationship between Han and other *minzu.* Historical ethnic conflicts are generally interpreted as being essentially class conflicts, sometimes initiated by previous unjust governments' oppression of ethnic minorities. The books discuss relations between two groups, the Han and "minorities" (i.e., all of the officially recognized minority *minzu* in Yunnan). Only in the case of major ethnic clashes, such as that involving the Hui in the late nineteenth century, are specific non-Han groups mentioned. Cultural influence and exchange is generally presented as a one-way process in which the developed Han people influence and develop an unspecified group of grateful "minorities." Thus, two sorts of culture are constructed and presented to the student: advanced Han culture and less advanced non-Han culture. This becomes explicit in the teaching of social evolution of humanity, which is presented as a scientifically proven, and therefore indisputable, theory:

All *minzu* [in Yunnan] live in different areas, and their economies are not equally well developed. Therefore, on the eve of Liberation, different developmental stages still existed: primitive society [*yuanshi shehui*], slave society [*nuli shehui*], serf society [*nongnu shehui*], and feudal society [*fengjian shehui*]. And therefore, Yunnan has long been called a "living history of social development." (*Yunnan difang shi* 1992: 64)

Students learn that some minorities still possess a worldview and system of values that belong to "primitive society" and that those with a "high cultural level" owe it to strong Han influence, such as that on the Bai during the time of the Dali kingdom (973–1283) (*Yunnan difang shi* 1992: 43). Large-scale immigration of Han into Yunnan during the Ming dynasty brought advanced agricultural tools and techniques. The dismissal of local hereditary chiefs during the Qing dynasty was greatly beneficial to the minorities because the previous system of granting power to local chiefs had blocked development of production, made society unstable, and prevented progress (*Yunnan difang shi* 1992: 59). When specific non-Han groups are mentioned it is not for their technical advancement but for their "prosperous minority cultures." Minority dances and music are used as examples of "mankind's earliest forms of singing." In this way, the books contrast a picture of technically and politically advanced Han against primitive but sensitive minorities. Students also learn about the establishment of education in Yunnan, but this is limited to Confucian education and early Chinese modern education, both of which "disseminated advanced Han culture," while nothing is mentioned about other groups' forms of education (*Yunnan difang shi* 1992: 47; and *Yunnan lishi* 1991: 47).

In other subjects, especially secondary school politics and history, the common national teaching material also emphasizes patriotic education and social evolution. The primary school course in ideology and morals (*sixiang pinde*) focuses on proper moral behavior, which includes love of the country, flag, CCP, and national anthem. The Yunnan Bureau of Education has edited a booklet meant for supplementary reading in ideology and morals that includes stories of heroic people (such as the famous revolutionary hero Lei Feng)[6] and the Communists' achievements in Yunnan. In a chapter called "Yunnan: The Home of National Harmony," children learn the names of the twenty-six *minzu* living in Yunnan, who before Liberation "did not trust each other" and fought against each other in this area where "production

---

6. In 1989, after the crushing of student demonstrations, the central government launched a national campaign for studying Lei Feng in schools all over China. The life of this PLA soldier, described in his fictitious "diary" created by the PLA, had been the center of a mass campaign in the early 1960s. Lei Feng was praised and studied for his unfailing devotion to his country, the revolution, his comrades, and Chairman Mao.

and economy was utterly backward" (*Sixiang pinde* 1991: 19). But then came Liberation:

> After Liberation all *minzu* in our country became equal. Socialist ethnic relations based upon equality, unity, and mutual aid were established. The country also granted special consideration to minorities. The formerly oppressed minorities became masters of the country. . . . The Party and the country were deeply concerned about the minorities in the border regions. They sent *minzu* work teams to the minority regions to help them develop trade, education, science, culture, and hygiene. . . . The Party's minority policy promoted unity of the *minzu,* so that former "enemies" [*yuanjia*] became "relatives" [*qinjia*]. All of the *minzu* in Yunnan lived in harmony and united to help each other and to develop and protect the borders of the fatherland. (*Sixiang pinde* 1991: 19–20)

In a following exercise pupils must memorize the names of the twenty-six *minzu* in Yunnan. They also have to fill in two key words from the text, namely that all *minzu* in China are "equal" and that they must "unite." The Han are not directly mentioned since the text speaks only about the Communist Party helping the minority *minzu,* who are depicted as backward and helpless peoples. Indirectly the Han appear as the majority, representing the Party, not (as a group) backward, and not in need of the same kind of help.

In secondary school the teaching of evolution and ethnic categories is intensified. Students learn, for instance, that "if we look at the whole country, the Han *minzu* constitutes the vast majority. Generally speaking, their level of development is also the highest, so with regard to equality and unity of *minzu,* the Han people carry the gravest responsibility" (*Sixiang zhengzhi* 1993, first year of junior secondary school, vol. 1: 57). In the second year of junior secondary school, students study in detail Morgan's and Engels's stages of social evolution. Below a picture of Beijing man from the Stone Age, they see a picture of contemporary men belonging to the Jinuo *minzu* (from Sipsong Panna) who are dividing meat into equal portions for villagers—a so-called remnant from primitive society. The book's rather dull descriptions of the stages of human social evolution are sometimes given life through examples of contemporary minorities whose methods of production and social organization are characteristic of particular evolutionary stages. For instance, the Yi in Liangshan are put forward as examples of how the extremely backward developmental stage of "slave society" still existed at the time of Liberation. Tibet is used as an example of a "feudal serf society" that existed until Liberation.

In classes on ideology and politics (*sixiang zhengzhi*) in the third year of senior secondary education, many more examples are put forward to illustrate the point that all of China's *minzu* have belonged to the same Chinese nation [*Zhonghua minzu*] since the time of Qin (221–206 B.C.E.) and that most represented different (low) stages of development before 1949. It is also repeatedly stated that minority areas are still culturally and economically backward, although they have an abundance of unexploited natural resources. With their higher level of development, the Han are obliged to help the minorities to develop. This, it is claimed, will even help the Han themselves because of the wealth that the harvesting of natural resources in minority areas will bring to the whole country (*Sixiang zhengzhi* 1993, third year of senior secondary school: 131–33).

Students may read one thing in textbooks and hear it from their teachers, but remember quite another. When I asked Naxi students or graduates what they had learned in school about their own *minzu,* most immediately answered, "Nothing" (*Mei you xue*). When asked more specifically if teachers sometimes taught about the Naxi, although not according to textbooks, many recalled that Naxi teachers sometimes told Naxi stories or a bit of Naxi history, such as why most Naxi are called either Mu or He. Many had also heard that the Naxi were always "good at studying" and at "learning from Han culture." All agreed that they had never learned anything about the Naxi from textbooks. When asked about what they had learned generally about the different *minzu* in China, virtually all mentioned descriptions of social evolution. All students without exception were well aware that minorities represented the most backward stages, and most believed this to be an indisputable fact, since it was never discussed in class but simply presented as the truth.

At present there are divergent opinions among educational administrators, teachers, and intellectuals in Lijiang as to whether students should learn more about local culture, language, and history. One of the secondary school headmasters in Lijiang, a Naxi himself, expressed his point of view in this way:

At that time [before the 1980s] there was no teaching material about the development of the various *minzu*. Now there are some books on this topic, but because there is no general agreement about matters such as how to present "*dongba* culture," it would be impossible anyway to teach about it in school. We teach from a broad perspective, and to stress the history or culture of certain *minzu* would be damaging for the unity of the *minzu*. We teach about the five-thousand-year history of the Chinese nation.

Naxi themselves do not agree on this subject, but many cadres, teachers, and intellectuals now think that Naxi ought to learn at least something in school about their own culture and history. There is very little interest in teaching about the other ethnic groups in Lijiang, probably because they are minorities there and do not have a strong intellectual elite. Most government officials, cadres, teachers, and educational administrators in Lijiang are Naxi themselves, and all tend to emphasize "*dongba* culture" as the most outstanding and valuable aspect of Naxi identity and culture.

The Naxi *minzu* is a rare example of a small minority that is mentioned briefly in the Yunnan history booklets cited above. Lijiang is used as an example of an area where the transference of local power in 1723 to Qing bureaucrats resulted in economic development (*Yunnan lishi* 1991: 40). In the Yunnan history book for the students at Yunnan's normal schools, the "*dongba* religion" of the Naxi is mentioned. This book explains that in accordance with the various stages of development, different "primitive religious beliefs" prevailed among the nationalities, and some, including the Naxi, had their own unique religion (*Yunnan difang shi* 1992: 68).

THE ROLE OF EDUCATION FOR NAXI IDENTITY TODAY: "IN EDUCATION WE NAXI ARE THE BEST"

Because of our geographical situation, we Naxi have always found it very easy to adopt cultures coming from the outside. With the Tibetans to the north and the Bai and Han to the south, we have been under strong influence from these cultures. We do not have a Naxi university, so we have to adapt well to Han culture [*Han wenhua*], and therefore we, of all the fifty-five minority *minzu* in China, have the most university students. (Forty-year-old teacher)

Pupils from the Naxi and Tuo'en ethnic groups in a village primary school in Lijiang. Like several other primary schools, this one receives government support as a semiboarding school, although it functions as a full boarding school. Pupils whose families live a half day's walk from the school stay during the week, bringing and cooking their own food.

Many small village schools have only one or two teachers, who simultaneously teach several grades of primary school. Here the class is divided into two grades facing separate blackboards.

Premi village primary school in Lijiang. Among the Premi, as well as the Naxi, there is officially no bilingual education. However, many local teachers use Naxi or, as in this school, Premi as their language for instruction during the first few years of primary education. (Photo by Koen Wellens)

The Mao Zedong poster in this teacher's training school classroom reads, "Have pride and self-respect; improve yourself and stand on your own feet."

Tai participant in a patriotic speech competition in Sipsong Panna.

Several monasteries in Sipsong Panna have started to teach novices mathematics, standard Thai, and Chinese in addition to traditional Buddhist subjects. This blackboard presents Thai, Chinese, and Tai equivalents of Arabic numerals.

Novices in front of a monastery in Sipsong Panna. (Photo by Koen Wellens)

Students in the dormitory of a secondary boarding school in Sipsong Panna. All Tai female students wear Tai clothing, whereas Akha female students are ashamed of the traditional Akha costume, which they (and the Tai students) associate with "backwardness" and poverty.

Rural lower primary school in an Akhe village in Sipsong Panna. Chinese work teams installed basketball courts in most villages in Sipsong Panna and other minority areas in the 1950s. According to one Han cadre who himself participated in such a project, courts were to serve as playgrounds, places for storing grain, and (most important) public spaces where work teams could gather villagers to inform them about the CCP's policy and reform work. (Photo by Koen Wellens)

Buddhist monastery and pagoda in Damenglong, Sipsong Panna.

Pupils between the ages of seven and fifteen in a village primary school with only one teacher in a Khmu village in Sipsong Panna. Like the Tai, the Khmu are Buddhists, but because they have no monk to teach their novices in the small village monastery, the few novices in the village attend primary school instead. (Photo by Koen Wellens)

Tai participants in a major festival in Damenglong, Sipsong Panna. (Photo by Koen Wellens)

Today the Naxi have a relatively high percentage of graduate and under-
graduate students compared to most other *minzu* in China. In 1993, 0.643
percent of Naxi had graduated from college (*benke*, four years) compared to
a national average of 0.543 percent. Among the Han, 0.558 percent were college graduates, the Mongols 0.757, the Koreans as much as 2.271, the Manchus
0.624, and the Hui 0.591. All of these *minzu* are known in China for having
a high level of Chinese education. In comparison only 0.107 percent of the
Dai *minzu* were college graduates.[7] Although technically some of the small
minorities have a higher number of college graduates than the Naxi, this is
often because each minority *minzu* is entitled to have members educated at
a higher level no matter how small the *minzu* is and no matter how low the
educational level of graduates from senior secondary school. When comparing
Lijiang with Sipsong Panna, is it clear that school enrollment and graduation percentages are not only higher in Lijiang, but surpass those in most
other areas in Yunnan. In 1988 for instance, when 94.5 percent of school-aged
children in Yunnan were enrolled in primary school, 86.5 percent were
enrolled in Sipsong Panna Prefecture, 78.3 percent in Menghai County (in
Sipsong Panna), and 96.4 percent in Lijiang County.[8] Most Naxi students
who continue beyond junior secondary school are from the town of Lijiang,
and the vast majority of Naxi students who continue into higher education
are graduates of the two best regular secondary schools in the town of Lijiang.

Due to the early establishment of Confucian education in Lijiang and the
relatively successful spread of modern education in Lijiang, the Naxi are often
described in Chinese media and publications as a *minzu* with a "high level
of education," a *minzu* that has proven "willing to learn from more advanced
cultures." This characterization has come to occupy a significant position in
Naxi identity, even to a certain degree in the countryside, where education
is less developed. It has even become an ethnic marker in the consciousness
of many Naxi, who consider it a typical Naxi feature, a sort of inherited inclination toward "love of learning" or "love of culture" (*ai wenhua*). In rural
Naxi villages many people explained that, unlike many other ethnic groups
(notably those higher up in the mountains), the Naxi are very interested in

7. From *Zhongguo tongji nianjian 1993:* 91
8. Based on *Yunnan jiaoyu sishi nian, 1949–1989* 1990: 32–37.

learning and that only economic limitations prevent more of them from receiving an education.

Most Naxi are very proud of the Naxi researchers, teachers, and Party and government officials who have positions in Kunming or other places in China. In spite of the fact that they are intellectuals whose way of living, customs, and occupation are profoundly different from those of most Naxi, they have nevertheless come to symbolize (even among many rural Naxi) the Naxi as a numerically small ethnic group capable of developing and manifesting itself in China. Many Naxi peasants and teachers in rural areas criticize the government in Lijiang Town for not paying enough attention to the rural situation in Lijiang. This, however, does not prevent many of them from talking about the intellectual Naxi as a Naxi subgroup (rather than as government representatives) who demonstrate the *minzu*'s intellectual capability and openness toward "advanced culture." Many intellectual Naxi, even those who live outside of Lijiang and have no plans to return there, express concern about economic development in Lijiang. Some of them have established the Society for Naxi Culture (Naxi Wenhua Xuehui) as a network mainly for Naxi intellectuals, those in high administrative positions, and business leaders. One of the purposes of the society is to influence and direct economic and cultural development in Lijiang, but most Naxi peasants are not aware of the existence of this rather exclusive group.

Since 1991 the Lijiang government has enforced the national policy of population control. Now all *minzu* in Lijiang with an urban household registration (*chengshi hukou*) may have one child, whereas peasants and other people with rural registration (*nongye hukou*) may have two. However, it is quite common for rural families to have more children. Since 1981 there have been policies in effect to control the number of children, and many Naxi in Lijiang Town have only one or two children. This seems also to have strenghtened parents' focus on their children's education. The wish of many Naxi parents to have at least one child continue into higher education is the most obvious reason why so many younger Naxi parents in Lijiang Town have decided to speak only Chinese at home. Since the only possible way to a higher education is through the Chinese language, many parents hope to facilitate their child's upward social mobility by teaching him or her Chinese from birth. The general attitude in the town of Lijiang is that "the children learn Naxi anyway on the street among their friends, so we had better prepare them for school as early as possible." This also explains why many Naxi intellectuals who are themselves occupied with Naxi history and culture, or who have strong opinions about the need for protecting and developing Naxi culture, find it necessary to teach their children Chinese only.

Although the main reason for teaching children Chinese at home while most parents speak Naxi with each other seems to be pragmatic, based on the form and content of Chinese school education, many interviewees emphasized what they saw as a common Naxi characteristic, "love of learning," as their reason for educating their children in Chinese. Since the Naxi "loved learning," and learning in schools happened to be Chinese learning, they were more motivated to bring up their children in the Chinese language than were most other minorities.

The Naxi's focus on "love of learning" as a specific ethnic characteristic is in my view closely related to the teaching of social evolution and to the pervasive conceptualization in China of minorities as backward. In one particular aspect the Naxi escape the label of being backward, namely in their historical adaptation of and to Chinese education. Thus, the focus on "love of learning" establishes the Naxi as a *minzu* fairly close to the Han on some levels of civilization while distinguishing them from the minorities in the mountains (and, to a certain degree, from the the Mosuo subgroup of the Naxi, who are not considered to share this characteristic).

Clearly the perception of "love of learning" as a typical Naxi feature is most widespread among Naxi with a higher education. It is mainly through education that the concept of "backward minorities" is impregnated in the minds of the students, often instilling feelings of cultural inferiority. The concept of backward minorities is one that is extremely difficult to escape in the Chinese context, because it not only saturates many levels of society, but is presented in schools as scientific, objective truth. Students are not encouraged to develop a critical approach to the content of school education and its textbooks, and therefore they rarely express doubt about the truth of what is written. In this way the official categorization of minorities as basically backward is reproduced in the minds of many educated minority members. They internalize to a certain degree this external interpretation of the content of their ethnic identity, so that the categorizers' definition becomes "true" and becomes part of their identity as a minority *minzu*.

A more positive side to the Chinese categorization of the Naxi has been the conception of them as a minority "willing to learn," which has existed at least since the Qing dynasty, when the royal Mu family was praised by Chinese bureaucrats for its openness toward Confucian education and culture. It has been repeated in publications of all kinds about the Naxi. It has also become a strategy in the Naxi's attempt to establish an alternative picture of themselves as a group that may have been backward at the time of the Communist takeover, but was so inclined toward learning that it always had the potential for development. In this regard, the more positive aspect of the Chinese categorization of the Naxi has come to play a significant role in the remaking of Naxi identity.

Naxi teachers in institutions of higher learning in Lijiang and Kunming in particular have turned out to be very influential in spreading the concept of the Naxi as an ethnic group that loves learning. Many Naxi students in Kunming mentioned that through the influence of Naxi teachers, they had come to change their perceptions of themselves as Naxi and of the Naxi as a group. Their teachers had not opposed the general theory of social evolution for all ethnic groups, but had presented alternative understandings of the presumed backward elements of Naxi culture. One of the positive features was "love of learning"; another was "*dongba* culture," which was presented as a strength, not as an example of "superstition" or "backwardness." Especially in recent years, alternative interpretations of cultural features previously considered backward have transformed and strengthened Naxi identity (see also Chao 1996).

THE *DONGBA:* FROM SUPERSTITION TO CULTURE

Anyone who travels to Lijiang (and many Chinese, Asian, and Western tourists now do so) inevitably encounters a wide range of local expressions of Naxi identity. Apart from local architecture, old women's blue costumes, and traditional *dongjing* musical performances, the visitor is certain to notice abundant representations of *dongba* script in the town of Lijiang. In the 1990s many shopkeepers started to paint *dongba* characters on their signs, several Naxi now paint and sell calligraphy with *dongba* characters, well-known Naxi artists incorporate *dongba* pictures into modern paintings, the local bookshop has a whole shelf reserved for publications about the Naxi and *dongba,* and two *dongba* museums are open for visitors. In the ongoing process of recreating and formulating a modern Naxi identity, various aspects of *dongba*—their script, rituals, recorded stories, and myths—have been combined and reworked into the concept of "*dongba* culture." *Dongba* culture has become, at the same time, a commodity and tourist attraction, and an effective means of pushing the Naxi *minzu* up the evolutionary ladder by showing that they have "civilization" and "culture" (*wenhua*). As argued by Emily Chao, "Similar to the process by which the Han have designated themselves as modern and scientific in contrast to the traditional, superstitious, and backward minorities, the creation of a 'civilized space' within a category 'Naxi' was an oppositional process that inherently drew on the marginalization of Naxi *femaleness, illiteracy,* and *superstition*" (Chao 1996: 234). Both inside and outside China an unprecedented interest in *dongba* script and rituals has developed in recent years, starting from the mid-1980s, when Lijiang opened up to foreigners. Many Naxi in the town of Lijiang agree that the tourists and researchers from outside Lijiang and China have stimulated and encouraged the Naxi's own interest in *dongba* script.

By 1949 there were *dongba* practicing only in the rural areas of Lijiang. We have no figures on the exact number, but, according to interviews, many Naxi villages at that time had a *dongba* or would invite one from a neighboring village. After the Communist takeover *dongba*'s activities were prohibited as expressions of feudal superstition (*mixin*), and, partly for this reason, there are few *dongba* today. The Institute of *Dongba* Cultural Research[9] (Dongba Wenhua Yanjiu Suo) in Lijiang was started in 1981 as a branch of the Yunnan Academy of Social Sciences with the purpose of promoting *dongba* research and translating *dongba* texts. The institute has employed a few *dongba* to assist in projects such as translation work and reconstruction of rituals. One *dongba* started to learn *dongba* rituals and script from his father when he was fourteen years old. At that time there were two *dongba* families in his village. He recalled,

> In 1949, when I was twenty-eight years old, it was forbidden to practice *dongba* rituals, so I stopped. Nobody asked me to come any more. Then

---

9. This is the institute's own translation.

in the 1980s people again started to invite me as a *dongba,* and later I was invited to Lijiang to work. My wife and kids were very much against my starting to practice again. Now they are not against it any more—they accept it because so many people are interested in it. . . . Previously *dongba* rituals were called "superstition"; now they are "culture."

The fact that *"dongba* superstition" has turned into *"dongba* culture" is manifested in the way more and more Naxi intellectuals describe the *dongba* as no longer representatives of feudal culture or peasants' superstitious belief, but as "the Naxi's own intellectuals" *(Naxizu de zhishifenzi). Dongba* culture has become central to Naxi identity as it is expressed publicly in China today. *Dongba* rituals are still performed in some Naxi villages, but that does not necessarily imply that the concept of a *dongba* culture plays a significant role in Naxi peasants' ethnic identity. In the early 1980s, after the end of the Cultural Revolution and with the renewed acceptance of religious and ethnic expression, it was mainly a relatively small group of Naxi intellectuals in Kunming who started to promote research into *dongba* activities and to focus on *dongba* culture as a specific feature of the Naxi as an ethnic group and a minority *minzu* in China. In the last ten to fifteen years this has gradually spread to other strata of the Naxi community in Lijiang and is developing rapidly. *Dongba* rituals are no longer merely objects of research. Recently some intellectual Naxi with official positions have even started to invite *dongba* to perform rituals at home in connection with family events, and some have initiated projects in which the modern use of *dongba* culture is combined directly with education in an attempt to spread knowledge of the *dongba,* to develop Naxi ethnic pride based on *dongba* culture, and to reject the construction of the Naxi as backward.

The Dalai Minority Culture and Ecology Village

Dalai is a small Naxi village some kilometers out of Lijiang Town. During the Qing dynasty the village had a private Confucian school, and when the Republic was established in 1911, a local public primary school took over all school-based education. The school was rather popular in the early 1930s and had about forty pupils, including a few girls. Before the 1950s there were two *dongba* families in the village, but the last *dongba* died in the late 1970s. In

1934 the local teachers started a "common peoples' school" where adults participated in Chinese literacy courses in the evening.

In 1995 the village was the center of a celebration honoring the Naxi's guardian spirit, Sanduo. A *dongba* was invited by prominent Naxi scholars and bureaucrats to perform a traditional ritual for the villagers and for *dongba* researchers from Japan. The event was an interesting mixture of photographing, filming, and making serious offerings to and honoring Sanduo. It was also part of a larger local project initiated by Mr. He, a former Naxi official who had returned to his village after retirement. The guiding idea behind Mr. He's Minority Culture and Ecology Village (Minzu Wenhua Shengtai Cun) was to promote "traditional Naxi culture," which he found was threatened by modernization. Mr. He's vision was to create a synthesis of old values and modern techniques, to combine "the Confucian *Analects, dongba* [practices], Communist propaganda, and computers" (He Wanbao 1995: 2). One of his major ideas, restarting a locally based "common people's school," the Peasants Evening School, a private initiative independent of government financial support, has already been realized. A small library was opened in connection with the evening school. Local peasants may freely attend the school, which arranges not only courses on agricultural techniques, animal breeding, and use of fertilizer, but also in Naxi romanized script and *dongba* characters. As Mr. He remarked, "The most important thing about this evening school is that people learn things they can really use in society." Naxi romanized script is taught because it is easy to learn and is used in collecting and recording local stories, myths, and songs.

When the school was just started in 1994, approximately seven locals attended the courses on *dongba* script taught by a *dongba,* as compared to around forty who took courses on agricultural techniques. The organizers expected a slow revival of *dongba* rituals, since a few younger *dongba* were being trained in neighboring villages, and more and more families planned to revive the tradition of inviting a *dongba* to perform rituals associated with life events such as death, marriage, and illness. The evening school has no connection with the regular primary school in the village. Only one of the two primary school teachers, both of whom are from nearby villages, had heard about the new evening school, which she considered a good initiative because "in this school [the regular primary school] children never learn anything about Naxi history or culture. We also never learned anything, so we do not know anything about it now."

Naxi Dongba *Cultural School of Lijiang*

The Naxi *Dongba* Cultural School (Naxi Dongba Wenhua Xuexiao),[10] another recent major local project, is directed both toward strengthening the role of "*dongba* culture" in the common Naxi identity and toward promoting the utilization of its economic potentials. This school was started in Lijiang in early 1995 in order to offer short-term education to people in Lijiang County who had at least graduated from junior secondary school. The first class enrolled forty students (all Naxi from the vicinity of Lijiang Town), who paid two hundred yuan for the course, during which they would learn to read and write one thousand *dongba* characters; learn about *dongba* history, rituals, and art; and study basic English for the purpose of future employment in the growing local tourist business. Some of the students were unemployed youth, some were primary school teachers, and some worked at local museums or travel agencies. Some wished to find work in the tourist industry, whereas others were simply interested in learning more about *dongba*. Approximately half of the students completed the course. The faculty was enthusiastic about the project and had visions for further development of the school. They hoped to raise money for a class of about fifty fourteen- to fifteen-year-old students from the poorest mountain areas, including those who had not continued their studies because their parents could not afford it. The plan was to build dormitories for these students, who would study for two years. A fund-raising leaflet described the project:

> Our purpose is to save "*dongba* culture" via living people, expand our *minzu* culture [*minzu wenhua*], stimulate our *minzu* spirit [*minzu jingshen*], and promote local economic development. After a period of practicing teaching, we want gradually to enroll more students, so that the school will turn into a cradle for qualified people who study and carry on "*dongba* culture." It will also become an international study institution for "*dongba* culture" and a center for *dongba* art. We are trying our best to achieve this great goal.

10. The English name is the school's own translation.

Some of the people connected to the school also expressed hope that it would be possible to start a *dongba* course in one of the established universities. As one person said, "The Tibetans, Koreans, and Mongols have their own universities, so why not we Naxi? Previously most Naxi thought that only Han culture was interesting and developed. Now many realize that we have a culture and a tradition with its own value."

Both of the schools described here are interesting because they show how intellectual Naxi engage in local economic development in Lijiang through the establishment of alternative education that incorporates (or is even built upon) the teaching of local Naxi culture and history, which is lacking in regular state education. Initially directed by a relatively small group of Naxi intellectuals, the concept of *dongba* practices as feudal "superstition" has evolved into that of a "culture," carrying implications of script, art, history, and civilization. Whereas "superstition" is perceived as a burden of backward people, "culture" is regarded as a force, a proof of civilization, and a justifier for demands of local influence and control of economic and cultural development. The concept of *dongba* culture as a unique Naxi ethnic marker undermines the powerful construction of the Naxi as a backward minority. It establishes the Naxi as a *minzu* with *wenhua* and solves the dilemma of how a *minzu* characterized by its "love of learning" and positive attitude toward "advanced cultures" nevertheless remained backward and resisted assimilation with the Han: *dongba* practices were not "superstition" but were a "culture" that was valuable as a refined expression of Naxi society. This culture was different from that of the Han and of other *minzu* in the area and elsewhere in China. The Naxi "loved learning from the advanced Han," but they also had their own characteristics. They had their own "culture" and even their own "*dongba* intellectuals."

Dongba ritual practice, only one of several religious practices among rural Naxi, for a long time did not even exist in the town of Lijiang. Nevertheless, the Naxi have succeeded in turning the various aspects of the *dongba* into a modern Naxi symbol. When directly asked, most Naxi today mention "*dongba*" or "*dongba* culture" as a major "Naxi feature." This is not because *dongba* culture, as such, plays an important role in most Naxi villages, but because the educated Naxi elite's formulation and strong voicing of Naxi identity is spreading into the countryside, where the same elite is regarded with respect and approval, as were the Confucian educated elite before them.

CONCLUDING REMARKS

The reason the Naxi have been so successful in turning public attention toward *dongba* as a culture and a strength, rather than as a form of superstition is, I believe, closely related to the relatively high educational level of the Naxi and their own belief in "love of learning" as a Naxi characteristic. The educated Naxi elite consists of a comparatively large number of people, many of whom hold prestigious and influential positions in Kunming or Lijiang. They are employed at all levels of government in Yunnan Province and Lijiang County, and considering the relatively small number of Naxi, many are influential teachers and researchers. Many come from families where the fathers and grandfathers were students in Confucian private schools, and they value education very highly. They have a well-developed network through groups such as the Society for Naxi Culture and so are able to organize themselves and express demands within the politically acceptable national framework.

Their level of Chinese state education has enabled the Naxi to establish local, alternative education that will most likely have more far-reaching consequences at the local level than will the more exclusive Society for Naxi Culture. Thanks to their own education, the Naxi who initiated these projects know how to play by the rules, so that this education is not regarded as a threat to regular state education but is supported by the local autonomous government and most heads of state schools in Lijiang (most of whom are Naxi). Even so, the creation of the new alternative schools in Lijiang represents a reaction against state education that almost completely ignores non-Han culture, language, and history and fails to show that minorities in China have more to offer than picturesque costumes, dancing, and singing. In fact, state education involuntarily supports—perhaps even creates—a focus on ethnic identity. Minority members can never escape their label as minorities, because they are officially classified as such and learn in school that the classification relies on objective, scientific proof. Neither can they escape the label of backwardness, because they learn that this, also, is a scientifically proven fact. Finally, through an education that ignores local history, language, stories, and religion, they indirectly learn that much of what they have experienced and learned at home is without value in the broad context of the People's Republic. Although this creates feelings of stigmatization for some educated minority people, education has, for the Naxi, been instrumental in the development of a stronger and forcefully expressed ethnic identity. This has been made possible by their relatively high percentage of educated members, their shared belief that "love of learning" is typical of Naxi, and the promotion of *dongba* script by their intellectual elite.

Many of the intellectual Naxi have themselves participated in the national project of defining *minzu* and disseminating theories of social evolution, but they have nevertheless begun to react against the perception of *themselves* as members of a group that is backward by definition. In this sense they are reacting to an external definition, an ethnic categorization, of what it implies to be Naxi. In other words, they do not (unlike the "Mosuo branch" of the Naxi) reject what Richard Jenkins has called the nominal aspect of ethnicity (the name or the boundary of the group), but they do reject the content of this name and seek to reinterpret it (Jenkins 1994). Since the nominal ethnic categorization was based upon an already existing social category with which most Naxi (excluding the Mosuo) already identified—they did not doubt that they were Naxi—this identity has been further strengthened. At the same time, it has become vitally important for Naxi intellectuals to redefine the content of the external ethnic categorization that was the public and official version of their experience as an ethnic group.

Education played several roles in the remaking of Naxi identity. First of all, it was one of the most significant media through which the officially sanctified categorization of the "backward minorities" and the definite *minzu* boundaries were communicated. Therefore, it was the educated Naxi who most strongly came to regard the Naxi *minzu* as "backward" and who experienced a strong contradiction between this and their perception of themselves as an ethnic group with a special potential for learning and development. Many experienced personal conflict because of the contradiction between the Naxi's success in education and their individual classification as members of a backward minority. Success in education, partly resulting from a high degree of integration into the Chinese state and nation and the adoption of the Chinese language and cultural values through lengthy contact with the Han, was in itself a factor that enabled the Naxi to reinterpret the content of the constructed ethnic categorization in a way that is acceptable in the present political climate in China. In this way ethnicity was remade partly through the reinterpretation of the original content of an external categorization.

Of course education alone does not explain why the recent strong expressions of ethnicity among the Naxi have neither met with political sanctions nor been regarded as a threat to state sovereignty. The Naxi are a very small ethnic group, they have no ethnic relations across national borders, and they have absolutely no aspirations to political independence. Their expressions of ethnicity, to the degree that they are directed by instrumentalist motives, seek to define the Naxi as a group that has adopted a lot from Han (Confucian) culture and language but has maintained its own culture. This also justifies further control over local resources and political decision-making, all clearly within the context of the Chinese state.

4 / History of Chinese Education in Sipsong Panna

The term "Tai" commonly refers to peoples in Thailand, Laos, Burma, south China, north Vietnam, and northeast India who speak a Tai language, whereas "Thai" refers to citizens of Thailand. One of the fifty-five officially recognized Chinese ethnic minorities is the Dai *minzu,* which comprises several, but not all, Tai-speaking groups in China (the Zhuang and the Dong *minzu,* for instance, speak Tai languages as well). The Dai category consists of different Tai people whom the Chinese called Baiyi prior to the ethnic classification in the 1950s. To distinguish among the different Baiyi, the Chinese applied names such as Dry Baiyi (Han Baiyi), Colorful-Waist Baiyi (Huayao Baiyi), and Water Baiyi (Shui Baiyi). These categories are still used by some Chinese, and some Tai also use these terms when speaking Chinese. The Dai *minzu* comprises Tai groups such as the Tai Nua, Tai Beng, Tai Duan, and Tai Lue (Lüe/Le). The Tai Lue are also called Xishuangbanna Dai or simply Xidai in Chinese, but they usually call themselves simply Tai, unless they need to distinguish themselves from other Tai groups. In 1992, 1,025,402 people in China were classified as part of the Dai *minzu.* The majority live in Yunnan Province, where they are the fourth-largest minority (together with the Zhuang), constituting 2.73 percent of the total population (1990) and 8 percent of the minority population (*Yunnan tongji nianjian* 1991: 96).

Chinese researchers distinguish four major Tai (Dai) dialects and scripts. The written language of the Tai Lue in Sipsong Panna is developed from a script closely related to Sanskrit (Pali script).[1] The script and spoken language of the Tai Lue and the other major Tai group in Dehong County (called the

---

1. See Gombrich 1995 [1988].

Tai Mao, Mao Shan, Chinese Shan, and Tai Nua) are mutually unintelligible. Today there are Tai Lue living in Laos, Burma, Thailand, and Vietnam, but the majority still live in Sipsong Panna.[2] Anthony Diller estimates that between five hundred thousand and one million people speak Tai Lue dialects (Diller 1994: 12). In the 1950s, when the Chinese government promoted the development of new scripts for minorities, the Tai Lue script was simplified and standardized. This "new Tai"(*xin Daiwen*) was used in schools, newspapers, and other local literature until the local government decided to revive and standardize the "old Tai" script (*lao Daiwen*) in 1987. This policy was reversed in 1996, when the government again returned to "new Tai." None of the other minorities in Sipsong Panna who speak different languages has a script. The Akha are officially classified as part of the Hani *minzu,* for whom a script was created in 1957, but this script was based on the Luchun dialect and is not used by the Akha in Sipsong Panna.

Sipsong Panna Tai [Chinese: Xishuangbanna Dai] Autonomous Prefecture was established in 1953 and comprises the counties of Menghai and Mengla and the city of Jinghong, where the prefectural government is seated.[3] Of the 798,086 people who live in the prefecture, almost 36 percent (278,955 people) belong the Dai *minzu,* while the second-largest group, the Han, constitutes 26 percent. It was only after 1949, when the CCP took complete control of Sipsong Panna, that Han immigration on a large scale commenced.[4] Thus the fact that the Han in Sipsong Panna today make up nearly one-third of the population, and more in the capital of Jinghong, is a recent development. The other major *minzu* are the Hani with 19 percent, Lahu with 6 percent, Bulang and Yi with 4 percent each, and Jinuo with 2 percent.[5] These *minzu* comprise peoples who have historically lived in Sipsong Panna with the Tai and use various self-appellations, such as Akha, Akhe, Jinuo, Lahu, Sanda, Phusa, Blang, and Khmu. The Tai historically inhabited the most prosperous plains in this subtropical region, while before 1950 other groups lived higher up in the moun-

2. See also Lebar et al. 1964: 206–14.
3. When the Communists took over Sipsong Panna at the end of the Republic, there were four counties: Cheli (Jinghong), Fohai (Menghai), Nanqiao (Mengzhe), and Zhenyue (Mengla).
4. See Hansen 1999a on Han Chinese migrations to Sipsong Panna after 1949.
5. All figures are from the prefectural Bureau of Statistics and are based upon a 1993 census.

tains and rarely interacted socially with the Tai, who regarded them as inferior *kha* (slaves).[6] As in the case of the Tai Lue in Ban Ping village in Thailand described by Michael Moerman in 1966, the primary ethnic distinction made by the Tai in Sipsong Panna was between hill and lowland people, paralleling the dichotomy of jungle and state. The groups exchanged commodity goods, such as Tai salt and rice for Akha cotton and noodles. Silver pieces had been exchangeable for goods since the seventeenth century, but commodity exchange was still important in the 1940s (Chen Han-Seng 1949: 54).

Theravada Buddhism became widespread in Sipsong Panna during the fourteenth century and is still the dominant religion today. Most Tai villages have a small Theravada temple and monastery, but, like other Tai Lue in Laos, Burma, and Thailand and the Siamese (Central Thai), the Tai Lue in Sipsong Panna also respect spirits (*phi*), such as household, personal, village, and *meeng* ("local principalities" governed by local Tai princes) spirits.[7] In China the Tai, Blang, A'chang, and Khmu in Sipsong Panna, Simao, Lancang, Dehong, and Baoshan are Theravada Buddhists.

Sipsong Panna is a subtropical region with a rainy season and fertile land, especially on the plains where the Tai live. According to official statistics, more than 80 percent of the population are peasants, and the most important crops include wet-rice, sugarcane, coffee, hemp, tea, fruit, and not the least rubber, which is cultivated on state farms established in the 1950s. The non-Tai ethnic groups live higher up in the mountains in villages that are generally more poor and where living conditions are harsh. Large forest areas have been logged to plant rubber trees, and this has often resulted in disputes between the Han employees at the state farms and the local Akha, who depended on hunting in the jungle. The area is still rich in teak, sandalwood, medicinal plants, and (dwindling numbers of) wild animals. Especially since the early 1990s, the tourist industry has been booming, as has foreign trade after the opening of the borders with Burma and Laos. Most tourists are Han, but international visitors from Taiwan and especially Thailand are on the increase.

6. *Kha* is a common Tai derogatory term for proto-Indochinese groups who speak various Mon-Khmer languages and live in the hills and highlands of Yunnan, Burma, Thailand, Vietnam, and Laos. The term probably means "servant," "attendant," or "slave" (Satyawadhna 1990: 75–76).

7. See also Moerman 1966 on spirits in Lue communities in Thailand, and Tanabe 1988.

Some Thai financially support the development of Buddhism in Sipsong Panna, and many seem to be on a nostalgic search for remnants of an "original" Tai culture. The most important festival of the Tai is New Year (now popularly known in China as the Water Splashing Festival), which traditionally started on the sixth day of the sixth month of the Tai calendar and continued until the sixth day of the seventh month.[8] Today the festival is celebrated for three days, during which hordes of tourists flock to Jinghong. Splashing water on one another is now allowed only on one official day. For tourist purposes, the local park (and even ethnic theme parks in other parts of China) arrange their own small Water Splashing Festivals as well as other staged exotic rituals, such as those of the Wa people.

A BRIEF HISTORY OF THE TAI IN SIPSONG PANNA

According to the recorded history of the Tai Lue, Chao Bhaya Cheeng was the king, the *chao phaendin,* who in 1180 first established the Tai kingdom called the Golden Palace of Jing Rung.[9] He was the ancestor of the following *chao phaendin,* who possessed the highest level of power in Sipsong Panna until the Chinese government abolished royal titles in 1950. Under the *chao phaendin* and the central government were the princes (*chao panna* and *chao meeng*), who ruled in twelve subdistricts called *panna* and subdivisional *meeng.* The princes, whose positions were also hereditary, ruled relatively independently in their districts.[10] The *chao meeng* ruled together with the *chao guan,* who were heads of the local governments, but whose positions were not hereditary. Villages also had other local headmen who were not members of the *chao* class, but whose positions were legitimized by the prince. The *chao meeng* were allowed to communicate directly with the Chinese government and to accept official Chinese titles. Attempting to secure control over the local princes' activities and government, the king had his own "middlemen" who

8. For a study of the Tai calendar, which starts in the year 638 of the Western calendar, see Gao Lishi 1992: 102–12.

9. On the history of the Tai in Sipsong Panna, see Hsieh 1989 and 1995; Jiang 1983; Gao 1992; and Chen Han-Seng 1949.

10. See *Daizu jianshi* 1986: 181 for a scheme of the hierarchical governing of the kingdom of Sipsong Panna, and *Daizu shehui lishi diaocha: Xishuangbanna* 1985, vol. 2: 31–43 for a more detailed study of the political system of the Tai.

lived in privileged villages outside *chao meeng* rule in order to keep an eye on the princes (Hsieh 1989: 111).

It is still a matter of dispute whether Sipsong Panna was an independent kingdom and state before the twentieth century and from what point it must be considered part of the Chinese state. Shih-chung Hsieh has argued that little attention has been paid to the state of Sipsong Panna because it was never recognized as a state by the leading imperial powers (Hsieh 1995: 302). The kingdom of Sipsong Panna was one of four small Tai kingdoms (Sipsong Panna, Lan Zhang, Keng Tung, and Lan Na) whose governments and populations had frequent and extensive contacts with one another. All of these neighboring states were designated as regions under administration of the Chinese empire, but their only obligations were to pay tribute to China and not attack the empire. With the creation of the modern nation-states in the twentieth century, they became part of four different states: Lan Na became part of Siam (later Thailand), and Lan Zhang first became part of the French colony of Indochina, then of the state of Laos. Keng Tung was first colonized by the British and then became part of Burma. And finally, Sipsong Panna was incorporated into the Chinese state, except for Meeng Wu and Wu De, which were occupied by France in 1895, annexed to French Indochina, and therefore later became part of Laos (Chen Han-Seng 1949: 4).

In the capital in Sipsong Panna, the king ruled together with a central government in which the local princes were represented at meetings. According to Hsieh, the kingdom of Sipsong Panna formed an effective and centralized government at least until the twentieth century. It was not a protectorate of China or Burma, and it had absolute rights in military and foreign affairs, economic activities, and internal governance (Hsieh 1995: 304). The kingdom also had its own recorded laws (in Tai script) concerning, for instance, criminals, penalties, and commoners' obligations toward the *chao* (Jiang 1983: 434–37). The Chinese imperial system during Yuan and Ming of appointing local hereditary chiefs (*tusi*) as local rulers was also employed in Sipsong Panna, but imperial authority was only nominal. Apart from six *panna* that the Tai king agreed to leave for direct rule by Chinese magistrates after revolts in 1728, the successive *chao phaendin* and the *chao meeng* remained the Tai rulers in the rest of Sipsong Panna. They also kept their officially appointed posts as *tusi* until Sipsong Panna was declared liberated by the Communists in 1950.

After the establishment of the Republic in 1911, the Chinese administration in Sipsong Panna expanded, and the area was divided into districts administered by Chinese magistrates. On lower levels of administration, the common *baojia* system was introduced as in other places in China. This was a hierarchic system in which one unit, the *bao*, consisted of ten *jia*, while one *jia* was made up of ten families. The local heads of *bao* and *jia* in Tai areas were normally Tai, and the system was intended to connect the magistrate's office above with the local level below. The Republican government also encouraged Chinese peasants and soldiers to settle in Sipsong Panna, and in 1940 it granted special privileges to Chinese peasants from Siam who wanted to grow tobacco in the area. During this period of increasing Chinese dominance, the establishment of Chinese schools became for the first time part of a strategy to integrate Sipsong Panna and its population into the Chinese state. The *chao phaendin* had lost much of his former power, and the local population was subjected to heavy tax burdens due to the double government system (Chen Han-Seng 1949: 25). In spite of several incidents of protest against Chinese rule and economic exploitation during the time of the Republic, there were no large-scale united revolts against the impositions of Chinese rule.

In 1944 the king of Sipsong Panna, Chao Mhoam Lhong Khong Gham, died and his stepson, Chao Mhoam Gham Le, became the last king.[11] At that time Chao Mhoam Gham Le (with the Chinese name Dao Shixun) was only fifteen years old and studied in a secondary school in Sichuan. Therefore, two brothers of the previous king were successively appointed as prince regents and given Chinese official status (Commission for Work with Historical Accounts of Sipsong Panna Tai Autonomous Prefecture, ed., 1987: vol. 1: 99–100). Members of the royal class and the Tai government of Sipsong Panna were deeply split by the political and ideological struggle between the Chinese Nationalists and Communists. Some of the *chao,* among them the regent prince, supported the Nationalists, who had allowed coexistence of the Tai political system and the Chinese administration, while other prominent *chao* supported the Communists. One of the most famous Communist supporters was Chao Tsengha (Zhao Cunxin), who was chairman of the external cabinet of the Tai government and who became the prefect of Sipsong Panna after the Communist victory. By 1950, when Sipsong Panna was declared "lib-

11. Many Chinese insist that the prince never actually became king.

erated," many Tai had fled to Thailand and Burma, where some took refuge with leading Chinese Nationalists.

The Communists adopted a successful strategy of cooperation with parts of the Tai upper strata, thereby avoiding large-scale revolts against the final abolition of royal titles and the traditional Tai government and political system. Chinese names of places and counties in Sipsong Panna based on the Tai's own names were adopted. In spite of protests from some members of the other ethnic groups in Sipsong Panna, the new local government was a Tai—not a Hani or Tai/Hani—autonomous government and the Tai name of the kingdom was adopted as the name of the new autonomous prefecture, which was established in 1953. Most likely this was an important part of the Chinese government's strategy to avoid major conflicts with the Tai in the early stages of the PRC. Many of the leading *chao* from the former Tai kingdom received government positions in the new autonomous prefecture. The last king never returned to live in Sipsong Panna, but continued to enjoy high prestige among the Tai. He obtained a position in the Chinese People's Political Consultative Conference in Yunnan, and his descendants were given very good employment and educational opportunities. While the government adopted a cooperative attitude toward the *chao phaendin, chao meeng,* and other important members of the central Tai government, local headmen maintained or even increased their authority in the villages when the *chao* lost local power. It was only in 1956, when campaigns for land reform were launched all over Sipsong Panna, that their power and authority were broken as well.

SCHOOLS DURING THE REPUBLIC: BUYING STUDENTS

Unlike in Lijiang, Confucian education never gained widespread influence in Sipsong Panna. Only members of the royal family participated in limited private Confucian education and one scholar mentions that there were two private Confucian schools in Mengla County by the end of the Qing in 1911 (Zou 1992: 1). Education of male novices (*pha*), however, in the local Buddhist monasteries (*wat*) was widespread and common among the Tai and Blang. When the Nationalist government created new districts and subdistricts in Sipsong Panna in 1911, it also set up the first Chinese schools. These schools were meant for children of both locals and Han immigrants. Through the teaching of Chinese, the government hoped to break the authority of the *chao* class and the influential Buddhist monks who conducted all education of Tai boys in the monasteries. Only some members of the ruling *chao* class—those who had contacts with the imposed Chinese rulers, and some of whom had private Chinese teachers as well—understood and spoke Chinese. The lack of knowledge of Chinese was regarded as a major obstacle for the imposition of Chinese rule, and already in 1912 the head of the Chinese government of Simao and Puer reported to the provincial government about the urgent need for developing Chinese education in Sipsong Panna (Xiao 1993: 125). After this the Nationalist government started primary "citizen schools" at the *bao* administrative levels. In 1935 a "simple normal school" (*jianyi shifan xuexiao*) was started in Fohai (Menghai), and in 1946 the first secondary school was established in Cheli (Jinghong).

In 1921 the Yunnan provincial government issued regulations for expanding border education in the hope that this would promote the integration of these areas and consolidate Chinese control. The new regulations had to be followed in all border regions where the majority ethnic groups were non-Han and where the cultural level was regarded as utterly backward. The goals of promoting education in border areas were very ambitious: all citizens between the ages of six and fifty who did not know Chinese were obliged to attend "border education" (*bianjing jiaoyu*); by 1943 education should be universal among all peoples in border areas; and between 1931 and 1937 all areas should establish primary, secondary, and simple normal schools, mainly to teach the Chinese language (Jiang 1950: 285–86). With regard to minority students, the Chinese administration in Sipsong Palma was obliged, in principle, to refrain from claiming tuition fees, to provide financial support for food and clothing, and to exempt Tai families who sent one or more children to school from paying the household tax.

However, the new schools had to be financed through the tax system, and the existence of the double government (Tai and Chinese) created heavy economic burdens on the population. There were taxes and fees for nearly everything—houses, leprosy prevention, the militia, magistrate's services, the *chao* government, slaughter, and so on. Among the heaviest burdens, according to Chen Han-Seng's study, were taxes that financed education: the general education tax for the establishment and maintenance of the schools, and the tax that supported boys attending Chinese schools. According to Chen, these two taxes constituted as much as 35 percent of the total household tribute (Chen Han-Seng 1949: 47–49).

Since few Tai voluntarily sent their children to the Chinese schools, a quota system was introduced forcing each medium-sized village to send at least one boy to school in the nearest larger village. This rule was very unpopular among the Tai, and in 1936 it sparked a revolt in Cheli. The government maintained the quota system but allowed the villages to choose whom to send away to school. This became an economic burden for Tai villagers, who started to pay boys from Han, Akha, or other local groups to fill their quota and go in their stead. Some poor Tai families would rent out a son to attend the unpopular Chinese school for fifty yuan and some unhusked rice (Chen Han-Seng 1949: 23). Most older interviewees recalled the Republican schools as very unpopular, and agreed that it was common to pay poor Tai—or, more often, Akha or Han—to attend them. One of the few interviewees who had himself attended a citizen school in Simao recalled,

> Everybody had to pay for the Nationalists' citizen schools and each small district was told how many students it had to send to the school. Our district had to provide six or seven students. I was sent, and the whole village paid my family for that. The Tai were the rulers and they sometimes paid other ethnic groups to go to the school. Nobody wanted to send their children to the school. They preferred that they worked at home, and people always said that children would turn Han if they went there. They feared that their children would become like the Han and maybe leave the village and the family. They feared assimilation [*tonghua*]. If children cried, parents would threaten them by saying, "The Han are coming!" and immediately the children would stop. Whenever Han people came to the villages, even in the 1950s, children would run away in fear.

Jiang Yingliang, the well-known researcher who was a magistrate in Cheli in 1945 and a member of a research group that had to prepare a plan for changing the local administration, points to additional reasons why Chinese education failed in this period: most schools were not started on the Tai plains but higher up in the mountains, where most Han lived in fear of malaria; the Tai students did not get the preferential treatment they were entitled to, and although the royal family supported Chinese education in public, it was in fact against it. Therefore, most students in the new schools were Han, many schools operated only on paper in order to get financial support, and, finally, in 1942 all schooling stopped in Sipsong Panna due to Japanese bombing of the area (Jiang 1950: 288–89).

Only among the royal family and the families of officials in the Tai government seat and palace (Xianyigai) of Jinghong did it become common to send children to the new schools. I interviewed one former student of the primary school connected to the palace, Mr. Dao.[12] Mr. Dao's father had been a high-ranking member of the central Tai government, and in 1933 Dao started in the primary school where about thirty boys and girls (many of them Han) studied Chinese. All teachers were Han except for one Tai official who taught Tai script. Like most other Tai boys at the time, Mr. Dao became a novice in the temple after he graduated from the school. In 1941 he was one of the few Tai who continued on to secondary education at the simple normal school in Menghai, where most students were local Han or Hui. All teachers were Han, and students studied for one year.

Jinghong was the area of Sipsong Panna where Chinese education was most developed in this period, though still very limited. According to official statistics from 1938, there were fourteen schools with a total of 696 students (Xiao 1993: 126). We do not know which ethnic groups the students belonged to, but all information points to a majority, or at least a large proportion, of Han students. In accordance with the Nationalist government's wish to promote education in border regions, Yunnan Province started one of its special border area schools, Southwest Border School (Xinan Bianjing Xuexiao), in Jinghong in 1947. This school consisted of a primary and a secondary school for educating minority cadres loyal to the Chinese state. Students were recruited mainly from the *chao* class, because the Chinese government needed the cooperation of the nobility and the local administration in order to gain the trust and loyalty of the common population. The school enrolled two hundred students, but due to serious political and financial instabilities, it func-

---

12. Members of the royal family and the central Tai government normally adopted the Chinese name Dao or Zhao, whereas Tai commoners have no surnames. Male Tai names start with Ai, and female names with Yi. Several interviewees said that when they went to school before 1949 the (Han) teachers would give them the "scholarly name" of Dao even if they did not belong to the *chao* class.

tioned for only a short time (Xiao 1993: 126–27). One of the few (incomplete) statistics on school attendance in Sipsong Panna during the Republic shows a generally very low number of students. In 1945, when Lijiang was reported to have 73 percent of children attending schools, the whole of Sipsong Panna had 15 percent and Fohai (Menghai County) only 1 percent (*YMJFG* 1992: 52).

A few American missionaries also worked in the area between 1913 and 1944. They did not succeed in converting many locals, who were firm believers in Buddhism and their own spirits. However, the *chao phaendin* and the Tai government agreed to rent some land for the missionaries to set up a hospital and school. The missionaries had language problems and indeed difficulty persuading people to convert, so they brought in a small group of Tai from outside Sipsong Panna who had already been converted and relied on them to spread the Christian message to the local Tai. There were around thirty to forty students in the school, which taught the Tai language in addition to English (Zha 1993: 142–49).

THE COMMUNIST PROJECT
OF SPREADING SCHOOL EDUCATION

After the PRC established control in Sipsong Panna in 1950, it sent large numbers of mostly Han cadres, teachers, and work teams to the area. By establishing friendly contacts with the locals, they were to disseminate knowledge of the CCP and its policy, set up a new government, initiate land reform, recruit adult students for cadre training, and start new schools. Special research teams conducted the economic and political investigations that later served as the basis for accomplishing land reform and provided the new Chinese government with its first thorough knowledge of the social and political system among the Tai in Sipsong Panna. Researchers concluded that socioeconomically, Sipsong Panna was mostly a "feudal manorial landlord system" (*fengjian lingzhu zhi*), a low evolutionary stage. Their finding of remnants of "primitive society" (in the form of collectively owned land in villages) and "slave society" convinced researchers that the mode of production among the Tai was more backward than that of the Naxi (and of course the Han).[13]

---

13. See *XDZG* 1986: 23–27; *Daizu shehui lishi diaocha: Xishuangbanna* 1985, vols. 1–10.

Especially in a border area such as Sipsong Panna, where knowledge of the Chinese language was so limited, where the former ruling class still possessed symbolic authority, and where Buddhist temples were the centers not only of religion but also of education, it was essential that the new Chinese government quickly foster loyal cadres who could act as connecting links between commoners and the government. For the same reasons, it provided special treatment for members of the upper class who did not flee the country (which quite a few did). Many of them received positions in the autonomous government established in 1953, when all previous royal titles and positions were abolished.

After 1950 an increasing number of Chinese migrants, most of whom were Han, came to Sipsong Panna. In spite of the trouble they encountered, most of these cadres, teachers, and workers on newly established state farms were convinced that their presence greatly benefited the Tai and the other *minzu* in the area. They saw their mission as developing, civilizing, and integrating this outpost of the PRC. One of them expressed very clearly the general point of view of Han immigrants at this time:

> Already in the 1960s the Tai were quite civilized [*kaihua*]. They welcomed us and wanted to learn Chinese. Many Han were sent from all over China to help develop Sipsong Panna. If we Han had not come, this place would not have developed. The Tai welcomed us because they realized that we, as a more advanced [*xianjin*] *minzu*, could help them develop this place. I believe that Sipsong Panna is the place in China where education has developed most rapidly because the sudden influence of Han culture was so strong.

Communist work teams (*gongzuo dui*) traveled all over Sipsong Panna and selected representatives from villages who would receive a short-term education, usually at the Normal School in Menghai (which moved to Jinghong in 1956) but sometimes at the Yunnan Institute of the Nationalities in Kunming. In villages, work teams usually chose a younger man who had been a monk and therefore knew Tai script. If somebody knew a bit of Chinese, this was also regarded as an advantage. Most of the young men who received short-term cadre training would return as local administrators at the village level. Members of the royal family in Jinghong and the central Tai government who agreed to cooperate with the new Chinese government received government positions, but in the countryside, work teams normally chose poorer peasants, rather than so-called landlords and headmen, to receive cadre or teacher education. However, in the first seven years of Communist rule in Sipsong Panna, until land reform started in 1956, work teams and Chinese cadres generally adopted a policy of cooperation with the village headmen. By doing so they were able to persuade the local population to participate in mass meetings and to let their children attend school. By 1956–57 most of the highest *chao meeng* had already been moved to Jinghong in order to break their local authority, which might obstruct the work teams' policies.

In 1953 the new prefectural government gathered all primary school teachers in Sipsong Panna for a one-week course in Tai script. Additionally, a special minority class was started in the Normal School to train teachers who knew enough Tai to communicate and teach the Tai script in schools. The hope at this time was that the introduction of the Tai language in schools would eventually cause people to abandon their tradition of sending boys to the monasteries. At this time there were twenty-three primary schools and one normal school in the whole of Sipsong Panna. Eighty percent of the students were non-Han. The first regular junior secondary schools were established in 1958 in each of the three counties (Jinghong, Menghai, and Mengla), and the first Blang and Jinuo primary schools were established in 1956.

In the first years of the People's Republic, Tai script was taught in many of the new primary schools in Tai villages and in the special minority class at the Normal School. Schools sometimes invited monks to teach Tai, because few teachers were able to do so. In the beginning the Tai script used in schools was the same as that used in monasteries. No other minority languages were taught, and in all non-Tai villages in Sipsong Panna the children learned only the Chinese language and script. The "old Tai script," as it was called by the Chinese, was not standardized, and in the early years of the PRC there was a great demand for Tai books. A few village schools experimented with teaching one class of Tai pupils in Chinese only and teaching another basic Tai before turning to Chinese studies. The teachers from that time whom I interviewed did not doubt that the students in the Tai class performed best in school. One of these schools resumed the experiment in 1993 and even used some of the teaching material in "old Tai" from the early 1950s.

In spite of these early attempts to establish education in old Tai, it was quickly decided to make a simplified version of the Tai script in line with the new government's wish to simplify Chinese characters and to create new scripts for minorities. In 1954 a few Tai who knew Chinese well and were proficient in the Tai script were asked to propose a simplified form of Tai script, the so-called "new Tai script." They also created a simple dictionary and some teaching material. The *Panna Newspaper,* written in new Tai, was started in 1957. Publication was suspended between 1966 and 1972, and between 1993 and 1996 the paper was printed in the old Tai script. Thus, by the mid-1950s three writing systems were taught to the Tai in Sipsong Panna: Chinese in all schools, new Tai in some schools, and old Tai in all monasteries. The locals' attitudes toward the new script were divided, as they are today. Some Tai argue that the simplified script is much easier to learn and therefore more practical, while others argue that since Buddhist texts and traditional Tai stories taught in the monasteries are in the old Tai form, children are cut off from their own tradition when they learn the new form of Tai. With the recent increase in contacts across Sipsong Panna's borders, some argue that the old Tai is advantageous for learning standard Thai.

If you have learned the old Tai script, it is very easy to learn the simplified version, whereas those who know only the new Tai script maintain that they are completely unable to read the old script. This is of course quite similar to the situation of readers who have learned only simplified Chinese characters. However, there is a gender-specific dimension to the difference between new and old Tai. Because only Tai boys studied in the local monasteries, they were also the only ones who learned old Tai. Those Tai girls who learned any Tai script at all always learned new Tai. The new and simplified Tai script that was taught in the schools was created to eradicate illiteracy, but it had the side effect of actually dividing the Tai, who no longer had one common script that at least most boys would study. Today a whole generation has learned only the new Tai script (and/or Chinese) in school and is unable to read old Tai, unless they are male and have had the opportunity to learn it in a monastery.

One of the Tai who participated in editing the first Tai teaching material was Zhao Xi,[14] who was born in 1933 and was a novice for nine years. He was

14. Like most other names of interviewees in this book, this is a pseudonym.

just about to become a monk when he decided to return to secular life in 1951 because the new government offered to give him a free education in the Normal School. Zhao's story gives a good picture of how the work teams propagated communism, the difficulty of starting new Chinese schools, and Tai commoners' attitudes toward the new administration in the early 1950s.

Zhao Xi's Story

I was a student in the Normal School from 1951 to 1952 in a special class for Tai. All students had to know Tai script, so most of us were former monks. We learned Chinese and studied the policy of the Communist Party and the new principles. We also studied geography—China's geography. We did not know that China [Zhongguo] was not a foreign country [*waiguo*]. For us Burma, Thailand, Laos, and China were all foreign countries, but in the villages people did not even know that there was a border between them and Burma or Laos. In the Normal School we learned that Sipsong Panna was part of China. [Then in 1954 Zhao was sent to be a teacher in a Tai village:] In the evenings the work team showed films from the Soviet Union about socialist society, about how the Soviet Union used machinery in agriculture and how education was necessary to achieve this kind of development. Therefore, many people wanted to try to go to school. They themselves built a thatched house for the school building.

On the first day of school, more than two hundred people attended the classes. They were between eight and nineteen years old. Some had been novices before, and some were still novices. There were more than fifty in each class. After a very short time, students did not show up anymore. They preferred to work in the fields, some married, the novices had no time for school work, and for some it was too far to walk. Every evening we teachers visited families to talk to the parents about this. We helped if somebody was sick, we arranged for old people to take care of cattle while the children were in school, and so on. Since I had been a novice myself, I understood the conditions in the temple. I knew that during the daytime, the novices did not study the Buddhist sutras. Therefore, I told the monks that the things *they* taught the children did not contradict what *we* taught them— that the teachings complemented each other. I told them that the Communist Party was not against their form of education or against their religion.

We also arranged activities such as ball games, singing, dancing, and so on to make the school more attractive. And nobody had to pay for anything — oh yes, only the few who were richer than the others, otherwise it was all free. Not like today, when it is so expensive to have a child in school. . . .

Society changed very, very slowly here. In the 1950s everybody still considered the *chao phaendin*, the *meeng*, and the *pia* [local headmen] to be the highest authorities. It was very important that people saw that the new government worked together with the local Tai leaders. That proved to them how important their local leaders were.[15]

The initiation of land reform in 1956 in Sipsong Panna politically marked the beginning of a period when powerful Party leaders considered the local minorities ripe for organized struggle against their former leaders. Unlike Central China, where struggle against landlords was supposed to be like a hurricane (*jifeng baoyu*), in the border areas redistribution of fields and deprivation of local landlords' power was adopted as a "peaceful consultation" (*heping xieshang*). The advantages of the reforms were carefully explained to the ruling class, who were to be treated leniently and allowed to keep some fields (XDZG 1986: 84–90). The struggle against local headmen was often carried out as a so-called "back-to-back struggle" (*bei dui bei douzheng*) in which the peasants did not face the headman directly, in order to avoid harming the "unity of the *minzu*." By 1957 land reform was completed, but had been resisted directly in at least one short-lived revolt by one of the former *chao meeng* in cooperation with Nationalists on the Burmese side of the border (Hsieh 1989: 214).

The period of land reform between 1956 and 1957 was presented by some interviewees as a brief "high tide" of Chinese education in Sipsong Panna. One mentioned that people were excited about the prospect of dividing fields among themselves and therefore cooperated with the work teams and teachers who wanted them to send their children to school. Other reasons were that people were freed from paying taxes if they let their children attend school. Some parents also thought that sending their children to school could prevent their own family from being criticized in the same way as other local headmen and landlords. However, apparently few people were convinced of

15. Extracts from 1994 interview.

the relevance of the content of the Chinese education, and many children quickly dropped out of school again.

The policy of conducting "peaceful consultative reforms" was firmly criticized in 1958 as an expression of a revisionist policy of cooperation with feudal lords and granting border areas special treatment. In the same year, the Great Leap Forward was launched and People's Communes were set up all over Sipsong Panna. The period from the land reform movement onward was marked by a number of political campaigns. The reidentification of classes during the "additional teaching of democratic reform" (*minzhu gaige buke*) in 1958 and the "four clean-ups" (*siqing yundong*) in 1964–65 caused a large number of Tai to flee the country. Former Tai leaders were criticized at mass meetings, all contacts across international borders were prohibited, and many monks and novices returned to secular life in response to antireligious policy. The palace of the *chao phaendin*, the Tai government building, and the nearby major temple of Sipsong Panna were completely ruined in 1957, and the area was converted to a state-owned rubber plantation.[16] Mr Zhao Xi recalled,

> It was all chaos! It was even more chaotic than the Cultural Revolution, which was carried out mainly in the cities. All contacts across the [international] borders, which had always been very common in Sipsong Panna, were forbidden. A lot of people were branded as spies because they had family members across the border. We could not marry Tai on the other side of the border any longer, or even write letters. Already in 1962 there were only a few monks left, and a lot of temples were destroyed. A lot of people escaped to other countries.

During this time the government also became more conscious of the content of the teaching material in minority languages. For instance, in 1959 the central government decided that all teaching material in minority languages should be directly based upon ideological teaching of "socialism, communism, and patriotism" (*YMJFG* 1992: 201). Although the Tai tradition of sending boys to the monasteries was criticized, many boys still became novices

---

16. This state farm is still functioning today. The temple is a complete ruin; its stones, pillars, and other materials as well as those from the palace have been used by the state farm. The government has now started to reconstruct the palace area as a tourist attraction.

for a time. For this reason, schools were dominated by female pupils. Before 1958 some schools tried to solve this problem by arranging special "novice classes" (*heshang ban*), in which novices were taught at a special time of the day or even inside the monastery. However, most teachers from this time recalled that Chinese education was still not popular. Students often came only every second or third day, or dropped out after a few months or years. Religious influence was especially strong south of the Mekong River, and school attendance was low. The Normal School had problems convincing its Tai students to complete their studies; one student from 1956–59 recalled that about half of the students in his class dropped out before graduation. Generally speaking, the number of students in schools was inversely proportional to the number of novices in temples. In times when religion was severely suppressed, school attendance also was strongly encouraged (or even enforced), so the number of novices fell while school enrollment rose. Thus, figures show that school attendance was relatively high in Sipsong Panna in 1958 and during the Cultural Revolution, and fell again when the political pressure to attend Chinese schools lessened. For instance, in Mengla County in 1953, in 15 schools with 950 students, the enrollment rate was 13.8 percent. In 1958 in 40 schools with 3,310 students, the enrollment rate was 50 percent. This fell to 28 percent in 1962, increased to 62 percent with the start of the Cultural Revolution in 1966, and increased again to 92 percent in 1975 (Li Guangpin 1992: 127).

In the whole of Sipsong Panna in 1950 there were 11 schools with 390 students and 22 teachers. In 1957 the number of schools had increased to more than 100, with more than 9,000 students, and in 1964 there were 400 schools, more than 35,000 students, and more than 1,000 teachers (Zhou Houkun 1992: 148). According to interviews, enrollment figures are exaggerated because schools and village authorities tended to over-report and did not subtract the many students who quickly dropped out. In line with decisions of the Yunnan provincial government concerning education in border regions, most of Sipsong Panna's schools at this time were part-time schools where students worked in the fields in the afternoon, or "simple reading schools" (*jianyi xuexiao*) where they studied only minority script, Chinese script, spoken Chinese, and mathematics (*YMJFG* 1992: 186). Until 1958, when each of the three counties in Sipsong Panna started a junior secondary school, the only post-primary school was the Normal School. From 1965 to 1968 there was also one "part-work part-study" school and an agricultural school.

However, the figures clearly show that the Chinese government put a lot of effort into establishing schools to spread knowledge of subjects such as Chinese language, culture, and history in order to integrate the people of Sipsong Panna into China and ensure the authority of the state.

Although Chinese education spread steadily throughout Sipsong Panna since the 1950s, it did not manage to pull the Tai boys out of the monasteries. The increased number of schools should be seen in relation to the large number of monasteries and of novices and monks studying Buddhist texts in the Tai language. In 1950, compared to the 11 Chinese schools and 390 students, there were 574 temples, 930 monks, and 5,550 novices registered. For the first time Tai girls were able to get a school education, but for most Tai parents, the prospect of having a child educated in a Chinese school was not economically or culturally attractive and was considered irrelevant to daily life. Nevertheless, the government, the work teams, and an increasing number of enthusiastic teachers (mainly from outside Sipsong Panna) managed to multiply the number of Chinese schools by ten within the first seven years of Communist rule, and for the first time in Sipsong Panna increasing numbers of Tai pupils in villages attended Chinese schools at least for a short period of time. However, the most dramatic increase in school attendance took place in periods when policy became very restrictive and antireligious. This forced large numbers of monks to return to secular life and prevented many boys from becoming novices. During these times more children attended schools because they had no alternative and because local cadres stressed the need to send children to Chinese schools. Buddhist training in the Tai language was regarded by the Chinese government as a direct obstruction to the development of the only real and proper form of education—that in Chinese schools.

PROHIBITION OF MONASTIC EDUCATION
DURING THE CULTURAL REVOLUTION

According to my interviews, the number of monks and novices fell dramatically as early as 1957, perhaps as much as 50 percent.[17] After the launch-

---

17. I have no exact figures; the interviewees estimated this on the basis of their own knowledge of the large number of monks who returned to lay lives.

ing of the Cultural Revolution in 1966, all novices and monks were compelled to discard their yellow robes and to resume a secular life, and many monks fled the country. Buddhist images and temples all over Sipsong Panna were smashed, and books written in Tai script were burned. Only a few temples were saved, because some people were able to convince Red Guards that they were useful for purposes such as storing grain. Some important books in Tai script were saved by people who buried them in the woods. For almost fourteen years no Tai novices were trained, and teaching of the old Tai script was conducted only in families where the father or grandfather secretly taught children to read.[18] The Tai reacted with tacit acceptance; most seem to have swallowed their anger and accepted the conditions. "We were angry, but there was nothing to do [*shengqi, mei banfa*]!" said one Tai man in his fifties.

In the initial phase of the Cultural Revolution, national policy demanded that border areas be treated with caution, but this view was quickly criticized, and struggles began in minority areas against rich peasants, landlords, members of the aristocracy, and monks. In Sipsong Panna large numbers of revolutionary work teams, students, and teachers arrived to carry out the revolution. Since most members of the local government belonged to the *chao* class, many of them were paraded on Nationalities Street, sent to the villages to work as peasants, and replaced by Han officials.[19]

One of the fiercest border-region campaigns was that to "politicize the frontiers" (*zhengzhi bianfang*) in Sipsong Panna between 1969 and 1971. Former stages of the Cultural Revolution in border areas had been severely criticized for upholding the revisionist ideas that these areas needed special treatment and that minorities were in some respect different from the Han:

> Yunnan is being polite at the frontiers, practicing revisionism at the frontiers, engaging in excessive peacefulness at the frontiers. This excessive peacefulness is just an excessive step toward capitalism. You are afraid that people will flee. Why be afraid of that? If bad people run away, let them do so. The

18. Although education in monasteries was, and still is, reserved for boys, quite a few girls have learned in their homes to read and write Tai.

19. See Hsieh 1989: 231–33 on the fate of *chao* during this time.

border areas engage only in culture and production. They have left class struggle and policy in order to engage in culture and production. How is that possible! (1968 report, quoted in *Yunnan minzu gongzuo, 40 nian:* 216)

The campaign brought a second round of establishing People's Communes in the border regions and provoked large-scale and violent struggles against so-called rich peasants, landlords, aristocracy, and "spies" among minorities. Due to the government's former strategy of cooperating with religious leaders and the nobility in minority areas, there remained many "remnants of feudal society." These were ferociously attacked and smashed in these areas. Sipsong Panna was no exception.

The Cultural Revolution was carried out most directly in Jinghong, where schools closed down and teachers (almost all Han) went to Simao to participate in revolutionary education for three months. Some students stayed in the secondary school to participate in the struggles; others returned home to their villages. In the countryside, primary schools continued to function, and new junior (and a few senior) secondary schools were started in production teams and communes after 1970. Many Buddhist and other texts in Tai (old and new) were burned, and the teaching of Tai in schools was prohibited. As in Lijiang and the rest of China, all teaching was now in Chinese, and the most important subject was the ideas and sayings of Mao Zedong. Some Tai interviewees who were teachers in small villages at that time recalled that they were not allowed to teach Tai script, but that they often used spoken Tai to explain. Otherwise, pupils would not understand. Most teachers were Han who came, or were sent, in large numbers from other places in China to "carry out revolution" or "learn from the peasants."

There were many pupils in schools during the Cultural Revolution when all religious activities were suppressed, but the number began falling immediately after the policy relaxed after 1979. According to Zou Zhenxie, as many as 102,017 students attended primary schools in Sipsong Panna in 1975 (Zou 1992: 3). In *A Survey of Sipsong Panna Tai Nationality Autonomous Prefecture* it is argued that 12,444 students started in primary schools in 1970, but 44 percent dropped out before graduation in 1975 (*XDZG* 1986: 147). Although my interviews confirmed that most children under eighteen attended school for short periods of time during the Cultural Revolution, the first figure is remarkably high considering that the entire population of Sipsong Panna was less than five hundred thousand at this time. Probably many schools over-reported enrollment and did not calculate those who dropped out.

The extremely repressive policy of the Cultural Revolution has been strongly criticized by the Chinese government since 1979. In publications and official reports about Sipsong Panna, the policy of this period is condemned for having harmed the "unity of the *minzu*" by suppressing religion, Tai script, and monastic education. Yet Han cadres and teachers engaged in education have always regarded the Buddhist education of boys in Sipsong Panna as the main obstacle to the development of Chinese education. Only the oppressive policy of the Cultural Revolution managed to abolish this kind of education, to stop the development of Buddhism and the spread of the Tai script, and to enroll large numbers of Tai students in Chinese schools. No Chinese cadres, teachers, or educators in Sipsong Panna would say that the policy of the Cultural Revolution was in any way a good policy. Nevertheless, it did bring about some of the changes that the central government and most Chinese cadres desired for Sipsong Panna: increased influence of Chinese language and culture and decline of Buddhist and Tai traditions.

5 / Education and Ethnic Identity in Sipsong Panna since 1980

By the end of 1982 most People's Communes in Yunnan's border areas had been abolished, and the peasants had contracted land under the new responsibility system. Many peasants in Sipsong Panna (and elsewhere) kept their children out of school to work in their new fields, and the new political atmosphere allowed for a more relaxed attitude toward religious practices. While the number of temples and novices in Sipsong Panna has steadily increased since 1982 in what some have called a "religious fever" (*zongjiao re*), the government established new minority schools, Tai classes, and special "novices classes" in order to attract more students.

THE REVIVAL OF BUDDHIST EDUCATION

Since the fourteenth century it has been common practice for Tai parents to send their sons to local Theravada temples to study the Buddhist sutras in Tai script. In many temples novices also read other material, such as traditional Tai stories and the history of the *chao phaendin*. Both the Nationalist and Communist Chinese governments have regarded this tradition as an obstruction to the spread of Chinese culture, language, and political rule, because it hindered the establishment of a successful Chinese educational system in Sipsong Panna. Monasteries were centers of education and religion, and virtually every Tai village had its own monastery, monks, and male novices. Novices studied for some years, after which most returned to secular lives. Some continued their Buddhist training and became monks when they were twenty years old. Normally monks enjoyed high prestige in the village, and elderly Tai today claim that it was very difficult for a man to get married if he had not been a novice.

Lay Buddhists, monks, and novices were all part of the *sangha,* the entire following of the Buddha:[1] "The Buddha conceived of the pursuit of Nibbana [Nirvana] by layman and monk as fully complementary and reciprocal—the layman pursuing the goal in such a way as to provide the material necessities of life to the monk and the monk giving of himself to the layman by way of maintaining and manifesting the inspiring ideal and teaching and guiding the layman" (Lester 1973: 47). The role of the Buddhist laymen in the villages of Sipsong Panna was identical to that of the Tai in Ban Ping village in Northern Thailand, who earned merit by avoiding wrong actions, attending the temple, and bringing offerings to the temple, its monks, and novices (Moerman 1966: 140). Before being accepted as novices in the local temples, Tai boys in Sipsong Panna went through a period of pre-study, in which they still did not live in the temple but often frequented it, studied Tai language, and prepared to become novices within a year (in the fourth month of the Tai calendar). Often a small group became temple boys together, mostly with support from their parents, who had a share in the merit their son would gain by becoming a novice. For the parents' afterlife it was essential that at least one son had been a novice. Each boy had a personal benefactor who supported his ordination. This person served as a kind of adoptive father and was responsible for instructing the boy about his life in the temple and making the necessary arrangements. At an important ordination ritual in the temple, the boys (who were mostly between seven and ten years old) became novices, received new names, and started wearing the yellow robe. All villagers contributed financially to the celebration in the temple, and most had parties at home as well. In the village the boys now enjoyed higher status and respect through their connection to the temple.

Between 1957 and 1980 this practice declined and even disappeared completely between 1966 and 1979 due to the repressive policy of the Chinese government. However, especially since 1982, religious expressions have returned to Sipsong Panna and with them the practice of training boys in the monasteries. In the part of Jinghong that is north of the Mekong River,

1. Though *sangha* may refer to all followers of Buddha, both lay and monastic, it often refers only to the monastic followers (Lester 1973: 48). According to Richard Gombrich, the term is ambiguous and commonly refers to those who are ordained (Gombrich 1995 [1988]: 2, 18–20).

Han influence and antireligious policies have been most persistent, and here only a few temples have been rebuilt, few boys today become novices, and school attendance is comparatively high. In other areas of Sipsong Panna, especially in the southern part of Jinghong and Mengla and the whole county of Menghai, the upsurge in religious activity has been strong.

According to several interviewees, the so-called "religious fever" began in 1982, when people finally dared to believe that they were free to restart their religious practices. However, because a whole generation had not studied in temples and monks had either fled the country or resumed lay life, the Tai faced the practical problem of finding monks who could teach the new novices in the local temples that they had started to rebuild, mostly with their own money. Most Tai families have relatives in Thailand or Burma, and, mainly through contacts with them, many villages were able to invite foreign monks to Sipsong Panna. The gradual improvement of the Tai peasants' economy also made possible the increasing number of temples, monks, and novices. In 1982 there were 145 temples, 36 monks, and 655 novices in the whole of Sipsong Panna. Twelve years later, in 1994, there were 435 temples, 509 monks, and 5,336 novices.[2] The largest increase took place between 1982 and 1984, according to the Sipsong Panna Prefecture Bureau of Religions.[3]

In the first years of the religious upsurge, when many villages still did not have a monk, novices were often alone in the monasteries with nobody to teach them and without any idea of how to lead a Buddhist life. Often an elderly villager who had been a monk or novice earlier in his life would try to guide the boys. Today there are still some poorer villages without a learned monk to teach their novices, and in some villages peasants complain that their monk is insufficiently educated. Thus, there are today considerable differences among villages. To the disapproval of many foreign and local monks, novices in these temples often spend their time smoking, playing pool, and enjoying their free time.

In the numerous villages where foreign monks (mostly from Thailand or Burma) serve as educators or where local monks have been properly trained

2. Temples have to report the number of novices to the Bureau of Religions, which keeps statistics on the numbers of monks, novices, and temples.

3. In 1987 the county government in Mengla "urged" all thirty-four foreign monks in the county to leave Sipsong Panna, in accordance with the prefectural government's policy.

as teachers, villagers express satisfaction with the situation. Most of those I talked to were happy to send their boys to the monastery and had high esteem for the monk. However, some parents explained that even if they would like their children to go to a Chinese school, they had no way of forcing boys who preferred the monasteries. I did not find this explanation very convincing, since most of the boys were only seven to ten years old when they became novices. Teachers, however, confirmed that this was an explanation commonly heard from parents. Probably it was a tactful way for some parents to excuse themselves for not insisting on keeping the boys in school when facing representatives of the Chinese educational system. Although I always tried to make the purpose of my interviews clear to interviewees, some villagers thought that I represented the Chinese school system and feared criticism for not sending boys to school. Some later told me that they had thought that I, a university graduate, would regard their temple education as backward and useless. These parents' reluctance to force their children to attend school illustrates that—even though most Tai have accepted the Chinese schools as part of village life and are mostly happy to have a school in their neighborhood—they do not consider such education essential. Most villagers I talked to felt that children should try the school for a few years, and if they did not like it or were not good enough, they might as well stop. If they had a good monk in the village, parents considered Buddhist education at least as good as Chinese school education in terms of learning how to read and write. More importantly, they regarded it as essential for moral training and for earning merit for their sons and themselves. The practice of sending boys to receive Buddhist education is a tradition built on religious belief and is a habitual practice for many Tai. It is a significant component of Tai ethnic identity and a practical way of transmitting Tai script, history, and cultural values. In comparison, the Chinese school in Sipsong Panna is a poor competitor.

However, due to the previous repressive policies of the Chinese government, a whole generation of men and fathers have not been novices themselves. Many consider it less important for boys today to become novices or find it sufficient for boys to study in the temple for a few months. Sometimes these men are urged by village elders to send their sons to the monasteries, and generally mothers tend to be more strongly in favor of upholding the tradition. Again, one of the most important factors determining local support for temple education is the quality of the teaching monk. A Tai mother of two sons remarked,

> [Concerning her sixteen-year-old son:] He attended the village school for two years. He passed the examination to the higher primary school [from third to sixth grade in a school three kilometers away], but he did not want to continue there. All his friends were to become novices, so he wanted that as well. Even if we had wanted him to go to school, we had no way. Now he has been a monk for three years. [Concerning the son of twelve:] He went to school for two years in the village and did not pass the examination to continue into higher primary school. He tried again, but failed. Then the teacher suggested that he should go instead to the monastery to learn Tai script, which is also very good. Education is very good, and it does not matter if it is in the school or the monastery. The monk we have now is very good. He has a lot of knowledge, and it is good for us to have him here. I hope our older son will first become a monk in four years [when he is twenty]. Then he can be a monk for four or five years, and then he can return to lay life and become a peasant. When they are twenty they are grown up and want to marry.

This mother came from a village that had invited a young monk from Thailand, who had also begun teaching Thai to all interested villagers and who planned to invite a Tai to teach Chinese to the novices. His understanding of the situation in the village corresponded to that of most of the parents I talked to: "There will be more and more novices in this village because now they can really gain knowledge here in the temple. When a monk can provide the children with knowledge, the parents are very happy to send them to the monastery. If they do not learn very much, parents will instead encourage them to go to school." In this village the school recruited new pupils every second year, and after two years of study the children participated in an examination that determined whether they could continue on to the primary school in the administrative village three kilometers away. In the summer of 1994 nineteen pupils graduated after two years of study in this village school, twelve continued on to the full primary school, six boys became novices and dropped out of school, and one boy dropped out without becoming a novice.[4] The only teacher in this school belonged to the Yi *minzu* and spoke and understood only Chinese. All children in the school spoke Tai and only a little Chinese. There was no possibility of learning Tai in school during these first two years.

In several monasteries, monks now teach mathematics, Thai language, and (more rarely) Chinese. The most important temple in Sipsong Panna, Wat Pa Jie Maharajatan in Manting Park, has recently begun offering higher education for novices and monks who are sent back to village temples after completing studies. In this way the temple has attempted to diminish the antagonism between school and monastery education. One monk expressed the problem thus: "In the temple, children do not learn modern knowledge. In school, they do not learn how to be a good human being." The temple in Manting was rebuilt in 1989 and reopened in 1990. In 1995 a huge building with teaching facilities was inaugurated, financed mainly by sponsors from Thailand but also with support from the prefectural government. In 1990 about twenty monks from Wat Pa Jie Maharajatan were in Thailand studying in Buddhist monasteries, and by the end of 1994 almost half had returned to start teaching in the temple. It was hoped that the capacity of twenty-five novices could be expanded to two or three hundred within the next few years. Most novices (Tai and a few Blang) came from poor villages, and many of them had parents who either could not afford or were not particularly interested in letting them continue in regular schools. In the temple they got a free education of one or three years, after which they were sent to village temples as monks. According to one of the monks in the temple, this was the first attempt in Sipsong Panna to set up a comprehensive Buddhist training that included the study of modern subjects:

> The influence of religion in Sipsong Panna is definitely less than before 1957. In total there might be more monks now, but they study for a shorter period of time and are less qualified. Therefore, we want to increase the teaching of knowledge within the monasteries. Before, there was no Buddhist school [*Fojiao xuexiao*]. Now we are starting one, a real temple

4. Among those from this particular village who continue on to the full primary school, only a few graduate. The rest drop out after a few years.

school [*simiao xuexiao*]. Here novices can go to school while studying Buddhism.

Apart from Buddhist studies in Tai script, the novices were taught Chinese by a Tai with a teacher's education, using Tai as the language of instruction. The government had given permission for establishment of the new school, insisting that Chinese should be taught with national teaching material. Thus, the novices studied Chinese-language materials intended for the first three years of primary school. One class had already graduated in Thai studies, and the temple planned to offer English classes when one of the monks returned from college. Students were also eventually supposed to receive education in mathematics, geography, and local history based upon Tai texts.

All monks and novices I talked to were very excited about the new school that would bridge the gap between Buddhist teaching and the demand for knowledge in modern subjects and Chinese language. Very few boys in Sipsong Panna who have been novices for more than a few months manage to get an education beyond the primary school level. There are several reasons for this: their level of Chinese is insufficient, it is difficult for them to attend school while studying in the monastery, they earn no credits for learning to read and write their own language, some parents consider it a waste of money to pay for a school education that does not lead to a job or further education, and many are not motivated to get a Chinese education at all. Therefore, the higher Buddhist education in the temple in Manting is a welcome alternative for the small percentage of novices who get a chance to study there.

In the early 1980s, religious activities in Sipsong Panna were centered on rebuilding temples and restarting the tradition of temple education from scratch. In the last few years, encouraged by increasing contacts across the international borders, attitudes toward temple education have been slowly changing. Even though most Tai in the mid-1980s wanted to educate at least one son in the temple for religious purposes, many had been influenced by the extensive government propaganda that insisted that only Chinese schools could promote economic modernization. Buddhist education and modern (i.e., Chinese school) education were presented as mutually exclusive. Through their contacts across the borders, more and more Tai people in Sipsong Panna learned that in Thailand there is a closer connection between schools and temples, monks sometimes participate in common teachers training courses, teachers in elementary schools may take a special course in teaching Buddhism, and larger temples offer courses for girls and boys who are not novices—and Thailand nevertheless has a developed economy. Thus, a number of interviewed Tai from south of the Mekong River questioned the thesis of the mutual exclusiveness of modern and Buddhist education.

CHINESE ATTITUDES TOWARD TEMPLE EDUCATION

Generally speaking, most Han cadres, teachers, and researchers in and outside Sipsong Panna continue to express negative views of the influence of Buddhist education on the Tai. A few researchers elsewhere in Yunnan (mostly belonging to minority *minzu* themselves, but also some Han) expressed a much more open view of temple education than did most local cadres and teachers in Sipsong Panna. Many local Tai schoolteachers and government officials trained in Chinese schools share the negative view, although elderly officials and teachers who have themselves been monks tend to be more positive. The most concrete criticism of temple education is that it employs backward teaching methods; because of the monks' low educational level, too many novices are illiterate after they leave the temples; and it prevents girls from learning to read and write. Some of the most highly educated Tai monks are attempting to solve these problems. Because Tai girls traditionally were never taught in monasteries, most monks feel that it would be impossible to extend education to girls and that female education is not their responsibility. Recently, however, some monks have tried to arrange courses in Tai or Thai for all villagers, including females. Other commonly raised objections against monastery training are far more extensive and directed toward the heart of temple education. It is said, for instance, that temple education obstructs modernization by preventing the spread of Chinese culture:

> But the Buddhist temple education is a religious, theological education, the purpose of which is to teach people to stand aloof from worldly affairs, detest life, and escape the present to jump out of the sea of bitterness and into Nirvana. It wants people to seek a passive life, not an active life. It gives people the knowledge of how to follow the way of Buddha, but not the strength to understand and change the world. . . . This kind of edu-

cation fosters, to a large extent, people who follow religion, the feudal ruling clique, and traditional culture. Their function is to defend feudal and
religious rule. This is a force that restrains and blocks development for Tai
society and culture and which faces a conflict with the historical tide of
modernization. (Sun Ruoqiong et al., eds. 1990: 266)

This text on minority education goes on to argue that the only way to promote
modern education in Sipsong Panna is to penetrate the traditional outlook of
the Tai, who tend to prefer the well-known, old-fashioned education. Forbidding
temple education is no solution; instead, ways must be found to convince
people that only in Chinese schools will their children be brought up to adapt
to the modernizing world. Buddhism, on the other hand, is held responsible for bringing up a population of self-centered and xenophobic people:

> From the perspective of cultural psychology, the ancient and once splen-
> did Buddhist culture has caused the religious Tibetans and Tai to create a
> feeling of cultural superiority that puts themselves in the center. This atti-
> tude of superiority is partly an expression of highly cherishing the concepts
> and behavior of their own *minzu*'s culture, and partly an expression of
> despising and excluding other cultures. (Ibid.: 268)

Recently, this objectification of so-called Tai psychological characteristics has
been criticized by a few Chinese researchers who are not dealing specifically
with education (see, e.g., Liu Yan 1993: 279). Zhang Shiya (1992) has made
a general and theoretical study of religious education in southwest China,
and, although he does not discuss education in Sipsong Panna in detail, he
is generally much more positive and analytical toward religious education
than are most Chinese researchers of Buddhist education in Sipsong Panna.
Many remain profoundly worried that Buddhism is obstructing the Tai's possibilities for development. The people within Sipsong Panna who are most
negative toward temple education and see no potential in it are the Han who
occupy high positions in school administration, headmasters, older teachers
in administrative posts, and Han cadres in the government education departments—people with great influence on local forms of education. They tend
to see Buddhist education as the main force preventing boys from having a
Chinese education, and they rarely acknowledge problems within the Chinese

educational system itself. Many are worried that the Tai might become "even more backward" than the minorities living in the mountains, who have always been considered to be most backward by the incoming Chinese and the Tai themselves.[5]

Many Tai teachers and cadres, especially those living in Jinghong City, share this critical view of the institution of temple education. The Tai who have a Chinese education themselves would never let their sons participate in Buddhist education, because it would prevent them from moving upward in Chinese society. However, they tend to be more open toward the idea of cooperation between schools and temples. In the early 1950s some monks were invited to teach in the new schools, but during the resurgence of religious activities since 1980, cooperation between monasteries and schools has been extremely limited. Usually monks and teachers are in contact with each other only when teachers go to monasteries to inform monks that novices must go to school, or when monks go to schools to obtain permission for novices in school to participate in temple activities. There is a strong conflict of interest between monks and teachers, which was expressed very clearly in a junior secondary school in a small town where the resurgence of religion has been very strong. In this school thirteen out of fifteen teachers were Han, whereas 40 percent of the students were Tai and only 10 percent were Han. When I visited the school, one of the most important Buddhist festivals in the township was under way, and Tai people came from all over the neighborhood to celebrate for two whole days. However, the students in the school had no time off. The teachers' attitudes toward this religious event were expressed clearly by a teacher who firmly stated, "This has nothing to do with us!"

A few highly educated Han and Tai in Sipsong Panna have a more positive view of temple education, mainly because they regard it is an opportunity for boys who cannot pass the examinations within the school system. However, with recent attempts by scholarly monks in Sipsong Panna to set up higher education for novices, a more respectful attitude toward temple

5. Although these government officials would paraphrase the official policy when talking in their office with other cadres walking in and out, many were more radical in their opposition to temple education when talking in private. A few (retired) cadres were, on the contrary, more positive when talking privately.

education seems to be slowly developing among some Tai with a higher Chinese education, who (mostly privately) acknowledge that Buddhist education has not prevented Thailand from modernizing, and that it is therefore wrong to blame the tradition of educating novices for slow economic development among the Tai in Sipsong Panna. By claiming that Buddhist education is changing, they indirectly reject the common Chinese view of temple education as static. However, it is beyond dispute that temple education today is an obstacle to the spread of Chinese education and thus Chinese culture, language, nationalism, and knowledge of Chinese history. This is the main reason why Chinese authorities, including cadres and teachers, are firmly against it.

RESPONSES TO "RELIGIOUS FEVER": SPECIAL "NOVICES CLASSES" AND REGULATIONS

Between 1980 and 1983 the government in Sipsong Panna faced a situation in which school attendance was less than 60 percent and the drop-out rate very high, especially south of the Mekong River. This was a result partly of the resumption of sending boys to the temples, and partly of the new system of contracting fields, which caused parents to keep their children home to work. Some schools were almost empty, some had only female pupils, and most boys dropped out after a few years. A number of measures were introduced to force parents to send their children to school, and today the education departments, teachers, and school administrators still discuss how to increase the number of graduates at all levels. Almost 90 percent of children start school in Sipsong Panna today, but only 55.5 percent complete five years of study (Sipsong Panna Prefecture Education Commission 1992: 2).[6] Although 67 percent of novices enrolled in school in 1994, few stayed there for more than a few years.

After the start of "religious fever," the government sent teachers, cadres, and representatives from the government-sponsored Buddhist Association

---

6. Primary school education in Sipsong Panna is six years, but in the countryside it usually is divided into four years of lower and two years of higher primary school. An examination after four years determines whether children are qualified to continue on to higher primary school.

to Tai villages to persuade parents to send their children to school. It was emphasized that boys were allowed to become novices only after graduation from primary school, but in practice this rule proved impossible to enforce. The government decided to make the local township governments responsible for finding methods to increase the school enrollment rate (*ruxue lü*) and the retention rate (*gonggu lü*) in the villages. Generally, it was decided that monks could wear their yellow robes in school, take a few days off for special Buddhist activities, and start school even after the usual age of seven. Today the rule is that novices are obliged to start school before they are twelve. They are also allowed special treatment in boarding schools, where, for instance, they share rooms with other novices or get upper bunks so that they do not have to sleep under the bunk of a layman. One Tai teacher explained,

> In the 1980s the novices did not want to go to school, so in 1987 the central government started to pay attention to this problem, and the government ruled that novices were obliged to go to school. In spite of enjoying wide religious freedom, the monks also have to follow the laws of the state, so they started to send their novices to school. Now they do come to school, but they do not study. They think it is enough to be in the temple, and they think they are like adults because of the high status they enjoy in their villages. Of course they all learn to read old Tai pretty well, but anyway they use it only for reading the Buddhist texts.

One of the most controversial experiments was carried out in Mengzhe Township in Menghai County, one of the areas where the religious influence is strongest. In 1980 only 71.5 percent of children started school there, so in 1987 the local government decided to set up a special "novices class" inside the main temple to teach novices Chinese and mathematics. In 1988 the class consisted of sixty novices between the ages of nine and nineteen from surrounding villages. The experiment lasted only two years. Although researchers and educators in Kunming spoke very positively of it, the local administration decided to abandon it because teaching was impossible when novices returned to lay life, and age differences made it impossible to accomplish the original, ambitious plan of teaching each student for five or six years.

Menghai is a poor county and lacked financial support for the experiment. Some local people also suggested that local monks might have been poorly motivated.

A few other experiments with special novices classes within schools were carried out in the mid- and late 1980s, but today there are no such classes in Sipsong Panna in temples or schools. Novices in schools are distributed among the regular classes and follow the regular curriculum. The temple that ran the experiment is located next to the village primary school, yet the monk I talked to did not know how many of the temple's thirty-six novices went to the school. He assumed that the novices were in a special class in the school, but in fact they were not. Out of seventy-two pupils in the school, seventeen were novices. According to one of the three teachers, novices study for only a few years. As in many village schools in Sipsong Panna, all three teachers were Han, and only one understood a little bit of Tai. All students were Tai and understood very little Chinese during their early years in school.

Teachers who have novices in their classes often complain that they are impossible to teach and run away as soon as they encounter problems. If one or two drop out, the rest quickly follow. One teacher explained: "The novices enjoy high status in the local society, and therefore they do not listen to the teachers. They listen only to the monks. When they are in the monastery, parents also do not interfere. Teachers are afraid to scold or demand anything from the novices, because then they are even more likely to run away from school." Economic pressure has proved to be the most efficient way of forcing parents and monks to send boys and novices to school, but it is still rare for a township government to decide to fine parents for not sending their sons to school. Mengzhe Township has high numbers of novices, monks, and temples. Approximately one thousand new pupils start school every year, but because only about 50 percent complete primary school, some administrative villages in Mengzhe began fining parents who do not send their children to school. One village decided that if parents want a son to become a novice (around the age of seven or eight), they must pay a deposit of fifty yuan to the village administration. If the boy graduates after six years of primary school, the parents get the money back. If a son manages to pass the examination to junior secondary school, the parents get an extra reward, but this rarely happens. Teachers now have to report to the county Bureau of Education every year about the number of novices in their village, how many of them go to school, and how many have dropped out during the last year. Approximately 50 percent of the novices in Menghai County today go to school.[7]

Currently there are eighty novices studying in Mengzhe Central Primary School (Mengzhe Zhongxin Xiaoxue),[8] and in village schools all over Sipsong Panna novices participate in the same classes as other pupils. However, beyond the primary school level, very few novices or monks attend school. Of the few boys who have been novices and manage to pass the examinations for further studies, most return to lay life before continuing their studies. However, there are exceptions, especially from Mengzhe Township, where in recent years some novices have continued on to secondary education and a few (fewer than five) have gone on to higher education.

REGULAR SCHOOLS, TAI CLASSES, AND MINORITY SCHOOLS

The provincial and central education departments have accepted that Sipsong Panna will achieve only six years of prefecture-wide compulsory education by the year 2000. Only the three county seats and a few townships in Sipsong Panna have already achieved this. In 1990 minority *minzu* represent 73.1 percent of the population and 76 percent of primary school students in Sipsong Panna. However, beyond primary school the proportion of non-Han students drops: in junior secondary school 58 percent are minorities, in senior secondary school 31.37 percent, in vocational schools 70.78 percent, and in specialized secondary schools 59.9 percent. In primary schools 60 percent of teachers belong to minority *minzu,* compared to only 35 percent of all Sipsong Panna's teachers and school administrators (Sipsong Panna Prefecture Education Commission 1992:2).

7. According to an interview with officials at the Menghai County Bureau of Education in 1994.

8. Each township has a *zhongxin xiaoxue,* which is a full primary school where pupils living in the township and the best pupils from surrounding villages can study for the last two years of primary school. Unlike the village schools, these central primary schools follow all regulations concerning curriculum. Their teachers are generally better educated, and they often have fewer students per teacher than do village primary schools. They often have boarding facilities for the students from the villages, who bring and cook their own food.

Regular Schools

The best regular schools in Sipsong Panna, in terms of educational level of teachers and the number of students who continue on to the next level, are the keypoint primary and secondary schools in Jinghong and schools located on state rubber plantations (state farms). The Bureau of Education does not administer the schools on state farms (*nongchang*), which have their own administration and policies on recruiting students and teachers. Since about 85 percent of the people living and working on state farms are Han immigrants and their families, most students in these schools are Han. Seventeen percent of the population in Sipsong Panna is connected to state farms, and most of the minorities on the farms (approximately 15 percent of the farm population) have been recruited outside of Panna or among the Akha.[9]

The biggest of the ten state farms is Jinghong State Farm, where more than thirty thousand people live. It has a full primary and secondary school with more than 1,700 students. The schools have 103 teachers, of whom one is Tai and the rest are Han. Normally students are recruited from within the state farm, but students from outside are allowed to enter if they pay four hundred yuan extra per year in primary school and seven hundred yuan in senior secondary school (in 1994). According to the headmaster, "very few" students in state farm schools are non-Han. The administration would not give exact figures, but other interviews showed that only occasionally does a Tai or other local non-Han from outside the farm enroll. This happens in cases where parents have a connection to a farm or when an outside school has an agreement with a state farm to send one or two of its best students to the state farm's school after graduation from primary school. State-farm schools have no lessons in Tai, which is considered completely irrelevant since there are no Tai students. As in other schools, there is no question of offering Tai lessons to non-Tai students, even though the Tai constitute the majority in Sipsong Panna and it is a Tai Autonomous Prefecture.

The two local keypoint schools, which have the best educational facilities and financial support outside the state farms, also have the highest percentage of Han students and teachers. Both schools were started in the mid-1950s and have had an increasingly high percentage of Han students, due to the

9. See also Hansen 1999a.

growing number of Han cadres in the capital, Jinghong. Students today need 280 points out of 600 to be admitted into a keypoint secondary school, as compared to 200 points for the other regular secondary school in Jinghong. Members of minority *minzu* get 10 extra points. All representatives of the secondary school's leadership and 78 out of 84 teachers are Han. In 1992 the school had 1,370 students, of which 227 were Tai and 830 were Han. Most minority students are the children of cadres in Jinghong, and many of the students classified as Dai have one Han parent. Mainly because of advantages within the educational system, all over China most children of mixed Han-minority marriages are registered as members of the minority *minzu* of the non-Han parent. In Sipsong Panna most children of interethnic marriages have a Han father and a Tai mother. From an educational point of view, they have the advantage of being brought up speaking the Chinese language while being able to exploit the favorable admission rules for minority students. Only a few of the non-Han students manage to continue on to higher education; in 1993 and 1994 not a single Tai graduate from the keypoint senior secondary school passed the university entrance examination. An administrator at the school explains this in terms of a common cultural deficiency of the Tai:

Han students generally work much harder than the Tai. The Tai are not like us Han, who find education extremely important. The Tai children are not good at "eating bitterness" [*chi ku*]. Their economy is rather good, they are satisfied with life, and they do not want to work hard for something. This is not like the Jinuo and the Hani, who are used to "eating bitterness." This is a Tai autonomous prefecture, and this problem has always existed. We are discussing what to do about it, how to help the Tai students. We want to make more efforts in our "family work" [*jiating gongzuo*], where we talk to parents and try to persuade them to support their children's going to school.

When the school was started in 1957, it had one special class for Tai students who learned new Tai, but this was quickly cancelled. Today there are no lessons in Tai, and the administration has no plans for restarting Tai classes, which are considered to be relevant only in villages where children do not know Chinese: "All of our students understand Chinese. We have no language problems and do not need to start any Tai lessons" (Han administrator).

A common attitude of teachers and administrators at the best Chinese schools is that the teaching of Tai language is necessary only to facilitate the learning of Chinese. It has no value in itself, nor is there any reason that Han students living in the Tai autonomous prefecture should learn the Tai language. It has no prestige, no practical function at higher levels of education, and teachers and cadres in Sipsong Panna often say that "Tai language is useless when crossing the Mekong River."

Tai Classes

Primary schools in Sipsong Panna may decide to offer classes in Tai language, and school teachers in Tai villages are encouraged by the Bureau of Education to use Tai to explain Chinese terms and sentences that students do not understand. In reality this is seldom practiced, due to the shortage of Tai teachers. This problem exists in other minority villages in Sipsong Panna as well where most teachers do not speak the local language. In principle, the Bureau of Education wants to appoint local primary school teachers who speak the language of the local pupils. However, such people still are in short supply, and so is outside funding to train more Tai teachers. The issue of bilingual education is normally addressed only in relation to the Tai, because other local ethnic groups—such as the Akha, Blang, and Jinuo—do not have scripts. Although a considerable number of them know Tai, they never participate in the Tai lessons in schools.

In the mid- and late 1980s several primary schools offered teaching in Tai language, but most stopped after a few years. Today many full primary schools in Tai administrative villages and county seats offer Tai lessons, but only to a very limited degree and for a small percentage of students. The major reasons for this are the poor financial situation of many schools, the shortage of Tai teachers versed in Tai script, and, not least, disagreement within the government and among school staff on the need for and utility of Tai lessons.

Most primary schools that offer Tai lessons have one class of students who, in addition to studying the regular curriculum, participate in one or two hours of Tai per week for the last one to three years of primary school. In 1986 the prefectural government decided to abandon the use and teaching of new Tai and return to a standardized version of old Tai. This created problems because a whole generation of Tai had learned only new Tai in schools. Girls and women who had attended schools or literacy courses since the mid-1950s, and boys and young men who had grown up when few were able to become novices and learn old Tai in the temples, had all learned new Tai or Chinese. The local newspaper, which had always used new Tai, started using old Tai in 1993. According to one of its editors, many people were against this because they were not able to read old Tai, and the journalists themselves had problems adapting to it. On the other hand, many of the Tai who had been against the reintroduction of old Tai in schools seemed by the mid-1990s to be gradually changing their opinions because of the increasing contact with Thailand, Burma, and Laos. Therefore, it was surprising that in 1996 the government decided once again to return to new Tai. Because, as before, teaching material had to be rewritten, all Tai classes seem to have been interrupted during the 1996–97 academic year, waiting for the new teaching material. Obviously this move will add to the confusion resulting from teaching two versions of the script, and traditional Tai will again be taught only to male novices in the monasteries.[10]

When the government decided to return to old Tai in 1986, new teaching material for Tai classes in primary schools had to be edited, and this was based on the first old Tai teaching material created in the early 1950s. All schools that offered teaching in Tai during my fieldwork in 1994–95 used old Tai. However, the majority of students in secondary schools had learned new Tai, if indeed they had learned Tai at all. Often teachers and even headmasters at schools were not aware that their own school had started teaching old Tai, and many teachers and cadres seemed to believe that Tai education was much more widespread than in fact it was. This was partly a reflection of a common tendency of teachers and administrators (especially the non-Tai) to regard bilingual education as unimportant. Some had never paid attention to the actual level and scope of Tai teaching in the area, while others believed (or wanted me to believe) that Tai teaching was very widespread as a result of the official policy of supporting Tai education in schools. The majority of pri-

---

10. It is still unclear what the consequences of the new decision will be. Informal talks with locals in 1996 suggested that some Tai teachers felt very confused about the decision. The only explanation I was given was that new Tai is easier to learn and to use for computer programming than is old Tai.

mary schools that teach Tai arrange one special Tai class. Pupils usually may decide themselves if they want to participate, and although Han and other *minzu* are allowed to attend these classes, they never do. Most Tai from these classes graduate with an examination that gives them extra points for the entrance into junior secondary school.[11] The keypoint primary school in Jinghong City has had so-called "bilingual classes" (*shuangyu ban*) since 1978. Most of the sixty pupils in the two Tai classes in 1994 came from the nearby village of Manjinglan, and only a few were from Jinghong. The Han students (42 percent of all pupils) never participated. The children in the "bilingual class" learn Tai for two hours a week from the third to the sixth year of primary school. According to the headmaster, "The bilingual class is not so important here, because there are so many Han, and the Tai quickly learn Chinese." A number of other primary schools started teaching Tai in the mid-1980s, but many of these classes stopped after a few years due to the lack of teachers or because a few hours of Tai did not prevent boys from going into the monasteries.

Most of the Tai students in secondary and higher education who came from the northern part of Sipsong Panna or from Jinghong had never learned Tai in school, whereas the majority of those from village schools and from south of the Mekong River had learned some Tai (either in school or at home). Some used it for writing letters and taking notes in class, but most of those who had not also been novices found that they had never learned to read and write Tai properly, or they had quickly forgotten it because they seldom used it after primary school.

One of the few primary schools that experimented with real bilingual education was situated in an administrative village in Jinghong. Here children in the bilingual class learned only Tai for the first year. In the second year they started to learn Chinese taught in Tai. From then on more and more teaching was conducted in Chinese, but children continued learning Tai throughout the six years of primary school. The first bilingual class started in 1989 and the second in 1994, and beginning in 1995 the school hoped to

---

11. Out of three hundred possible points, participation in the Tai classes and examination contribute between ten and thirty extra. Regular subjects contribute up to one hundred points at the examination.

start a new Tai class each year. However, this experiment was interrupted in 1996 with the decision to return again to new Tai, and it was unclear whether the school would find financial support to continue the bilingual classes at all. Only two out of ten classes in 1994–95 were bilingual Tai classes, but the normal classes also received two hours of Tai per week from the third year onward. Ninety-eight percent of the students and half of the teachers in this school were Tai. Most of the Tai I talked to in the six villages in this district were very positive toward bilingual education, including those whose own children did not participate in it. The county Bureau of Education still considered these to be experimental classes, and there was strong disagreement on whether to continue and expand them.

The only school beyond the primary level that teaches Tai in Sipsong Panna is the Normal School, which offers one bilingual Tai class a year, the purpose of which is to train teachers to instruct in the Tai language and to teach Tai script in primary schools. At the Normal School 28.7 percent of students (and 18 percent of teachers) are Tai. When the first Tai classes after the Cultural Revolution started in 1984, all students had to participate. According to one of the teachers and to administrators, however, students did not attend these classes. They considered it a waste of time and too difficult when they did not know spoken Tai. In response, the school substituted a bilingual Tai class (first in new Tai, then in old Tai in 1990–97, and again in new Tai thereafter).[12] The textbooks for the study of Tai language were edited in the prefecture. They contained texts about the history of Sipsong Panna, the chronology of the *chao phaendin,* Han and Tai traditional stories, and instructions on writing letters, applications, and so on. Students themselves could not choose between the bilingual Tai class and regular classes, but all who were admitted to the bilingual class had to understand spoken Tai when they started. The attitude of students and graduates from the bilingual Tai classes toward their education was generally very positive, and several hoped to be able to start up evening courses in Tai for adults in the villages where they would be sent as teachers after graduation. Although most students criticized the tradition of sending boys to the monasteries, they maintained that the novices at least had the advantage of learning Tai script: "It is both good and bad

12. Some students and teachers from the regular classes suggested that all students at the Normal School ought to learn spoken Tai, but so far this has not been implemented.

that most boys become novices. The bad thing is that they often stay at the monasteries and do not go home to help, that they are too sluggish and do not learn enough. On the other hand it is difficult to learn Tai in school, and in the monastery they at least have the chance to learn it" (Tai female student). The only other institution in China where the Tai language is taught beyond the primary school level is the Yunnan Institute of the Nationalities, which has a four-year university course in Sipsong Panna Tai (and in Dehong Tai).[13] Most of the Tai from Sipsong Panna who graduate from this department are sent back to Panna as teachers, translators, or employees of the government, local television station, or newspaper. Some find work in private companies, which tend to pay higher wages.

Whereas most interviewed people in Sipsong Panna agreed on the usefulness of the Tai course at the Yunnan Institute of the Nationalities and the necessity for the bilingual class at the Normal School, they disagreed on the issues of bilingual education and of the teaching of Tai in regular primary and secondary schools. Teachers, school administrators, and members of the Bureau of Education in the three counties and the prefecture were roughly divided between a majority who saw the teaching of Tai as a temporary necessity, and a minority who wanted expansion and improvement of Tai-language instruction in primary schools, in examinations, and in secondary education. The main arguments for maintaining but not expanding Tai lessons in primary schools were that they were considered necessary only until Tai understood and read Chinese, and that they provided a means of persuading Tai parents to send their children, especially their boys, to participate in Chinese education. Therefore, some administrators emphasized that the goal of the bilingual Tai class in the Normal School was not to spread the knowledge of Tai language and culture, but to facilitate its gradual, natural, and voluntary disappearance:

The final goal is to make all people in China speak Chinese [*putonghua*]. So the final goal of the bilingual class is to make everybody in Sipsong Panna speak our mother tongue. They can use Tai to explain in schools when necessary, but the idea is certainly not that everybody should learn Tai script

13. Most students in the Tai department at YIN also take two years of standard Thai which has become very popular because of the increasing business contacts with Thailand.

or that Tai language should be spread further. There are too many languages in China—it would be impossible to teach them all. Teachers in primary schools may themselves decide when it is necessary to speak Tai. They have to teach Tai script, but not to all the pupils. (Han Chinese teacher and administrator in a secondary school)

Some cadres feared that because the Tai were concerned about learning their own script, they risked becoming "more backward" than the minorities from the mountains, who had always been considered the most backward. They saw the rapid development of Chinese education among the small Jinuo minority, in particular, as proof of the educational advantages and civilizing effects of teaching more Chinese and less Tai. Another common argument was that the Tai language was simply not useful in a modernizing society: "You see, it would be impossible anyway to teach everything in Tai. Take for instance this fountain pen. The Tai do not have a word for 'fountain pen,' and this is even more so the case in modern science. So the Tai language is too backward to use as a medium for teaching" (Han teacher). One of the monks I interviewed, who also had a Chinese education, agreed that the Tai language had not modernized, but argued that this was due to previous repressive government policies. He expressed the fear that Tai would turn into a purely religious script unless serious attempts were made to expand its teaching and use in schools. In this respect he put into words what several other Tai intellectuals and monks expressed indirectly:

Tai script has become too backward. For years old Tai was forbidden and people were forced to learn the revised script. But new Tai is useless and impractical. Even if you have learned it you cannot read the old texts. Because the Tai script was said to be a "feudal reactionary script" [*fengjian fandong wen*], it did not have any chance to develop. Today only a few use it for writing, and it is very confusing to find out how to write or translate new words like "television," for instance. In this way it risks becoming a script used only for religious purposes and for telling the old stories.

A small but growing number of Tai teachers, cadres, and students had started to raise (mostly in private) the question of introducing the Tai language into secondary schools, expanding its use in primary schools, and making the study of Tai history and culture part of the common school curriculum and examinations. They criticized the fact that parents were forced to send their boys to the temples if they wanted them to learn Tai, and some believed that schools would be much more attractive to the common people if they were based on the Tai language and included Tai history and literature in the curriculum. Others had a more practical point of view and argued that schools would become relevant and successful among the Tai peasants only when they taught useful knowledge of agriculture in the Tai language, or guaranteed graduates attractive job opportunities. Some of the more pragmatic Han cadres felt that teaching the Tai language in schools should be extended mainly so that parents would not send their boys to the temples.

In the meantime many peasants continue to send their boys to the monasteries, although this does not necessarily imply that they are directly against their children's receiving a Chinese education. However, due to the lack of cooperation between monasteries and schools and to the rejection of Buddhism and Tai language, history, and culture inherent in the Chinese educational system, Chinese schools are less attractive. This is, of course, further influenced by the fact that parents must pay for school, children sometimes must travel far to attend school, and many parents consider it a waste when their children do not continue in the school system, do not get a job, and end up as peasants who have not learned anything about peasantry during their years in school.

Boarding and Minority Schools

Since 1980 the central Ministry of Education has required that boarding and semiboarding[14] schools be promoted in mountainous and border areas in order to solve the problem of low attendance and high drop-out rates and to make sure that students attend full-time, standardized schools. As in the rest of China, the boarding-school system is praised in Sipsong Panna today not only for being a practical and economic solution in a poor rural area, but also for

14. In a semiboarding school, students may stay at the school for lunch. Each student gets financial support of seven yuan per month.

preventing students from dropping out of school and for making them do their homework. In addition, several Han cadres and educators in Sipsong Panna are very direct in describing the boarding-school system as an effective way of changing Tai customs and the "traditional way of thinking" (*chuantong de sixiang*). Most educators in Sipsong Panna were sincerely concerned about developing Chinese education among the Tai and saw the boarding system as the only way:

> The minority children's surroundings have to be changed if we are to manage to educate them. When they come here, they learn more, see new things, and develop their culture. Therefore it is good to have a boarding school for them in the city. It is much better for the children to develop here. If you do not change their environment, they do not change, but continue their habit of sending boys to the temples and living in the old way. (Han headmaster at a minority school)

There are four minority secondary schools in Sipsong Panna, and all students at these schools live there. In addition, some boarding students from rural areas attend regular secondary schools. Several full primary schools offer boarding facilities for higher primary students from villages.

Students of all ethnic groups whom I talked to at the minority schools looked, for the most part, positively on the boarding system, although for reasons other than those mentioned above. They were happy that they did not have to participate in work at home and therefore had more time to study. They found it hard to be able to visit home only once every six months, but had established close friendships with other students and were happy for the support they got from teachers in their spare time. During their education, many changed their perceptions of their religion, of other ethnic groups in China, and of their Tai identity.

All minority schools have rules about how many students should be Tai, and each year a number of students from all local *minzu* must be accepted, even though their points are not high enough. These schools are popular mainly because students get financial support from the government. However, because it is still a financial burden for many families to have a child in secondary school, they often find it a waste if children do not manage to continue on to higher education or to a specialized secondary school that guarantees a job.[15]

Students from regular middle schools tended to look down upon minority schools as second-rate, and many teachers complained about the difficulties of teaching in these schools, where less than 5 percent of students are Han and the vast majority come from villages where knowledge of Chinese is limited. Many students from the other schools held the erroneous view that, unlike themselves, students in the minority schools took special courses on the different *minzu* in Sipsong Panna and on Tai language. The minority schools in Sipsong Panna follow exactly the same standard curriculum as the regular secondary schools. The differences lie in the method of recruiting students, the special support for the schools, the fact that all students live at school, and of course the fact that minority *minzu* from rural areas constitute the vast majority of students. The minority schools were criticized by some teachers and cadres for isolating minorities and thereby preventing them from adapting to Chinese language and being influenced by "the more advanced" Han. On the other hand, if more minority students were to attend the regular secondary schools, admission rates would have to be lowered, special language considerations would have to be adopted, and economic support would have to be granted to these students. Most cadres in Jinghong and the other county capitals want their own children to get the best possible Chinese education to ensure their further studies and job opportunities. They would be unlikely to accept what they would regard as lowered standards for the sake of more minority students from the villages, and there is no question of introducing Tai language in these schools, because it would only make studies more difficult

15. The Prefectural Minority School (Xishuangbanna Zhou Minzu Zhongxue) has the best facilities and the most financial support, and has received donations from Japan. In recent years, state support for the school was reduced so that in 1994 parents had to pay about fifty yuan per month for food and living expenses. In all minority schools (as in regular schools) students have to pay for books, clothing, and medicine, and since 1995 students in all senior secondary schools have had to pay twenty yuan per month for tuition. Financial support for boarding-school students varies, but since 1992 each school has divided the money according to students' academic effort, participation in cleaning up, obedience, etc. In secondary boarding schools, on the other hand, students may get from seven yuan (for students with the lowest support in a minority school) to fifty yuan (for students with the maximum support in a specialized secondary school).

for the non-Tai students. Therefore, the system of special minority schools with no special curriculum is likely to continue.

CREATING BACKWARDNESS:
TAI CULTURE IN SCHOOL EDUCATION

Except for the Tai in the bilingual class at the Normal School, minority students in Sipsong Panna study the same textbooks as the Naxi and most other students in the rest of China. Together with other students in Yunnan, they also study Yunnan history, and some classes in secondary education in Sipsong Panna study the recent, locally edited *Geography of Sipsong Panna* (Xishuangbanna dili). When asked directly what they have learned about their own ethnic group's history, literature, and religion in school, most students in Sipsong Panna, like those in Lijiang, answered without hesitation, "Nothing." However, when they talked more generally about what they knew about the different *minzu* in China, and when I read their textbooks and listened to some of their classes, it was clear that they do learn about their own *minzu*. However, most of what they learn is presented indirectly and tends to convey a negative image of their own cultural heritage. For instance, the fact that Tai language and literature do not have any place in secondary education transmits to students the message that they are not important subjects, not relevant for modern education or even in opposition to it.

Like Naxi students, the Tai are imbued, through their school education, with the official construction of the fifty-six *minzu* in China and, not least, their respective levels of development. The Tai students often realize for the first time that their classification as Dai links them with Tai people in other parts of China with whom they have no contact and of whom they know nothing. All of the Tai students I talked to were (sometimes painfully) aware that they belong to what is considered a backward minority group. Some found a certain comfort in the fact that the other minorities in Sipsong Panna were considered even more backward because they had no script or "real" religion and were poor. Before entering school, Tai students from villages had not been used to interacting with the minorities from the mountains, and many of them tended to regard these groups as inferior to themselves. This view is to a certain extent confirmed when they encounter the official textbook descriptions of the social evolution of the *minzu*. The following dialogue is from a class on politics for the second year of junior secondary school in 1994. The subject was "the era of civilization" (*wenming shidai*). Approximately half of the students were Tai. The other half belonged to various other ethnic groups in Sipsong Panna such as Akha, Blang, Jinuo, and Lahu, who have generally been described in Chinese publications as occupying the low evolutionary stage of "primitive society" at the time of the Communist takeover in 1949. These non-Tai students belong to minorities without a script:

> TEACHER: What is the characteristic of a "primitive society"?
> CLASS (in unison): It has no script.
> TEACHER: Right. Therefore mankind in primitive society had not yet entered the era of civilization. At the time of slave society, mankind entered the era of civilization. Before the time of slave society, people had no culture [*wenhua*], no science [*kexue*]. The most important characteristic of the era of civilization is the existence of script. In primitive society, people used knots, carvings on wood, and so forth to remember things. Genuine script developed from pictographic script. Therefore we have the following stages: from no script, to knots and carvings, to pictographic script, and finally to genuine script. Then, why was there no division between physical labor [*tili laodong*] and mental labor [*naoli laodong*] in primitive society?
> CLASS: Because there was no script.

The Tai students learn that the other *minzu* in Sipsong Panna were more backward than themselves at the time of Liberation, but they also learn that they belong to a group more backward than the majority. They learn that (together with such groups as Tibetans and Uygurs) they were still at the stage of "feudal serf society" (*fengjian nongnu zhidu*) in 1949 and that today the area they inhabit is still considered economically and culturally backward.[16] This was put very directly by a junior secondary school teacher in 1994 who was lecturing on the unequal economic development in China to a third-year class

---

16. See also chapter 5 in connection with education in Lijiang. On the different stages of the evolution of the *minzu*, see, e.g., *Sixiang zhengzhi* 1993: 119–21 for the third year of senior secondary school.

in a junior secondary school. Although the economy was the main subject, it was implicitly understood that cultural development was always directly related to the level of economic development. It was also obvious that groups' respective levels were directly connected to political and administrative hierarchies. Thus, the provincial capital would definitely be more "developed" than, for instance, a village. The teacher made the point that "backwardness" is a relative term:

TEACHER: Is there a gap between our Panna [Sipsong Panna] and Kunming?
CLASS [shouting]: Yes.
TEACHER: Right. Our Panna is very backward. Is there a gap between Jinghong City and Menghai County?
CLASS: Yes.
TEACHER: Right. Menghai is more backward. Is there a gap between Menghai County and the small villages?
CLASS: Yes.
TEACHER: Right. We all know which is most backward.

The methods of teaching leave no room for discussion or questioning of textbook interpretations of *minzu* and cultural development. The most common way of teaching is to follow the book strictly, with students answering questions by repeating sentences from the book, usually in unison. As mentioned earlier in connection with the Naxi, the classification of *minzu* is presented as a scientific truth, and students learn it by heart without questioning the origin and validity of the criteria for classification. Their previous conceptions of the various local ethnic groups were not as strict and definite as those they now come to perceive as scientifically proven and final.

At the same time, students learn about the Chinese government's minority policy, which advocates equality of the *minzu* and equal rights to economic development and education. They learn how the government established autonomous minority regions to ensure minorities' rights to self-determination, and how the government even helped certain minorities "to jump over some stages of history in their development" (*Sixiang zhengzhi* 1993: third year of senior secondary school, 127). The language in the books is generally positive and presents a picture of the *minzu* as part of "one family" that makes up a common nation or nationality—the *Zhonghua minzu*—to which all *minzu* have contributed: the Han mainly with science, and the minorities mainly with songs, dances, and medicinal herbs (e.g., ibid.: 123). Indirectly the positive language and the interpretation of relationships among the *minzu* make it clear and unquestionable that not only the Chinese government, but also the advanced Han as a whole, have helped the more backward minorities to develop. Before Liberation the Mongols with all their leather were not able to produce leather shoes, the Tibetans with all their timber could not make matches, some minorities still practiced slash-and-burn agriculture, minority areas had no institutions of higher education, and areas such as Tibet did not have one public road. However, the text continues, "today the differences between the levels of cultural and economic development in the minority areas and the Han areas are decreasing" (ibid.: 130).

The Tai students, like those in the rest of China, do not have any specific courses in religion, but teaching about religion is part of the political lessons. Because most Tai students (with the exception of some in Jinghong City) have been brought up as Buddhists, it is not surprising that antireligious teaching in the schools seems to have affected many Tai students' and graduates' self-esteem and perception of their own religion, history, and customs. Many Tai students found a certain relief in the fact that they are described as having a "real" religion that is acceptable in China and not just "superstition," which is more "backward" and not publicly tolerated. Unfortunately for the other minorities in Sipsong Panna, their religious practices are not considered to be related to one of the world religions and may easily fall under the category of "superstition." In junior secondary school, pupils learn that superstitious people believe in gods (*shen*) and spirits (*gui*) that "do not really exist" (*Sixiang zhengzhi* 1993: first year of junior secondary school, 67). Superstition (unlike China's "five major religions" of Islam, Buddhism, Catholicism, Protestantism, and Daoism) is "a result of human ignorance" (*yumei wuzhi*) in earlier human society, when peoples' ability to reflect upon things was developing but they were not capable of producing scientific knowledge (ibid.: 67). According to the political material taught in school, superstition prevents the development of modern science and keeps people in ignorance and poverty. In senior secondary school, students read about the characteristics of "primitive religion" (*yuanshi zongjiao*), but it remains unclear what the actual difference is between this and "superstition." According to the book *Ideology and Politics* (Sixiang zhengzhi; 1993) the characteristics of religion are use of religious texts, teaching of doctrine, use of a church or temple building, and existence of priests or monks. These are not regarded as characteristic of "primitive religion," which has more in common with "superstition." All of the Akha, Blang, and Jinuo students I talked to were very embarrassed about the religious practices in their villages, which they themselves called "superstition." The Tai students, on the other hand, were very conscious that theirs was a world religion accepted by the government.

The students are presented with a very simple, basically Marxist analysis that describes religion as a social phenomenon that evolved in the class society and functioned as a means of suppressing the working people, who used it to escape poverty and misery. Therefore, religion in the long run is doomed to disappear in the socialist society where the exploiting class has been eradicated and where science, political consciousness, and human cognition continue to develop (*Sixiang zhengzhi* 1993: third year of senior secondary school, 139). On a general level, the political teaching material explains, religion in socialist Chinese society is no longer directly connected to a small, exploiting class except in the few cases where members of minorities advocate secession from China and use religion for this purpose (ibid.: 147–48). It refers to the constitution, which guarantees freedom to believe or not to believe in religion and—of greatest relevance for the Tai—which maintains that religion is not allowed to interfere with or obstruct the national education system. Thus, the students study the Communist interpretation of why religions still exist in the socialist society, how they will eventually disappear, why the government allows freedom of religion, and what this freedom implies. Students learn nothing about the teachings of the various religions, and when asked what they have learned about their own religion, most Tai students answer "nothing" or that "religion is free in China."

The government has realized the potential of tourism in Sipsong Panna, and this has resulted in the establishment of a one-year "tourism class" at the prefectural minority school, where students learn a bit more about their own area. Students are junior-secondary-school graduates who pay tuition (1,442 yuan in 1994) to learn minority dances, additional Chinese, a bit of Thai, botany, travel psychology (*lüyou xinlixue*), norms of behavior (*xingwei guifan*), etiquette (*liyi*), and hygiene. Most graduates from this class become staff in the new tourist hotels or tour guides for the numerous groups that visit the area for a few days. Ironically, one of the things the students learn is "customs of the Tai," which one Tai girl from this class described as "very useful because otherwise we would not know what our own customs and culture are."

THE NATIONAL MESSAGE:
"MOTHERLAND, I LOVE YOU FOREVER!"

Since the early 1980s patriotic education has been given high priority in the minority areas on the borders of the People's Republic. As in the rest of China, it has been reinforced after the crushing of the demonstrations in Tiananmen Square in 1989 and the government's subsequent campaign against "counter-revolutionary rebellion." Nationalism has become a dominant theme in official Chinese rhetoric, media, and education. It has become a means to strengthen China vis-à-vis the international community and to erode actual or potential internal ethnic conflicts. In Yunnan Province, where one-third of the population belong to minority *minzu,* the government has put great effort into spreading and extending patriotic education, especially in higher education and in the areas closest to international borders. Since Sipsong Panna borders on Burma and Laos, and the ethnic groups there have strong and historically close ethnic and cultural relationships across the borders, patriotic education is vigorously promoted in the area:

> Our prefecture is a "border minority area" with a border nearly one thousand kilometers long. With further reforms and an opening to the outside world, all kinds of corrupt capitalist thoughts and pornographic garbage might sneak into the prefecture in the wake of economic exchange. It is a reality of our prefecture that this may adversely affect young people. Combining this fact with the [Confucian] spirit of "putting morality first and giving all kinds of education their right position,"[17] we have launched patriotic education as the essence of our ideological and political work. We have closely combined the students' way of thinking with the realities of

17. *Daode wei shou, ge yu dao wei.*

society; we have combined patriotism with the conditions of the country, province, prefecture, and county; we have combined patriotism with love of socialism and love of the Chinese Communist Party. By doing so we have achieved striking results. (Sipsong Panna Prefecture Education Commission 1992: 5)

After the crushing of the democracy movement in June 1989, the local government held several large meetings for all the secondary school students in Sipsong Panna to inform them about what had happened in Beijing and to make clear that political and ideological work would now be strengthened among them. Most students had heard only rumors about the demonstrations in addition to the official versions, and few had heard objective reports about what had taken place. Apart from being told of the campaign to study Lei Feng and other revolutionary heroes, all schools and teachers were informed of the need to strengthen patriotic education as the main element in political and ideological work. The introduction of a course in Sipsong Panna geography in secondary schools was a direct result of the central guidelines for conducting patriotic education in minority areas, which advised that "love of the local area" was fundamental for "love of the country." Therefore, the book *Geography of Sipsong Panna* also has a short chapter about the history of Sipsong Panna, in which it is repeatedly emphasized that Sipsong Panna has always been part of the Chinese state. Furthermore, it describes the climate, natural resources, and development since 1949 and has a special section about the tourist spots. This book (taught for a total of ten lessons during the six years of secondary school) is the only material about their own area that students in some (not all) of the regular secondary schools study. Thus, the most important reason why teaching about local conditions is gaining ground in the educational system today is its role in patriotic education.

Patriotic education is incorporated into politics and history classes, and in recent years the government has arranged special "speech competitions," with patriotism as the topic. When I was in Sipsong Panna, the secondary school students took part in a competition for the best patriotic speech in standard Chinese (as opposed to the local Yunnan dialect). A number of local competitions were set up in secondary schools, and the winners from each school in the prefecture competed against one another. The other students also wrote essays about patriotism, and many blackboard messages in schools had patriotism as their theme. Since it was just after the 1994 Asian Games in Japan, many of the patriotic speeches concerned China's greatness as reflected in its number of gold and silver medals. Otherwise, speeches and short essays were much alike in their highly emotional way of repeating the official, nationalist rhetoric of textbooks, such as, "I love my own China. Some people from outside have asked me if I am a Korean or Japanese just because, being an Aini *minzu* [*sic*], my skin is dark. I answered, 'I AM A PURE CHINESE! [*dididaodao de Zhongguoren*]'" (female Akha participant in the competition). A central element in patriotic education is that all *minzu* should be convinced that they belong to, and together make up, the Chinese *minzu*, the *Zhonghua minzu*. Furthermore, it is promulgated that all *minzu* have contributed to the history and development of China and that therefore "the Han can never depart from the minorities, the minorities never from the Han, and the minorities never from each other." Thus, the nationalistic content in education focuses on the common history and common political/economic/cultural interests of all people within China. Common symbols are the mythical Yellow Emperor; the Olympic sports heroes; and the national flag, emblem, and anthem:

> TEACHER: What is the subject today?
> CLASS: The national flag, the national emblem, and the national anthem.
> TEACHER: What should all citizens do?
> CLASS: Love the national flag, love the national emblem, and love the national anthem.
> TEACHER: The national emblem symbolizes the union of all people under the leadership of the great Communist Party. How should we treat our national emblem?
> CLASS: We shall all love and respect our national emblem.
> TEACHER: We have to love our fatherland and love socialism. Can love of the fatherland and love of socialism be separated?
> CLASS: No.
>
> (1995, junior secondary school)

In published directions on how to conduct patriotic education among minorities, it is often emphasized that teachers should take care to avoid Han chauvinism and avoid giving the minorities the impression that they are backward.[18] In order to prevent minorities from turning against China and becoming "local nationalists," they should be convinced of their contribution to and role in the socialist Chinese state as minorities. Thus, by promoting the creation of local teaching material the government attempts to address the contradiction between official propaganda and policy, which praise *minzu* equality, and the minorities' practical experiences, which demonstrate the low valuation of their own languages, histories, and religions. Within the educational system there is a clear conflict between the government's wish to show how *minzu* contributed equally to the history of China, and presentations of the alleged scientifically proven backwardness of minorities. The last is needed to construct a developed Han majority vis-à-vis the less-developed, childlike minorities—a counterimage that legitimizes paternalistic help to improve so-called backward customs. That Tai students seem to be more influenced by the construction of themselves as members of a backward group than by superficial statements about their contribution to Chinese history and society suggests that the government's own presentations of minorities to a large extent undermine its nationalistic propaganda among them.

TAI STUDENTS' ETHNIC IDENTITY: THE CONFLICT BETWEEN FAMILY AND SCHOOL EDUCATION

Most Tai students in Sipsong Panna have learned at least some Tai script in primary school, so that they can recognize consonants and vowels. Only a few have learned enough to be able to read and write Tai fluently. Apart from the students in the bilingual class at the Normal School, the only course about Sipsong Panna is a brief Sipsong Panna geography course, which is taught only in some secondary schools. As compared to the Naxi, the Tai, because of the small percentage of Tai teachers, have heard much less about their own history, stories, traditions, and language from individual teachers in school. Students from other ethnic groups in Sipsong Panna have learned even less about their own history and culture, and only a small minority of them has

18. See, e.g., Xie Benshu et al., eds. 1994; and Yunnan Province History Society et al., eds., 1990.

ever been taught in their own language. With very few exceptions, these students expressed regret about this. Nevertheless, whereas many Naxi intellectuals were critical about the absence of curriculum that is directly relevant to their understanding of their own culture, the Tai students at higher levels of education were less concerned about this. Compared to the Naxi, who often explicitly expressed pride in their cultural heritage, many Tai students beyond the level of junior secondary school were ashamed and critical of the "backward habits of their family," the "tradition of sending boys to temples," and the "low level of education among Tai."

There is, however, one aspect of ethnicity that Tai students repeatedly mentioned as a source of pride, namely their script. One reason for this might be that their school education allows them to view their script as a proof of "relative development" and "literary tradition." Their religious practices, on the other hand, are presented as "obstructing modernization," their belief in spirits is labeled as "superstition," and the history of the *chao phaendin* and the independent state of Sipsong Panna is not likely to be part of the curriculum at all. Thus, while many Tai students at higher levels of education attempted to disassociate themselves from the cultural practices of their Tai families in the villages, they retained the Tai script as an accepted ethnic marker. In his study of Tai history and ethnicity, Shih-chung Hsieh found that the institution of the Tai king, the *chao phaendin,* was the most crucial factor in Tai ethnic identity and solidarity (Hsieh 1995). My fieldwork convinced me that the *chao phaendin*'s role in the ethnic identification of the Tai has been profoundly challenged during the last forty years, when the Tai increasingly have been forced to identify themselves in relation to the Chinese rather than to other Tai people south of Sipsong Panna. The *chao phaendin,* who has been physically absent from Sipsong Panna for the last fifty-odd years, has cooperated with the Communist government and has not attempted to maintain his influence in the Tai community. Furthermore, school education presents the Tai students with an interpretation of history that minimizes the role of the *chao phaendin* and makes clear that a Tai identity focusing on the previous king would run counter to the interests of the Chinese state. All of the students I talked to knew that historically Sipsong Panna was ruled by the *chao phaendin.* Many knew that the *chao phaendin* was in Kunming (although some thought he was long dead), but most had no idea why he was in Kunming and not in Sipsong Panna. To the younger generations of Tai today, the *chao phaendin* does not seem to play a significant role in their identification as Tai. Whereas the *chao phaendin* (and other living *chao* as well) still enjoys very high status among the Tai, I found that it was mainly among monks and Tai over the age of fifty that the *chao phaendin* was a major symbol of Tai identity. For most Tai it primarily was language, script, and religion that identified them as Tai in China and in contrast to the Han.

All Tai students were interested in learning their script, and they often emphasized that they would have participated in training in their own language even if it was not part of the examination. The majority realized that learning standard Chinese was indispensable for increasing their chances of further education, but at the same time they maintained that learning Tai ought to be part of school education. Students from the other ethnic groups without a script felt that learning Chinese was the most important task and that studying a local language would be a waste of time. Partly for this reason, local teachers generally praised ethnic groups such as the Akha and Jinuo for being more open than the Tai toward the Han and for putting more effort into learning Chinese and succeeding in school. Unlike the Tai, the Akha and Jinuo regarded school as the only way to escape poverty and backwardness. Many local minorities in Sipsong Panna know some colloquial Tai, but thought that learning Tai script would be merely an extra burden. It would not help them within the educational system or in getting a job later on. In this respect there was a conflict of interest between the Tai (one-third of the population) and the other minorities (one-third of the population combined), and on these grounds many cadres argued that the Tai language has no place in secondary education or in any of the non-Tai villages (villages in Sipsong Panna tend to be ethnically homogenous).

Compared to the Naxi intellectuals and students I talked to, the Tai who had attended Chinese schools at a higher level were generally much less explicit and demanding in their wishes to strengthen the position of Tai culture within education. In contrast to the Naxi, the Tai intellectuals have no "Society of Tai Culture," they have very few researchers, and they have less influence at decisive administrative and political levels. Except for the few students who were novices or monks, they tended to disassociate themselves from their cultural heritage and upbringing in their villages to the point of expressing embarrassment about their religious practices and the poor knowledge of

Chinese in their villages. It is mainly in the course of their education beyond primary school that they experience a contradiction between the things they learn during their childhood in the Tai villages and the content of school education. In their families, religion constitutes a significant part of village life, the only language employed is Tai, novices and monks enjoy high status, and most of them have heard stories of the Tai king and his kingdom from parents and grandparents. In school all of these aspects of Tai village life are repudiated as being worthless or even an impediment to modernization and the students' own careers. Most students therefore feel that they have no choice but to disassociate themselves from village traditions.

Whereas students in the bilingual classes at the Normal School (approximately forty students per year) and in the Tai classes at the Yunnan Institute of the Nationalities (approximately fifteen students per year) are well trained in their own script, the only Tai students in secondary and higher education who have a profound knowledge of their own language and history are those few male students who also are novices or monks. One of the things teachers and monks agree on is that it is a very heavy burden to be a novice while also attempting to perform sufficiently well in primary school to pass the qualifying examination for secondary school. Therefore, the few student novices who do succeed and wish to continue into secondary or higher education are normally very hardworking and highly motivated to study. All monks today are aware of the law of compulsory education in China, and many of the better educated among them want their novices to learn mathematics, history, and other languages in addition to Tai. Some monks now support novices in higher Chinese education, in the hope that they will return to the temple afterward as qualified teachers. However, other monks support their novices' going to school mainly because they have no other options, and they would rarely force them to stay in school against their will. The novices in school have to follow two full study programs. The knowledge they gain in the temples is by and large irrelevant in the Chinese school.

The few novices who had made it into secondary education had all attended a central primary school during the last two years of their studies, and they did not get extra points at the examination. Although they agreed that it was very difficult to pass the examination, none expressed regret at having been a novice, and all spoke with affection about the education they received in the temple. They emphasized that all of their knowledge of Tai language, history, religion, and literature had been acquired in the temple or from their grandparents, not in school. They considered it a great advantage to have learned Tai script so well, and they used it for taking notes in school, for transcribing Chinese and English words, and for writing letters home.

Some novices who had continued into secondary education had met with resistance from their grandparents, other elderly villagers, and some of the monks, whereas their parents were generally happy that they had continued in school:

> The old people in our village do not want us to become like the Han [Hanhua], nor do they want us to learn modern things. . . . After I had studied for three years in the monastery, I was curious to learn new things about the world and other languages. . . . Therefore, I wanted to go to school. But I felt at home in the monastery. I like reading the Buddhist sutras, so I also wanted to remain a novice and perhaps become a monk. Although some of the monks were against my going to a Han school, they still wanted me to remain a monk while attending school.

The few novices and monks who continued into secondary education encountered contradictions between their religious belief and the content of education in the Chinese schools. They were also faced with a basic indifference toward their religion in daily life at the boarding school. They came from an environment where their lives were centered around temple activities to a school that ignored the Buddhist festivals held in all Tai villages and that basically regarded their religious activities as a waste of time and a hindrance to development. During secondary education the monks and novices learned that in China all *minzu* have the right to have their own religious beliefs. But at the same time they were taught that religion teaches people to escape life and prevents them from modernizing their economy. Still, the novices and monks in secondary and higher education whom I have talked to denied that school education had in any way influenced their opinion of their religion. Their previous temple education and continued ties with other novices and monks made them less inclined than the other students to deviate from previous beliefs and opinions about their own cultural background: "During my education all teachers taught according to Marxism and dialectical materialism. I always disagreed with their viewpoints on religion and history. I have learned a lot of new things, but I do not agree with everything and I have not changed my mind about my own religion" (twenty-year-old monk and student). And in the words of another student and novice, "Before starting in school we already knew what it meant to be a Tai and believe in Buddhism. No school can ever change this." However, since Chinese schools have a negative attitude toward religion, and Tai language has no place in the Chinese educational system beyond primary school, many monks who want an education prefer to obtain it in Thailand, where "they really appreciate us monks," as several told me. Every year ten monks receive official scholarships to study in Thailand, but in fact a much larger number leave—some to visit family members and some to do business. Monks may go freely to Thailand, and every year several monks and older novices from Sipsong Panna manage to raise private financial support toward education in Thai temples.[19] Therefore, for boys, Chinese education is no longer the only alternative to education in the temples in Sipsong Panna, and with the improved economy and increasing contacts with Thailand, more novices and monks will probably look for educational opportunities there. Many parents regard the temple education in Thailand as a higher (sort of secondary) education after training in the local monastery.

Obviously, the novice and monk students were very positive toward the institution of temple education, but among the other students this topic often sparked heated discussions. During my interviews it became increasingly clear that young students in junior secondary school were much more sympathetic toward the customs of their own family and other villagers than were students in senior secondary school. This was especially so in regard to religion. A question that never failed to arouse laughter, giggling, and lively discussion was whether a female student would prefer her boyfriend to have been a novice and whether she would let any future son become a novice:

GIRL A: I would prefer my husband to have been a novice, because then he could teach our children Tai script.
GIRL B: I would also rather marry a novice.

19. When monks want to go to Thailand, they need permission from the Bureau of Religion. Since 1994 this permission has been relatively easy to obtain.

GIRL C: Sure, I would prefer to marry somebody who had been a novice. We Tai believe in superstition [*sic!*], and if a boyfriend has not been a novice, he might say nasty things and behave badly.

ALL: Certainly! It is best to marry a man who has learned something in the temple.

INTERVIEWER: What if you have a son?

GIRL B: My son has to be a novice!

INTERVIEWER: Why?

GIRL A: Boys should be novices. They can study at the same time — it's no problem.

GIRL B: Or he can become a novice after he finishes primary school. Many boys do that.

> (Three thirteen-year-old Tai girls,
> first year of junior secondary school)

GIRL A: I do not want a boyfriend who has been a novice, because that would mean that he has not been to school for a very long time and therefore does not know enough. Still, I would prefer a Tai to a Han, as long as he has not been a novice.

GIRL B: That is not true, as of course a novice can go to school as well. Now novices can also continue into middle school and even college. I think it is good to have a boyfriend who has been a novice. They learn a lot and they know Tai script.

GIRL C: I do not care if he has been a novice or not. The most important is that he has studied in school. If he has not been to school I definitely do not want him. He could learn Tai script and read the Buddhist scripts in an evening school.

> (Three Tai girls, first year of senior secondary school)

Generally students were very realistic in their attitude toward temple education and their own school education. They were all very much aware of the fact that Tai language, culture, and history play no role whatsoever in success within the educational system. While saying that they would welcome more Tai training in schools, they emphasized that schools would never expand Tai education as long as it was useless for obtaining higher education, for the Chinese state as a whole, and therefore also for their own ambitions. A sixteen-year-old female student remarked, "How could I have a boyfriend who had been a novice? Then he would not have been a good student in school, would he? The most important thing is to study, and, as it is now, the things you learn as a novice are of no use in school. Therefore it is damaging to your school education if you spend time being a novice. You simply won't get a good job!" Another female student was conscious of the role the school played in reducing the importance of Tai language and knowledge:

> A boy can be a novice and also go to school. I think that is the best way. They get more knowledge if they are novices for a period of time and they learn our own language. . . . We Tai have become more and more like the Han [*yue lai yue duo Hanhua*], especially here in the city. We often try to become like the Han. There are many more Han than Tai, and therefore they will never become like the Tai [*Daihua*]. Furthermore, we study Chinese and Han culture in school. They do not learn our language and know nothing about our customs.

The majority of female students in junior secondary school were positive toward temple education, whereas most older female students firmly stated that they did not want a boyfriend who had been a novice and that they would certainly never let their son become one. Male students tended to be more positive toward temple education. All had friends and close relatives who were or had been novices, and many had to make what they thought was a difficult choice between school and monastery. Again, the youngest male students were most positive toward temple education. Of course, age-related differences, such as level of reflection and the ability to express one's own thoughts, between students in junior and senior secondary school explain some of the variety in response. However, the students' increasing repudiation of their own cultural background could also be partly explained by their long-term stay in boarding schools, which prevented them from participating in village life, and by the curriculum.

The majority of Tai students who graduate from higher, specialized secondary or higher education have lived in city boarding schools since they were thirteen years old, sometimes even since they were eleven (since higher primary school). For six or seven years (in secondary school) and an additional three or four years (in college or university), most visit their families only once every six months, they speak Tai only with fellow Tai students, and they stop participating in religious activities. In order to succeed within the school system, students need to disassociate themselves from their religious background, their language, the things they have learned from elderly people about Tai history, and their own assumptions that they belong to a dominant group with valuable traditions. Only when putting aside what they have learned at home and realizing the overwhelming importance of learning Chinese, studying Chinese history, criticizing backwardness, propagating the *Zhonghua minzu,* and repeating the nationalist/patriotic messages will they have a chance to continue in the educational system. Therefore, most Tai intellectuals and students who have ambitions to continue into higher education are more preoccupied with adapting to the cultural values supported by schools and propagated in the broader context of Chinese society than with struggling to win a place for Tai culture within this system. The conflict between family and school is much more intrusive than for the Naxi and requires a choice from the students. This also helps to explain why the number of Tai students who manage to study beyond junior secondary school is still so small.

To a certain extent the hopes of many officials and school administrators of changing the cultural habits of the Tai by placing them in the "new surroundings" of boarding schools have been fulfilled. Students do start to have doubts about their religious background and play down the role and significance of their own experiences in their Tai villages, their history, and their language. Therefore, the Chinese-educated intellectual Tai have no contacts and no feelings of shared interest with the other strata of educated Tai, the monks. Many of the Tai students and intellectuals feel stigmatized and express embarrassment about their cultural heritage to the point of rejecting it. However, some students, particularly those past their mid-twenties, have recently started to express regret and discontent at not having had the opportunity to study their own language properly or to develop a modern Tai vocabulary, and at having been taught that Buddhism is incompatible with modernization. They have started to question the thesis that the Tai are a xenophobic, slowly developing people. However, these are a small group of individuals without scholarly or official positions to enable them to raise and push these questions within the Chinese political system.

ACCEPTING THE LABEL OF BACKWARDNESS?
AKHA AND JINUO IN CHINESE SCHOOLS

Although minority schools are sometimes criticized for isolating minorities and preventing them from raising their academic level through close contact with Han students, they do have some positive effects on Tai students' ethnic self-esteem. Outside class students mostly speak Tai with Tai classmates, with whom they also share their religious upbringing. In boarding schools most Tai students for the first time in their life make friends with youth from the other minorities. The Tai are aware that many teachers find the minorities from the mountains to be more hardworking and conscientious in school than themselves. This does not seem to diminish their sense of superiority resulting from the historic Tai dominance in Sipsong Panna. With very few exceptions Tai students also admitted that in spite of having Akha, Jinuo, Blang, or Lahu friends in the school, very few would marry one of them. Even if they wanted to, their parents would not accept it. As one eighteen-year-old female Tai student said, "If I fell in love with an Akha and wanted to marry him, my parents and grandparents would definitely object to it, but then. . . . I never could fall in love with an Akha."

The first school for the Jinuo *minzu* (approximately eleven thousand people, most of them living on Jinuo Mountain) was started in 1956, and it was also during the mid-1950s that the first primary schools were started in Akha villages, mainly with Han teachers from outside Sipsong Panna. These teachers did not speak the local language and met with many problems. The Akha and Jinuo were suspicious of the newcomers who settled in their villages and tried to convince them to build schools. They were very poor and saw no use in letting their children attend school rather than work. Hunting became another issue of dispute when farmers and cadres from farther inland in China were sent to Panna to start rubber-producing state farms. Before planting rubber trees, the new farmers needed to cut down vast tracts of jungle, and because the Akha and the other ethnic groups in the mountains depended on the jungle for their hunting, this often resulted in clashes between locals and incoming Han farmers. This did not work in favor of the Han who tried to start new schools.

Gradually though, Chinese primary schools became common in many Akha and Jinuo (and other) villages. Today most Akha and Jinuo children attend primary school for the first four years. But then most need to pass an examination to continue on to the fifth grade (around age eleven), and they have to go to a higher primary school in a nearby village, often walking several hours to and from school every day or staying at a boarding primary school. It is also very difficult for them to follow an education based entirely on Chinese language, and as a result many drop out after a few years. Only in those Akha and Jinuo villages where teachers are local and speak the local language do they explain in the children's own mother tongue. It is, however, hard to get teachers who are able to do this. There are not enough Akha with a teacher's education, and most teachers who are sent to a poor village try to get a transfer to a more developed village or township as soon as possible. Some of the Akha students I interviewed emphasized that the Akha villages might be less developed and less attractive than Tai villages, but "at least the Blang villages were even more backward." In this way, it seemed that everybody was able to find somebody whom they considered worse off than themselves and whom they could consider to be more backward. As one Akha said, to the great amusement and agreement of other students present, "I do not want to be a teacher in the poorest places, in a Blang or Lahu village, for example. . . . Just imagine, they know even less about science and have less knowledge than we Akha do!"

During the Chinese government's *minzu* fieldwork project in the 1950s, researchers reached the conclusion that the Jinuo and the Akha in Sipsong Panna could to different degrees be characterized as belonging to so-called "primitive societies" (although some Akha areas were described as having developed private land ownership). Most of the Akha and all of the Jinuo were described as being influenced by a sort of primitive communism, in which people shared everything, practiced slash-and-burn agriculture, practiced a form of "primitive nature religion," and the Jinuo lived in large clan houses with as many as one hundred family members. Through the teaching of the theory of social evolution, so vividly adopted by the Communists, existing local ethnic hierarchies in Sipsong Panna were in some respects cemented and confirmed. In the broader context of the entire People's Republic, groups from other areas were of course added to the hierarchy, and the Han were found at the top of the evolutionary ladder, but at the local level the form and content of education confirmed the Tai's historical experience and memory of who were rulers and who were subjects, who was associated with the state and who with the jungle, who were Buddhists and who were not.

Tai, Akha, and Jinuo boarding-school students live, eat, and study in the same place and have much more social interaction across ethnic affiliation than most of their parents or grandparents ever did. Many of them make friends, but at the same time they often express strong opinions about one another's customs and cultural practices—opinions that are influenced by the content of the Chinese education. One of the things that Akha and Jinuo students often mentioned to me as typical of the relationship between Tai and other local groups was their different attitude toward language. Most Akha who have not been to school, and especially those over thirty, can speak or at least understand Tai. However, when I asked students if Tai also understood the Akha language, they always laughed or looked at me with curiosity. "Of course the Tai do not speak Akha," I was told. Many students said that, in fact, many more Han than Tai learn Akha—not those Han employed on the rubber plantations or working as cadres, but Han who live and work in Akha villages, especially those who have married Akha women. I often heard Akha and Jinuo students say that whereas Akha are interested in learning other languages, the Tai are not.

Another issue that often resulted in discussions (sometimes rather heated ones) between Tai and other students was religion. The reason for this, I believe, was that due to their Chinese school education, which emphasized how religion and superstition obstruct modernization, students felt that it was very important to disassociate themselves from religious practices in their villages. Because they were aware that superstition was regarded as worse than religion—as more backward, more obstructive toward development—it was always important for them to fight back when members of other ethnic groups attacked their superstitious practices. One of the discussions I overheard in this connection demonstrated this very clearly. I was interviewing three Akha girls, and slowly, as often happened, other students came by to watch and listen. The Tai audience became provoked by some of the things the Akha said, and a discussion developed among them.[20] One Akha girl said that a major difference among the Tai, Akha, and Han was that the Tai were especially "eager to perform superstitious activities." She said that because

20. The discussion was in Chinese because the Tai and the Akha did not understand each other's languages.

the Tai believe in Buddhism, "they have a lot of superstitious activities." This made one of the Tai jump to her feet and announce that since the Tai believe in Buddhism, their religious activities are precisely *religious* activities and not superstitious ones, and that in fact it is the Akha themselves who practic super-stition. Another Tai girl then asked the Akha in the room to tell about their own superstitions, and one Akha girl started to tell, clearly embarrassed, about the *nipha* (female shaman) in their village. She told about how the *nipha* tried to cure sick people and how she could see in her dreams which girls from the village should become her students. The Tai students corrected the girl dur-ing her story; for instance, when the Akha girl said, "The *nipha* knows about medicinal herbs," a Tai girl said, "She only knows a little, though." The dis-cussion went on for some time, until one Tai loudly exclaimed, "This is really superstition," and the discussion was taken over by the Tai, who exchanged horrified memories of how they had seen a *nipha* perform her rituals on tele-vision. The Akha clearly felt bad about this, and several tried to say that their father or uncle or someone else in the family did not believe in the *nipha* any-more, whereas most admitted that their mother still insisted on calling for the *nipha* in times of sickness. The discussion more or less ended when one Akha concluded that "women are much more superstitious than men. Men are more open, I do not know why!"

On other occasions, too, I found it striking how eager many Tai students and intellectuals were to defend their own position against the minorities from the mountains — to stress their history as a dominant ethnic group with a script, a religion and a recorded history (of which they in fact knew very little). The dominant Chinese discourse on the historically unequal relationship between the minority *minzu* and the Han — with their objectified position as the most developed and modern ethnic group, and therefore in charge of major political decisions — seemed to have a profound influence on Tai in the educational system. They felt under pressure from the propagation of athe-ism, modernism, and development, which to a large extent force them to disassociate themselves from learned valued and beliefs, from their socialization as Tai. They felt that they were in fact "backward" compared to what they had learned about the Han. At the same time, many of them found it impor-tant to defend their position against the Akha and Jinuo, whom teachers often praised for being more engaged and sincere in their studies than the Tai. In fact, the Akha have a quite low percentage of students in school compared to the Tai, mainly because many Akha villages are poor, isolated, without electricity, and sometimes without enough food. Often less than 10 percent of Akha children in a village primary school continue on to fifth grade. Still, teachers in schools all over Sipsong Panna and most cadres engaged in education say that the Akha and Jinuo perform better than the Tai in school— or rather, that they come from less but achieve more. One headmaster of a *minzu* minority school expressed a prejudiced view commonly heard among teachers:

> Tai students are very intelligent, but they are not as industrious and good at studying as the minorities from the higher mountains. The Tai have a better economy, they have an easier life, they do not need to work so hard. I have faced this problem for twenty years now. The Akha, for instance, have a very hard life and are not so intelligent. Therefore, they are very eager to study hard, to learn, to escape such a hard life. Generally speaking, the Tai are more lazy. The minorities from the mountains learn the Han language faster than the Tai do. They mix more with the Han, whereas the Tai live more concentrated together and have their own script. They think that their own language and script are really good. They think they do not need to learn Chinese. The Akha realize the need for and advantages of learning Chinese.

Many Han teachers told me that by rejecting Chinese state education, the Tai "risk becoming even more backward than the minorities from the mountains." The fact that the Akha and Jinuo are praised by Han teachers and cadres for being willing to work hard and try to perform well in school provides them with status and the possibility of being regarded as "almost" more developed than the Tai. The Akha and Jinuo have no alternatives to the Chinese education, and they have few educated members, yet they are represented by teachers as hardworking, diligent people who are more open toward cultural change than are the Tai. This appraisal is possible because they seem to accept the presentation of themselves as backward and welcome the state's attempt to educate and civilize them in the Chinese school system. The Akha and Jinuo students and graduates apparently (at least for the time being) find it easier to accept that they learn only Chinese in school and not their own language, and that they are considered a backward group. If Akha or Jinuo students do not perform well in school, they tend to blame themselves and the backward conditions in their villages, whereas the Tai are more likely to blame the school system for not teaching their own language and for making it impossible for boys to study at the monastery and school at the same time. The Akha students I talked to were also much more embarrassed about their family and village than were the Tai. Some even told me that they were jealous of the Tai girls' traditional costume, which they considered much more beautiful than those worn by the women in their own villages—costumes that symbolized poverty and backwardness to themselves and to the Tai.

By accepting both the school's construction of their own ethnic group as backward and the need to discard their cultural habits and the importance of learned values, educated members of groups such as the Akha and Jinuo may in fact manage to challenge their own peripheral and subordinate position within the local ethnic hierarchy. In this respect, their assimilation may be regarded as a political strategy.

CONCLUDING REMARKS

Chinese authorities have encountered huge problems in their efforts to establish state education in Sipsong Panna. As in other minority areas of China, the basic goal is literacy in Chinese, so that the local population can participate in political administration and in modernizing the economy. Ideologically, the education of minorities is perceived as uniting the people of China in an atmosphere of ethnic brotherhood, as playing down and ultimately eradicating ethnic differences while promoting Chinese language, culture, and history. Education in the post–Cultural Revolution era must demonstrate, especially to minority *minzu* in border areas, that only participation in modern school education based upon Chinese language and history, socialism, patriotism, and atheism will bring about the desired economic development. Minority languages are granted a place in the educational system only when they facilitate the learning of Chinese or when doing so is considered an inevitable necessity to persuade people to attend the schools. Local history and culture are incorporated only to the degree that they help promote the supra-national identity of the *Zhonghua minzu*.

Due to scarce resources and limited national financial support at the local level, the lack of teachers with a knowledge of Tai language, and disagreement among cadres on the issue of bilingual education, most Tai children receive all of their primary education in Chinese, which few speak when they start school. The language problem is one important reason for the low percentage of Tai with a secondary or higher education. Some researchers, local teachers, and cadres argue that the introduction of Tai courses in more schools will not only make it easier for Tai children to learn Chinese, but will also result in more Tai boys attending school instead of participating in temple education. However, sporadic Tai training in school would not eliminate the fundamental contradiction between the content and form of the Chinese school system and the Tai people's cultural religious practices. Neither would it convince rural Tai parents that future employment, an improved economy, or higher local status would result from their children's advancing in the Chinese school system. Indeed, many Tai girls with a junior (sometimes even a senior) secondary education manage to find jobs only in the tourist industry—jobs that are despised by many Tai.

Intellectual Tai with a higher Chinese education constitute a very small part of the Tai population, and they are much more passive and aloof than Naxi intellectuals in their expressions of ethnic identity. They tend to distance themselves from aspects of Tai cultural identity that are in direct conflict with their Chinese education. Tai who have received a longer Chinese education focus most on language, less on religion, and not at all on the king and the kingdom when expressing their Tai identity. Because a Tai ethnic identity centered around the king and the history of the kingdom would oppose and offend Chinese propaganda about the *Zhonghua minzu* and its historically legitimized power in Sipsong Panna, this particular aspect of Tai ethnicity is probably the most sensitive and politically unacceptable. Furthermore, the direct collision of Tai temple education with Chinese education makes the religious aspect of their ethnicity problematic for Tai intellectuals to defend. Tai script, on the other hand, plays an important symbolic role as proof of a "high culture" and as a transmitter of religion, history, and traditional Tai literature. However, it also has a practical value in the villages, where many parents want their children to know the script that they themselves have at least a modest knowledge of. This means that a focus on Tai script and language in fact also runs counter to the promotion of Chinese education, which emphasizes the need to abandon one's own language in favor of Chinese. Thus it seems that for the minority of Tai who participate beyond secondary level, Chinese education to a certain extent causes them to abandon their religion, accept the construction of themselves as members of a backward group, disregard their history as a kingdom, and support the thesis of the uselessness of the Tai language. However, a number of factors have begun to pull Tai intellectuals and students in the opposite direction. Increasing contacts with Thailand and Burma have shown them that their language is useful outside Tai villages. Many express the wish to continue their studies in Thailand. Furthermore, they find in Thailand proof that Buddhism does not necessarily exclude economic development. As a consequence, some younger Tai students and intellectuals have started to see new potential in their own language and religion, and some are developing a new, growing solidarity with Tai peasants and monks.

Very few Tai go through the educational system at all, and most drop out after primary school or at least junior secondary school. For the vast majority of Tai living in the villages, Chinese school education has little impact on ethnic identity and cultural practices. To increase the influence of school education, the government would probably have to change the form and content of school education to make it directly relevant to the Tai's language, religious beliefs, and economic conditions. But many cadres and teachers fear that this would defeat the ideological purpose of school education in that it would support the already strong Tai identity rather than attempting to break it. Running counter to the government's intentions, the Chinese educational system in Sipsong Panna excludes many Tai. The resulting low level of Chinese education makes the Tai largely incapable of strongly and efficiently formulating and promoting their own cultural, political, and economic interests within the context of the Chinese state. At the same time, by insisting upon an educational system that excludes all aspects of Tai culture and diminishes its value, Chinese policy involuntarily strengthens ethnicity among the vast majority of Tai who do not participate in this education. Realizing that their language and religion are the main reasons for their exclusion from Chinese education, many seek alternatives that support, rather than reject, their way of life by turning toward monks, improving temple education, and strengthening connections with other Tai and Buddhists outside China. Those who participate in long-term Chinese education and become affected by its assimilative intentions tend to become stigmatized, and therefore they, too, welcome alternative explanations—such as those derived from cultural contacts in Thailand—of their culture as valuable and useful.

Conclusion

Through the state educational system, the Chinese government transmits its ideology of the nation and of the relationships among the peoples in China who have become categorized into static ethnic groups. Education of minorities plays a central role in implicitly reproducing notions of cultural inequality while explicitly promoting the "unity of the *minzu*." Students learn the names of the officially recognized *minzu*, as well as what it implies to belong to a minority *minzu* or to the majority, as indisputable, scientific facts. Thus, the classroom is an arena where processes of ethnic identification become highly relevant when minority students inevitably are confronted with the government's monopolizing interpretation of their identity. Equally important for students' self-perception as members of minority *minzu* are issues that remain unspoken, that are not communicated in school because they are considered irrelevant to state school education. Thus, a study of the impact of Chinese minority education on ethnic minorities' ethnic self-perceptions and identities has to take into account the fact that most non-Han students experience that their language, history, religion, and customs are considered useless (or at least less significant) knowledge in the Chinese school system. The influence of state education on the process of ethnic identification among different ethnic minorities is obviously ambiguous, and it is impossible to isolate education from other factors contributing to this process. Chinese state education is important for the government's hegemonic project to modernize society and define the Chinese nation, and as such it plays a definite role in the current resurgence of ethnic identities all over China. The perspective in this book has been local, focusing on Chinese education among two minorities and on its role in directing the form and content of their ethnic identity. I have tried to analyze what minority students in China learn about themselves as members of an ethnic group during their education and thus what role education plays in directing and forming ethnic and national identity in China today.

All over China education is highly standardized in terms of curriculum in primary and secondary schools, length of study, extracurricular activities, and so forth. Some students have additional teaching in their own language, but the content of education rarely deviates from the national standard. Teachers know which books to use and what to teach. They rarely have the opportunity and are hardly ever forced to select other teaching materials. Students belonging to different ethnic minorities in China and living in the peripheral areas of the Chinese state are thus presented with a definite set of interpretations and perceptions of themselves as members of minority *minzu*. These are often confirmed by shared experiences obtained through this education. Students learn that almost all of the minority *minzu* were more "backward" in terms of economy and culture than the majority Han at the time of Liberation. They learn that the Communist Party then helped them to develop so that all *minzu* in China became united in a multiethnic, socialist society. They became part of the Chinese family of brother *minzu*. This unity was made possible not merely because of the Communist Party. The more profound and comprehensive reason, they learn, is that all *minzu* in fact have a common history, are descendants of the Yellow Emperor, and thus have shared identity as part of the "Chinese nation," the *Zhonghua minzu*. Students also learn that within the framework of the Chinese state and constitution, all *minzu* in the "New China" have equal rights to develop their languages, maintain their cultural traditions, and believe in their own religions. More indirectly, though not less powerfully, Chinese education fosters in many students a perception of themselves as members of a "backward minority" simply because it denies the usefulness (sometimes even the existence) of the minorities' own languages, histories, religions, forms of education, customs, marriage practices, values, ethics, and so forth. Sporadic attempts to introduce brief volumes about "minority culture" (*minzu wenhua*) outside the common curriculum in local schools are insufficient to change this tendency. True bilingual education (not merely one or two hours per week of voluntary extra teaching in the minority language) is one of the methods that might increase students' acceptance of the value of their own language. However, this effect is often neutralized when the mother tongue, the minority language, is realized to be worthless for continued education. The possibility of continuing on to secondary and higher education is completely dependent on the student's level of Chinese, not on her ability to speak or write a minority language. Bilingual education probably facilitates the learning of Chinese, but when presented as a necessity only in villages where minority children do not speak Chinese well enough to attend "regular school," it is understandable that many students come to regard it as a method employed for the "most backward," not for the value of the language itself. In the province of Yunnan, where twenty-five minority *minzu* (one-third of the population) live mainly in rural areas, this is very often the case.

Chinese state education promotes cultural homogenization in order to facilitate communication, to ensure the integration of minority areas into the Chinese state, to promote patriotism and loyalty to the CCP, and, in a broader sense, to "enhance the cultural quality" (*tigao wenhua suzhi*) — to civilize — the more "backward" groups. Although rural Han are also sometimes described in these terms, there is inevitably an ethnic dimension to the description when it is applied to minority *minzu* whose "backwardness" is often explained as a result of cultural deficiencies. Often the languages, cultural practices, and economic life of ethnic minorities are described in texts, media, and oral communication as obstructing the development and modernization of the areas they inhabit. Belief in the civilizing and homogenizing effects of education in China is still very strong, as it was among many officials and educators promoting Confucian education among the "barbarians" on the periphery of the Chinese empire, especially during the Qing dynasty (1644–1911). But the degree to which present-day education actually manages to homogenize the population remains a question. The research presented here suggests that one result of an education directed at achieving cultural homogenization may well, at least in the long run, be fragmentation and increased focus on ethnic identity. While reducing cultural differences in order to adapt to the demands in the state education system, those under the heaviest pressure to assimilate may react with increased focus on ethnic identity. This is a process evident among ethnic groups all over the world and is part of a global process of modernist homogenization that often results in ethnic and cultural fragmentation (e.g., Friedman 1990 and 1991). As an institution with the built-in purpose of mainstreaming cultural behavior and directing national sentiment and loyalty toward the state, state education plays a vital role in this process in China. Thus comparison of different ethnic groups' responses to state education in China sheds light on how and why a standardized education system, intended to reduce or eliminate ethnic identities, can produce the opposite effect.

Naxi children in Lijiang and Tai and other children in Sipsong Panna study the same textbooks. The methods of teaching in both areas are very similar, as is the structural arrangement of minority education and boarding schools. However, although Chinese education has been quite successful among the Naxi, it has failed to reach the majority of the Tai, and Naxi and Tai local responses to Chinese state education are profoundly different from each other. Whereas Naxi intellectuals utilize education to promote a Naxi identity, many Tai with a Chinese education are culturally stigmatized and Tai peasants with no Chinese education cannot raise ethnic, political, and economic demands within the state. Through Chinese standardized education, a powerful discourse on what it means to be a member of a minority *minzu* and of the Chinese nation is transmitted. For several historic, cultural, and political reasons, this has been received differently among the two groups and has produced different reactions in terms of ethnic identification.

During the Qing dynasty, private and charitable Confucian schools became the prime institutions of learning among the Naxi in Lijiang. The Naxi elite who participated in this education gradually adopted it as their own, and most teachers and students in these schools were Naxi. Chinese/Confucian-educated scholars and teachers enjoyed high status in the Naxi community, especially around Lijiang Town. In a Ming dynasty chronicle, the ruling Naxi lineage already was praised for its ability to study Confucian ethics, and Lijiang was completely integrated into the Chinese empire during the Qing Dynasty. After initial suspicion toward the modern Chinese schools established in the early twentieth century, the Naxi gradually came to accept them as the most important local institutions of learning and as the ladder to influence and prestige. Today the Naxi minority is still singled out in Chinese sources as a group of people who have proven to be willing and able to learn from "more advanced" *minzu*. Many Naxi have come to think of themselves as belonging to a group characterized by its "love of learning," and in spite of many serious financial problems in schools in rural Naxi areas, most Naxi parents want at least one child (preferably a son) to obtain an education beyond primary school. They regard Chinese education as their own, and most teachers, principals, and cadres in local bureaus of education (as in local government in general) are indeed Naxi themselves. The Naxi elite who received a Chinese Confucian—and later Communist—education seemed for a long time to adopt as much as possible of the dominant cultural values of the Chinese center. Educated Naxi participated actively in the state's civilizing projects (Harrell 1995a) as carried out among the peoples living on the state's geographical, cultural, and political periphery. Education was a significant element in this project, and due to the fact that it denied the values of local Naxi customs, religion, history, and language, many Naxi came to feel embarrassed by their own ethnic affiliation. Existent or potential feelings of cultural stigmatization were sometimes reinforced by the state's political suppression of ethnic identity during different periods of the 1950s, 1960s, and 1970s and by its insistent demonstration of the backwardness of minority *minzu*.

Since the 1980s members of the Naxi intellectual elite have become spokesmen for a renewed focus on Naxi identity. This is taking place in a changing political climate that allows some expression of ethnic identity and in a modernizing society that is more open toward the outside world than before and informed about the processes of ethnic fragmentation elsewhere. A relatively high percentage of Naxi are intellectuals, cadres with positions in the local and provincial governments, teachers, and researchers. Many of them are reacting against their own stigmatization by seeking to express their identity as Naxi within the framework of the Chinese state. Intellectual Naxi enjoy high prestige in the Naxi community, as did Naxi with a Confucian education in the past. Today intellectual Naxi are utilizing their Chinese education to reformulate the content of the external categorization of themselves. They have reshaped their previously vilified "*dongba* superstition" into celebrated "*dongba* culture," and they are using their high level of Chinese education to expand their own influence in schools, alternative education, exhibitions, and research contacts in their native area of Lijiang. This project is gaining ground in the local community outside the small intellectual circles, and many Naxi peasants today talk with pride, rather than shame, about the time when they still had a *dongba* in their village. Even Naxi students in secondary and higher education tell of how they had been ashamed of the backwardness of their own *minzu*, but now feel sorry for other local minorities whom they consider to be much more backward than the Naxi, having fewer educated members and lacking "a culture of their own" (*mei you ziji de wenhua*), as several students expressed it. Belief in the existence of different degrees of civilization has not been abandoned as such, but by using their knowledge of the Chinese language, their high positions gained through participation in state education, and their acquaintance with the Chinese educational and political system, the Naxi have successfully established themselves as a group with their "own culture" (*ziji de wenhua*), less backward than previously assumed.

Although education in itself obviously does not explain the Naxi's renewed emphasis on ethnic identity and their reformulation of the content of their external categorization as a minority *minzu,* it certainly influences the process and directs the way in which their ethnicity is expressed. A relatively successful education (good participation and graduation rates) has provided the Naxi with the necessary tools (such as language, degrees, cadre positions, and the possibility of being taken seriously in political life) to establish and express themselves competently as a group in China. They are able to utilize the educational system for promoting their own position as a minority *minzu,* to create alternative education, and even to slowly influence—and possibly eventually change—the very content of state education. Chinese education, conducted in various forms during hundreds of years in Lijiang, has facilitated the integration of the Naxi into the Chinese state and helped them adapt to Chinese/Confucian, Nationalist, and Communist ethics and values. In this process they reduced a number of cultural differences and adapted not only to the Chinese state's pressure for cultural assimilation but also to general global demands for cultural homogenization in a modernizing world. When the political climate in China allowed it, the educated Naxi elite reacted against the pressure to homogenize, by increasingly emphasizing characteristics that they defined as specifically Naxi, as core characteristics of a Naxi identity. Due to their historically close relationship with central China and their successful participation in state education, this concern with ethnic identity is in many ways less controversial than that encountered among the Tai. Naxi identity, however strongly expressed, does not oppose the Chinese supraidentity of the *Zhonghua minzu* so vigorously promoted by the government. The Naxi elite find ways and room for expressing their identity as a minority *minzu* within the acceptable political framework, and, partly for this reason, the modern Naxi elite's identity may be able to slowly transform state institutions, such as education, from the inside. Therefore, the seemingly controlled and well-organized way of expressing Naxi identity today might, in the long run, have consequences for Chinese society that are more far-reaching than they immediately seem.

The situation among the Tai in Sipsong Panna is profoundly different. Their first encounter with Chinese schools took place after 1911, when the Republican government established the first primary and short-term teachers training schools in the area. But the Tai already had their own institutions for learning, the monasteries, which most boys attended for a few years, learning to read the Buddhist sutras in their own script. The Chinese schools in the area had their own Chinese teachers, who taught in Chinese, understood little Tai, and taught subjects considered irrelevant by most Tai at the time. In Sipsong Panna, Chinese education resembled colonial style education in other parts of the world in the sense that it was imposed on the Tai by an external political power mainly attempting to expand its own cultural, political, and economic spheres of control. Today Chinese education is more widespread in Sipsong Panna than ever before, and the custom of sending boys to the local monasteries is changing, though not really declining, so that boys are novices for a shorter time and attend Chinese school for at least a few years as well. Still, the local authorities engaged in spreading Chinese education encounter a wide range of problems when trying to persuade Tai parents to send their children to the schools and to make sure that they stay there. They have not succeeded in stopping the Tai's practice of sending boys to the monasteries, and Buddhism is again developing vigorously in the area in step with the improved economy of the Tai and their increased contacts with monks and relatives in Thailand.

The relatively few Tai from Sipsong Panna who do get an education beyond junior secondary school tend to dissociate themselves from their village's cultural heritage. In only a few primary schools do Tai children learn Tai, and this is useless (some say a hindrance) anyway for continuing on to secondary or higher education, where all teaching is based upon the Chinese language. In addition, their religion, their history as a kingdom, and their myths, stories, and songs are worthless in state schools and may even be interpreted as running counter to the schools' and government's promotion of the common *Zhonghua minzu* identity and the common history of China as a unified nation. This produces in many Tai students and graduates a feeling of cultural stigmatization—it makes them express embarrassment at their own background, the religious practices in their families, the poor knowledge of Chinese in Tai villages, and the low number of Tai graduates beyond the level of junior secondary school.

Unlike the Naxi, the Chinese-educated Tai intellectuals tend to play down their ethnic identity and stand aloof from whatever they associate with Tai identity and culture. They find little space within the Chinese educational system for an ethnic identity that almost inevitably risks becoming politically sensitive, due to its strong connection with religion, alternative schooling in monasteries, and the history of the Tai as the rulers of a kingdom. It is difficult for them to succeed within an educational system that gives almost no consideration to their own language and demands that most students leave their village surroundings at the age of thirteen to live in a boarding school based on moral values and cultural practices significantly different from those they have been brought up with. This, I believe, is one of the reasons why Chinese education still has little bearing on the lives of most Tai—either they simply do not participate in it or they let their children attend school for only a few years. As a result, most Tai are unable to formulate their own political, economic, and cultural interests within the context of the Chinese political system. Unlike the Naxi, they do not have a strong (Chinese-trained) elite that is able to promote their interests as a minority group in China. One of the main arguments used by the government to persuade the Tai to send their children to school is that it is the only way to modernize the economy and improve living standards. This is not convincing for those who have contacts with relatives and friends in Thailand, because they realize that modern education in other parts of the world does not necessarily imply rejection of Buddhism or other religions. Leading monks in Sipsong Panna are cooperating with monks in Thailand and Burma to improve and expand the Buddhist education of boys in Sipsong Panna, and many rural Tai welcome this as a positive way of combining modern education and Buddhism for their sons. Because the only educational option open to Tai girls remains the state schools, parents who have only daughters tend to be more interested in the Chinese schools than are parents with sons.

If the purpose of state education in Sipsong Panna is to direct loyalties toward the state and promote the supraidentity of the *Zhonghua minzu* while diminishing local ethnic identity and eradicating major cultural differences, it does to a large extent succeed among those Tai who participate—at least for the time being. However, the majority of Tai do not attend Chinese school for more than a few years, partly for the very reason that the schools ignore and even reject their history and their own cultural and economic life. In the aftermath of the cultural and political suppression during the Cultural Revolution, many Tai have revitalized religious practices and developed contacts with Tai in other countries as a direct result of renewed economic and cultural contacts across the borders with Burma, Laos, and Thailand. State education fails to provide most Tai with tools to express themselves as a group and as individuals in the Chinese state. The few experiments in Sipsong Panna with extended bilingual education, combined with the data collected during my fieldword, suggest that only an education taking Tai language, culture, and history seriously; cooperating closely with monasteries; providing students with knowledge of direct relevance to the daily economic life of rural Tai; and providing real training for jobs will attract more Tai to Chinese secondary schools. Although some Chinese researchers and cadres have reached the same conclusion, most still fear that this kind of education will spark a stronger focus on Tai ethnic identity and thus run counter to one of the foremost cultural purposes of state education, namely homogenization. One could argue that by keeping the majority of the Tai outside the schools, the educational system indirectly fosters a strong ethnic identification that is just not formulated within the framework of the state and therefore poses a greater political threat.

The Chinese concept of "minority education" implies education that is specifically directed towards the ninety million people who officially do not belong to the Han majority. They are "national minorities," and in the Chinese debate on minority education there is a tendency to regard them as one relatively homogenous group of people in need of more or less uniform special considerations within education. It is widely believed in China that standardized education will acculturate these people — with their various languages, religions, family structures, customs, and economic lives — to the degree that their ethnic identities will be of only minor significance in the Chinese state and society. Thus, the Chinese government and many cadres engaged in education continue to trust that by emphasizing a common Chinese language, history, and culture, while largely ignoring ethnic and cultural differences, standardized education can replace local ethnic identities with national sentiments of unity. Education may incorporate the teaching of local languages to the degree that is deemed necessary for achieving popular participation. It is feared, however, that a relaxed attitude toward centralized control of curriculum might result in increased focus on ethnic identity and local political demands.

My research concerning Akha and Jinuo responses to Chinese education has been less comprehensive, and my conclusions in that respect are therefore only preliminary. It appears that, due to the historically low position of the non-Tai in Sipsong Panna, some minorities from the mountains find in Chinese education a way to refute the prejudice against them that is still prevalent among Tai students and peasants. The number of Akha and Jinuo who participate and succeed in education is still relatively low due to poverty and a lack of proper schools in their villages, but they are nevertheless praised by cadres and teachers for being more industrious than the Tai and more interested "in learning from more advanced *minzu*"—that is, the Han. This praise of the Akha and Jinuo clearly has an impact on students' self-perception, and although the school education demonstrates to them that in the Chinese context they are regarded as even more backward than the Tai, many seemed to accept this image of themselves as backward more easily than did most Tai. They are used to being looked down upon by the Tai, know that the area they inhabit historically was ruled by a Tai king and government, and may see in Chinese education a means of combating their traditional low status and limited power. Many Akha villages celebrate when a student continues on to secondary—and especially higher or specialized secondary—school, and there seems to be a more determined attitude among the Akha and Jinuo students not to return to their villages as peasants after graduation. Thus, a local, historically inherited, ethnic hierarchy can play an important role in determining responses to state education, and some groups apparently see assimilation as a strategy for changing their own position within the local community, government, and administration.

In sum, the evidence demonstrates that belief in the Chinese state educational system's ability to control ethnic identity is not justified. The standardized educational system cannot by itself instill in students an identification with the state, nation, and CCP that eliminates the importance of their feelings of ethnic affiliation. By diminishing the cultural and political values of minorities' own languages, customs, and histories, while at the same time transmitting hegemonic interpretations of what it implies to be a minority *minzu* in the Chinese nation, the educational system in fact risks producing among ethnic minorities an *increased* emphasis on ethnic identity and cultural differences. Local factors such as the historical relationship with central China, ethnic connections across borders, religion, language, and personalities of individuals make possible a wide range of responses to the standardized education. Standardized state-controlled education is in no way capable of eradicating the importance of these factors, but it plays a role in determining the direction and form of ethnic identity processes. Most groups who adapt well to Chinese state education have been well integrated into the state for a long time and are relatively well adapted to the dominant culture. They are thus able to utilize succesful participation in the educational system to express ethnic demands within the framework of state institutions and the media. They may be able to use their Chinese education to bring about new forms of institutionalized learning that give more room for expression of the group's own interpretation of its history and culture. In comparison, those minorities who fail to adapt to the school system and tend to have fewer highly educated members from the state schools have often historically experienced a stronger form of cultural and political peripheralization within the state. When these people engage in activities such as ethnic and cultural relationships across the borders, their ethnic identification and expressions may conflict with the political interests of the state. Contacts based on an ethnic or religious sense of community across the political borders of the PRC may constitute a positive alternative for an ethnic group that experiences a high degree of cultural and political peripheralization in the Chinese state. However, groups with no such international ethnic or religious contacts have fewer alternative ways of expressing themselves and finding support for cultural practices that are incompatible with the political, ideological, and educational systems in China. Cultural homogenization is not necessarily achieved by insisting upon a strictly standardized education that leaves no room for cultural values and practices that are not officially promoted by the government.

Glossary

ai wenhua 爱文化

ai xuexi 爱学习

aiguozhuyi jiaoyu 爱国主义教育

baihua 白话

Baijiaxing 百家姓

Baiyi 摆夷

Baizu 白族

bao 保

bao guomin xuexiao 保国民学校

baosong 保送

bei dui bei douzheng 背对背斗争

benke 本科

Bian Duo Dushu Hui 边铎读书会

bianjing jiaoyu 边境教育

Caizheng Xuexiao 财政学校

Cheli Junmin Xuanweisi 车里军民宣慰司

chuantong de sixiang 传统的思想

chuji xiaoxue 初级小学

chuzhong 初中

da Hanzuzhuyi 大汉族主义

Daihua 傣化

dadui 大队

Daizu 傣族

Dayan Zhen 大研镇

difang minzuzhuyi 地方民族主义

dizhu 地主

dongba 东巴

dongba wenhua 东巴文化

Dongba Wenhua Yanjiu Suo 东巴文化研究所

dongjing 洞经

duanwujie 端午节

fengjian fandong wen 封建反动文

fengjian lingzhu zhidu 封建领主制度

fengjian nongnu zhidu 封建农奴制度

fengjian shehui 封建社会

fenpei zhidu 分配制度

Fojiao xuexiao 佛教学校

fushe zhongxue 附社中学

gailiang tuyu 改良土语

gaitu guiliu 改土归流

gaoji xiaoxue 高级小学

gaozhong 高中

gonggulü 巩固率

gongmin ke 公民课

gongshe 公社

gongzuo dui 工作队

gui 鬼

guizu ban 贵族班

guoli shifan xuexiao 国立师范
学校

guomin xuexiao 国民学校

guoyu 国语

guozijian 国子监

guwen 古文

Han 汉

han Baiyi 旱摆夷

Hanhua (become like the Han)
汉化

Hanhua (Han language) 汉话

Hani 哈尼

Hanren 汉人

Hanyu 汉语

Hanzu de wenhua 汉族的文化

heping xieshang 和平协商

heshang ban 和尚班

huayao Baiyi 花腰摆夷

jianyi shifan xuexiao 简易师范
学校

jianyi xuexiao 简易学校

jiating gongzuo 家庭公作

jifeng baoyu 急风暴雨

jinshi 进士

Jinzhi tuyu 禁止土语

juren 举人

kaihua 开化

kaiming 开明

kexue 科学

lao Daiwen 老傣文

Lijiang Baihua Bao 丽江白话报

Lijiang Diqu 丽江地区

Lijiang Diqu Zhongxue 丽江地区
中学

Lijiang Fu 丽江府

Lijiang Fu Gaodeng Xiaoxuetang
丽江府高等小学堂

Lijiang Fu Zhongxuetang 丽江府
中学堂

Lijiang Naxizu Zizhi Xian 丽江纳
西族自治县

Lijiang Renmin Zhongxue 丽江人
民中学

Lijiang Shifan Xuexiao 丽江师范
学校

Lijiang Xian Minzu Zhongxue 丽
江县民族中学

Liu Xian Lianhe Zhongxue 六县
联合中学

luohou 落后

mei you xue 没有学

Mengzhe Zhongxin Xiaoxue 勐遮
中心小学

Miaozu 苗族

minban 民办

minzhong xuexiao 民中学校

minzhu gaige buke 民主改革
补课

minzu 民族
minzu ban 民族办
Minzu Daxue 民族大学
minzu ganbu 民族干部
minzu gongzuo 民族工作
minzu jiaoyu 民族教育
minzu jingshen 民族精神
minzu tuanjie 民族团结
minzu wenhua 民族文化
Minzu Wenhua Shengtai Cun 民族
  文化生态村
minzu xiaoxue 民族小学
minzu xuexiao 民族学校
minzu xueyuan 民族学院
Minzu Yuwen Xi 民族语文系
minzu zhongxue 民族中学
mixin 迷信
muxizhi 母系制

na lai na qu 那来那去
naoli laodong 脑力劳动
Naxi 纳西
Naxizu 纳西族
Naxi Dongba Wenhua Xuexiao 纳
  西东巴文化学校
Naxi Wenhua Xuehui 纳西文化
  学会
nongchang 农场
nongnu shehui 农奴社会
Nongye Daxue 农业大学
nuli shehui 奴隶社会
nüzi chu xiaoxuetang 女子初小
  学堂

peitong 陪同
putonghua 普通话

Qianziwen 千字文
qinjia 亲家

ronghe 融合
ruxue lü 入学率

sanlun 三论
san tong 三同
Sanminzhuyi 三民主义
Sanzijing 三字经
shangshan xiaxiang 上山
  下乡
shaoshu minzu 少数民族
shen 神
shifan xuexiao 师范学校
shuangyu ban 双语班
shuangyu jiaoyu 双语教育
Shui Baiyi 水摆夷
simiao xuexiao 寺庙学校
siqing yundong 四清运动
sishu 私塾
sixiang gaizao 思想改造
sixiang pinde 思想品德
sixiang zhengzhi 思想政治

tili laodong 体力劳动
tonghua 同化
tongyi de duo minzu guojia 统一
  的多民族国家
tumin jianyi shizi xueshu 土民简
  议识字学塾
tusi 土司

waiguo 外国
Weisheng Xuexiao 卫生学校
wenge gongzuo dui 文革工作队

wenhua 文化

wenhua ban 文化班

wenhua shuiping 文化水平

wenming shidai 文明时代

xian li zhongxue 县立中学

xiang 乡

xiangtu jiaocai 乡土教材

xiaoxue 小学

xianjin 先进

xiaoxue tang 小学堂

xin Daiwen 新傣文

Xin Lijiang Dushu Hui 新丽江读书会

Xinan Bianjing Xuexiao 西南边境学校

xingzheng cun 行政村

xin xue 新学

xiongdi minzu wenzi 兄弟民族文字

Xishuangbanna Daizu Zizhi Zhou 西双版纳傣族自治州

Xishuangbanna Zhou Minzu Zhongxue 西双版纳州民族中学

xuewei 学位

Yanbian Xuewu Ju 沿边学务局

yi 夷

yixue 夷学

yumei wuzhi 愚昧无知

yuanjia 冤家

yuanshi shehui 原始社会

yuanshi zongjiao 原始宗教

Yunnan Sheng Li Jianyi Shifan Xuexiao 云南省立简易师范学校

Yunnan Sheng Li Di San Zhong Xue 云南省立第三中学

zhengfeng yundong 整风运动

zhengguihua 正规化

zhengmian jiaoyu 正面教育

zhengzhi bianfang 政治边防

zhishi qingnian 知识青年

zhongdian xuexiao 重点学校

Zhongguo 中国

Zhongguoren 中国人

Zhonghua minzu 中华民族

zhongxin xiaoxue 中心小学

zhongxin xuexiao 中心学校

zhongxue 中学

zhongzhuan 中专

zhou 州

ziran cun 自然村

zongjiao re 宗教热

zuguo guannian 祖国观念

zuxue 族学

Bibliography

ABBREVIATIONS

CLNAC	Commission of Lijiang Naxi Autonomous County for Editing the Annals, ed.
LNZG	*Lijiang Naxizu Zizhi Xian gaikuang*
XDZG	*Xishuangbanna Daizu Zizhi Zhou gaikuang*
YMJFG	*Yunnan minzu jiaoyu fazhan gaikuang*

An Tai et al., eds.

    1990   *Yunnan minzu jiaoyu gaige shixian yu tansuo* (Exploration and implementation of the reforms of minority education in Yunnan). Kunming: Yunnan Minzu Chubanshe.

Anagnost, Ann S.

    1993   "Cultural Nationalism and Chinese Modernity." In Harumi Befu, ed., *Cultural Nationalism in East Asia*. Berkeley: University of California Press.

    1994   "The Politics of Ritual Displacement." In Charles F. Keyes, Laurel Kendall, and Helen Hardacre, eds., *Asian Visions of Authority: Religion and the Modern States of East and Southeast Asia*. Honolulu: University of Hawaii Press.

Bacot, James

    1913   *Les Mo-so* (The Mo-so). Leiden: N.p.

Bailey, Paul

    1990   *Reform the People*. Edinburgh: Edinburgh University Press.

Banks, James A., and James Lynch, eds.

    1986   *Multicultural Education in Western Societies*. London: Holt, Rinehart and Winston.

Bastid, Marianne

    1984   "Chinese Educational Policies in the 1980s and Economic Development." *China Quarterly* 98: 189–219.

1987   "Servitude or Liberation? The Introduction of Foreign Educational Practices and Systems to China from 1840 to the Present." In Ruth Hayhoe and Marianne Bastid, eds., *China's Education and the Industrialized World*. New York/London: M. E. Sharpe, Inc.

Bentley, Carter

1987   "Ethnicity and Practice." *Comparative Studies in Society and History* 29 (1): 24–55.

Bernstein, Thomas P.

1977   *Up to the Mountains and Down to the Villages*. New Haven/London: Yale University Press.

Borchiged, Wurlig

1995   "The Impact of Urban Ethnic Education on Modern Mongolian Ethnicity, 1949–1966." In Stevan Harrell, ed., 1995a.

Borthwick, Sally

1983   *Education and Social Change in China*. Stanford, Calif.: Hoover Institution Press.

Bourdieu, Pierre, and Jean-Claude Passeron

1990   *Reproduction in Education, Society and Culture*. London: Sage Publications.

Brown, Melissa J., ed.

1996   *Negotiating Ethnicities in China and Taiwan*. Berkeley: Institute of East Asian Studies, University of California.

Byram, Michael

1991   "Bilingualism in Minority Education: The Conflict of Interest between Minorities and Their Members." In Keen Jaespert and Sjaak Kroon, eds., *Ethnic Minority Languages and Education*. Amsterdam: Swets & Zeitlinger.

Cai Hua

1997   *Une société sans père ni mari: Les Na de Chine*. Paris: Presse universitaire de France.

Cao Chengzhang

1986   *Daizu nongnuzhi he zongjiao hunyin* (The serf system and religious marriage of the Dai). Beijing: Zhongguo Shehui Kexue Chubanshe.

Cao Xiang

1990   "Yingyong Yunnan difang minzu shi jinxing aiguozhuyi jiaoyu"

(Using Yunnan local *minzu* histories to conduct patriotic edu-.
cation). In Yunnan Province History Society et. al., eds., 1990.

Carnoy, Martin

1974   *Education as Cultural Imperialism.* New York: David McKay
Company, Inc.

Chan Hoiman

1992   "Modernity and Revolution in Chinese Education: Towards an
Analytical Agenda of the Great Leap Forward and the Cultural
Revolution." In Ruth Hayhoe, ed., *Education and Modernization:
The Chinese Experience.* Oxford: Pergamon Press.

Chao, Emily

1996   "Hegemony, Agency, and Re-presenting the Past: The Invention
of Dongba Culture among the Naxi of Southwest China." In
Brown 1996.

Chen Han-Seng

1949   *Frontier Land Systems in Southernmost China.* New York: Insitute
of Pacific Relations.

Chen Hongtao et al., eds.

1989   *Yunnan minzu jiaoyu yanjiu* (Research on minority education in
Yunnan). Beijing: Zhongyang Minzu Xueyuan Chubanshe.

Chinese Ethnological Society, ed.

1981–91   *Minzuxue yanjiu* (Ethnological research), nos. 1–10. Beijing:
Minzu Chubanshe.

Churchill, Stacy

1985   *The Education of Linguistic and Cultural Minorities in the OECD
Countries.* Clevedon, England: Multilingual Matters.

Cleverley, John

1991 [1985]   *The Schooling of China.* North Sydney: Allen & Unwin.

Colquhoun, A. R.

1970 [1985]   *Amongst the Shans.* New York: Paragon Book Reprint Corp.

Comaroff, John L.

1987   "Of Totemism and Ethnicity." *Ethnos* 52 (3–4): 301–23.

Commission for Historical Accounts of the Chinese People's Political Consultative
Conference, Jinghong Commission, ed.

1993   *Jinghong wenshi ziliao xuanji* (Collection of historical material
from Jinghong). Jinghong: N.p.

Commission for Work with Historical Accounts of Sipsong Panna Tai Auton-
        omous Prefecture, ed.

1987   *Banna wenshi ziliao xuanji* (Collection of historical material from
           Sipsong Panna). Vols. 1–8. Jinghong: N.p.

Commission of Lijiang Naxi Autonomous County for Editing the Annals, ed.

1995   *Jiaoyu zhi* (Educational gazetteer). Unpublished draft.

Connor, Walker

1984   *The National Question in Marxist-Leninist Theory and Strategy.*
           Princeton: Princeton University Press.

Conze, Edward

1959   *Buddhism.* New York: Harper and Brothers.

Crossley, Pamela K.

1990   "Thinking about Ethnicity in Early Modern China." *Late Imperial*
           China 11, no. 1 (June): 1–34.

Cummins, Jim, and Tove Skutnabb-Kangas, eds.

1988   *Minority Education: From Shame to Struggle.* Clevedon, England/
           Philadelphia: Multilingual Matters.

Daizu jian shi (A brief history of the Dai)

1986   Kunming: Yunnan Renmin Chubanshe.

Daizu shehui lishi diaocha, Xishuangbanna (Investigation of the social history of
        the Dai, Sipsong Panna), vols. 1–10

1985   Kunming: Yunnan Minzu Chubanshe.

Dangdai Zhongguo de minzu gongzuo (*Minzu* work in contemporary China), vols.
        1–2

1993   Beijing: Dangdai Zhongguo Chubanshe.

Dao Yongming, ed.

1989a   *Cheli Xuanweishi Shi Si jijie* (A collected annotated genealogy of
           the Pacification Commisioner of Cheli). Kunming: Yunnan Min-
           zu Chubanshe.

1989b   *Zhongguo Daizu shilian jiyao* (An abstract of historical material
           concerning the Dai in China). Kunming: Yunnan Minzu
           Chubanshe.

Davies, H. R.

1970 [1909] *Yunnan, the Link between India and the Yangtze.* Taipei: Ch'eng
           Wen Publishing Company.

de Beauclair, Inez

1970   *Tribal Cultures of Southwest China*. Taipei: Orient Cultural Service.

De Lauretis, Teresa, ed.

1986   *Feminist Studies/Cultural Studies*. London: Macmillan.

Diamond, Norma

1995   "Defining the Miao: Ming, Qing, and Contemporary Views." In Harrell, ed., 1995a.

1996   "Christianity and the Hua Miao." In Daniel H. Bays, ed., *Christianity in China: From the Eighteenth Century to the Present*. Stanford: Stanford University Press.

Dikötter, Frank

1992   *The Discourse of Race in Modern China*. Hong Kong: Hong Kong University Press.

Diller, Anthony

1994   "Tai Languages: Varieties and Subgroup Terms." *Thai-Yunnan Project Newsletter* 25 (June): 8–17.

Dodd, William Clifton

1923   *The Tai Race—Elder Brother of the Chinese: Results of Experience, Exploration and Research of William Clifton Dodd*. Cedar Rapids, Iowa: N.p.

Dreyer, June Teufel

1976   *China's Forty Millions*. Cambridge, Mass./London: Harvard University Press.

Duara, Prasenjit

1993   "De-constructing the Chinese Nation." *Australian Journal of Chinese Affairs* 30 (July): 1–26.

Engels, Friedrich

1972 [1883] *The Origin of the Family, Private Property, and the State*. New York: International Publishers.

Enwall, Joakim

1994   *A Myth Become Reality: History and Development of the Miao Written Language*. Stockholm's East Asian Monographs no. 5, vols. 1 and 2. Stockholm: Institute of Oriental Languages, Stockholm University.

Eriksen, Thomas Hylland

 1993   *Ethnicity and Nationalism: Anthropological Perspectives.* London/
      Boulder, Colo.: Pluto Press.

Fei Xiaotong

 1981   "Ethnic Identification in China." In Fei Xiaotong, ed., *Toward a
      People's Anthropology.* Beijing: New World Press.

Feng Chunlin

 1989   "Qiantan Yunnan minzu jiaoyu de tedian ji qi fazhan yuanze" (A
      brief discussion of the characteristics of Yunnan's minority edu-
      cation and the principles for its development). In Chen Hongtao
      et al., eds., 1989.

Fishman, Joshua A.

 1989   *Language and Ethnicity in Minority Sociolinguistic Perspective.*
      Clevedon, England/Philadelphia: Multilingual Matters.

FitzGerald, C. P.

 1972   *The Southern Expansion of the Chinese People.* London: Barry and
      Jenkins.

Fong, Rowena, and Paul R. Spickard

 1994   "Ethnic Relations in the People's Republic of China: Images and
      Social Distance between Han Chinese and Minority and Foreign
      Nationalities." *Journal of Northeast Asian Studies,* Spring: 27–48.

Friedman, Jonathan

 1990   "Being in the World: Globalization and Localization." In Mike
      Featherstone, ed., *Global Culture: Nationalism, Globalization,
      and Modernity.* Special issue of *Theory, Culture and Society.* Lon-
      don: Sage Publications.

 1991   "Narcissism, Roots and Postmodernity: The Constitution of
      Selfhood in the Global Crisis." In Jonathan Friedman and Scott
      Lash, eds., *Modernity and Identity.* Oxford: Blackwell.

Gao Lishi

 1992   *Xishuangbanna Daizu de lishi yu wenhua* (The history and cul-
      ture of the Dai in Sipsong Panna). Kunming: Yunnan Minzu
      Chubanshe.

Gladney, Dru C.

 1991   *Muslim Chinese: Ethnic Nationalism in the People's Republic.*
      Cambridge, Mass.: Harvard University Press.

1994   "Representing Nationality in China: Refiguring Majority/
              Minority Identities." *Journal of Asian Studies* 1 (Feb.): 92–123.

Goldstein-Kyaga, Katrin

1993   *The Tibetans—School for Survival or Submission*. Stockholm: HLS
              Forlag.

Gombrich, Richard

1995 [1988]   *Theravada Buddhism: A Social History from Ancient Benares to
              Modern Colombo*. London/New York: Routledge.

Gong Yin

1992   *Zhongguo tusi zhidu* (The *tusi* system in China). Kunming:
              Yunnan Minzu Chubanshe.

Gong Youde

1993   *Ruxue yu Yunnan shaoshu minzu wenhua* (Confucianism and the
              cultures of the minority *minzu* in Yunnan). Kunming: Yunnan
              Renmin Chubanshe.

Goodman, Nelson

1972   *Problems and Projects*. Indianapolis/New York: Bobbs-Merrill
              Company, Inc.

Gosth, Ratna, and Abdulaziz Talbani

1992   "Inequality and Education in India: The Case of the Scheduled
              Castes." In D. Ray and D. H. Poonwassie, eds., *Education and
              Cultural Differences*. New York/London: Garland Publishing,
              Inc.

Goullart, Peter

1955   *Forgotten Kingdom*. London: John Murray.

Guan Jian

1993   "The Indigenous Religion and Theravada Buddhism in Ban Da
              Tiu, a Dai Lue Village in Yunnan (China)." *Southeast Asian Review*
              17, nos. 1 and 2 (Jan.–Dec.).

Guo Dalie

1983   "Lüe lun Naxizu xinli suzhi tedian ji qi bianyi yinsu" (A brief
              account of the Naxi's special psychological makeup and its
              various elements). In Chinese Ethnological Society, ed., *Min-
              zuxue yanjiu* (Ethnological research), no. 5. Kunming: Minzu
              Chubanshe.

1987   "Naxi wenhua xuehui de tedian he gongneng" (The characteristics and aims of the Society of Naxi Culture). *Minzuxue yu xiandai-hua* (Ethnology and modernization) 1: 22–25.

Guo Dalie and Yang Shiguang, eds.

1985, 1991   Dongba wenhua lunji (Anthology of dongba culture). Vols. 1–2. Kunming: Yunnan Renmin Chubanshe.

Guo Xiaolin

1990   "Review of Chinese Research on the Yongning Naxi Matriliny." *Stockholm Journal of East Asian Studies* 2: 77–90.

Hagendoorn, Louk

1993   "Ethnic Categorization and Outgroup Exclusion: Cultural Values and Social Stereotypes in the Construction of Ethnic Hierachies." *Ethnic and Racial Studies* 16 (1): 26–51.

Hansen, Mette Halskov

1998   "Fostering 'Love of Learning': Naxi Responses to Ethnic Images in Chinese State Education." In Kjeld-Erik Broedsgaard and David Strand, eds., *Reconstructing Twentieth-Century China: Social Control, Civil Society and National Identity.* Oxford: Oxford University Press.

1999a   "The Call of Mao or Money: Discourses on Resettlement among Han Chinese Migrants on China's Southwestern Borders." *China Quarterly.* Forthcoming, June, no. 158.

1999b   "Teaching Backwardness or Equality? Chinese State Education among the Tai in Sipsong Panna." In Postiglione and Stites, eds., 1999. Forthcoming.

Harrell, Stevan, ed.

1995a   *Cultural Encounters on China's Ethnic Frontiers.* Seattle/London: University of Washington Press.

1995b   "Introduction: Civilizing Projects and the Reaction to Them." In Harrell, ed., 1995a.

Hayhoe, Ruth

1992   "Cultural Tradition and Educational Modernization: Lessons from the Republican Era." In Ruth Hayhoe, ed., *Education and Modernization: The Chinese Experience.* Oxford: Pergamon Press.

He Hongchang

1990   "Lun pinkun minzu diqu de jiaoyu wenti" (A discussion of edu-

cational problems in poor minority areas). *Minzuxue* (Ethnology)
1: 54–58.

He Rugong

1988   "Lijiang ge shiqi de xuexiao" (Schools in Lijiang in the different
historical periods). In *Naxizu shehui lishi diaocha* (Investigation
of the social history of the Naxi), vol. 3. Kunming: Yunnan
Renmin Chubanshe.

He Shaoying

1995   "Qian lun Zang wenhua yu Naxi wenhua zhi jiao hui" (An
elementary discussion of the relationship and convergence of
Naxi and Tibetan culture). *Minzu yanjiu* (*Minzu* research)
1: 27–33

He Wanbao

1995   "Guanyu Dalai Minzu Wenhua Shengtai Cun shexiang." (The
idea behind Dalai Minority Culture and Ecology Village).
Unpublished leaflet.

He Zairui et al., eds.

1993   *Lijiang wenshi ziliao* (Lijiang historical accounts). Vols. 1–12.
Lijiang: Lijiang Xian Zhengxie Wenshi Ziliao Weiyuanhui.

He Zhonghua

1995   *Where the Goddesses Live: The Naxis.* Kunming: Yunnan Jiaoyu
Chubanshe.

Heberer, Thomas

1989   *China and Its National Minorities.* Armonk, N.Y.: M. E. Sharpe.

Hobart, Mark

1987   "Summer's Days and Salad Days: The Coming of Age of Anthropology?" In Holy Ladislav, ed., *Comparative Anthropology.*
Oxford: Basil Blackwell.

Hsieh, Shih-Chung

1989   *Ethnic-Political Adaptation and Ethnic Change of the Sipsong Panna
Tai: An Ethnohistorical Analysis.* Ph.D. diss., University of Michigan.

1995   "On the Dynamics of Tai/Dai-Lue Ethnicity." In Harrell, ed.,
1995a.

Hutchinson, John, and Anthony D. Smith, eds.

1994   *Nationalism.* Oxford: Oxford University Press.

Jackson, Anthony

1979   *Na-khi Religion: An Analytical Appraisal of the Na-khi Ritual Texts.* The Hague: Mouton.

Jaspaert, Koen, and Sjaak Kroon

1991   "Ethnic Minority Language Teaching and Language Policy: Introductory Remarks." In Koen Jaspaert and Sjaak Kroon, eds., *Ethnic Minority Languages and Education.* Amsterdam: Swets & Zeitlinger.

Jenkins, Richard

1994   "Rethinking Ethnicity: Identity, Categorization and Power." *Ethnic and Racial Studies* 17 (2): 197–223.

Jiang Yingliang

1950   *Baiyi de shenghuo wenhua* (The cultural life of the Baiyi). Shanghai: Zhonghua Shuju Yinxing.

1983   *Daizu shi* (A history of the Dai). Chengdu: Sichuan Minzu Chubanshe.

Jinghong County Bureau of Education

1993a   "Jinghong Xian jiaoyu gongzuo zonghe jiangbao cailiao" (A summarizing report on Jinghong County's work with education). Unpublished report.

1993b   "Jinghong Xian minzu jiaoyu qingkuang" (The situation concerning minority education in Jinghong County). Unpublished document.

Keyes, Charles F.

1979   "Introduction." In Charles F. Keyes, ed., *Ethnic Adaptation and Identity: The Karen on the Thai Frontier with Burma.* Philadelphia: Institute for the Study of Human Issues.

1981   "The Dialectics of Ethnic Change." In Charles Keyes, ed., *Ethnic Change.* Seattle: University of Washington Press.

1983   "Economic Action and Buddhist Morality in a Thai Village." *Journal of Asian Studies* 42 (4): 851–68.

1996   "Who Are the Tai? Reflections on the Invention of Identities." In Lola Romanucci-Ross and George A. De Vos, eds., *Ethnic Identity.* Walnut Creek/London/New Delhi: Alta Mira Press.

Knödel, Susanne

1995   *Die Matrilinearen Mosuo von Yongning.* Münster: Lit Verlag.

Kwong, Julia, ed.

1989   *Chinese Education* (special edition on education of minorities) 22 (1).

———, and Hong Xiao

1989   "Educational Equality among China's Minorities." *Comparative Education* 25 (2): 229–43.

Leach, Edmund R.

1954   *Political Systems of Highland Burma.* Cambridge, Mass.: Harvard University Press.

Lebar, Frank M., Gerald C. Hickey, and John K. Musgrave

1964   *Ethnic Groups of Mainland Southeast Asia.* New Haven: Human Relations Area Files Press.

Lee, Chae-jin

1986   *China's Korean Minority: The Politics of Ethnic Education.* Boulder, Colo./London: Westview Press.

Lester, Robert C.

1973   *Theravada Buddhism in Southeast Asia.* Ann Arbor: University of Michigan Press.

Lewin, Keith M., Xui Hui, Angela W. Little, and Zheng Jiwei

1994   *Educational Innovation in China: Tracing the Impact of the 1985 Reforms.* Essex: Longman.

Li Foyi

n.d.   *Shier Banna jinian* (A chronology of Sipsong Panna). Taipei: N.p.

1955   *Shier Banna zhi* (Sipsong Panna historical gazetteer). Taipei: Zhengzhong.

Li Guangpin

1992   "Mengla Xian minzu jiaoyu qingkuang diaocha" (Report on the condition of minority education in Mengla County). In Yan Sanlong et al., eds., *Xishuangbanna minzu jiaoyu* (Minority education in Sipsong Panna). Kunming: Yunnan Minzu Chubanshe.

Li Jinchun and Wang Chengquan

1984   *Naxizu* (The Naxi). Kunming: Yunnan Minzu Chubanshe.

Li Li et al., eds.

1991   *Yunnan Minzu Xueyuan sishi nian, 1951–1991* (Forty years of the Yunnan Institute of the Nationalities, 1951–1991). Kunming: Yunnan Daxue Chubanshe.

Li Lin-ts'an

1984 *Mosuo yanjiu lunwen ji* (Collected essays on Mosuo research). Taipei: Gugong Bowuyuan.

Li Ping

1989 "Shilun Yunnan minzu jiaoyu shiye fazhan de teshuxing he ying caiqu de cuoshi" (A discussion of the special features of the development of minority education in Yunnan and of which methods to employ). *Minzuxue* (Ethnology) 2: 74–77.

Li Ruoyu

1988 "Wo de muxiao Yunnan Shengli Lijiang Zhongxue" (My alma mater, Yunnan Provincial Lijiang Middle School). In *Naxizu shehui lishi diaocha,* vol. 3.

Li Shizong

1988 "Naxizu Diqu di yi suo zhongxue de chuangli he fazhan" (The founding and development of the first middle school in Naxi Prefecture). In *Naxizu shehui lishi diaocha,* vol. 3.

Li Zhaolun et al., eds.

1990 *Shaoshu minzu ganbu de xuanze yu peiyang* (The selection and training of minority cadres). Kunming: Yunnan Minzu Chubanshe.

Liang Jiaji

1988 "Huiyi Lijiang he Lijiang Sheng Zhong" (Recalling Lijiang and Lijiang Provincial Middle School). In *Naxizu shehui lishi diaocha,* vol. 3.

Lijiang County Bureau of Education

1994 "Kefu kunnan, yi fa zhi jiao, jiji shishi liu nian yiwu jiaoyu" (Overcome difficulties, manage education according to the law, strive for the practice of six years of compulsory education). Unpublished report.

———, et al., eds.

1991 *Yanjiu yu tantao: Jiaoyu lunwen* (Research and inquiries: Essays on education), 1–2. Lijiang County Government. N.p.

1995 *Lijiang Naxizu Zizhi Xian zhong xiao xuexiao deyu difang xiangtu jiaocai* (Local moral teaching material for middle and primary schools in Lijiang Naxi Autonomous County). Unpublished draft.

Lijiang Minzu Zhongxue shi nian (Ten years of Lijiang Minority Middle School)

1991 Unpublished report.

Lijiang Naxizu Zizhi Xian gaikuang (A survey of Lijiang Naxi Autonomous
County) (*LNZG*)
1986   Kunming: Yunnan Renmin Chubanshe.

Lin Yaohua
1987   "Zhongguo xinan diqu de minzu shibie" (Ethnic identification
            in southwest China). In *Yunnan shaoshu minzu shehui lishi diaocha
            ziliao huibian* (Collection of materials from historical and socio-
            logical investigations of minority *minzu* in Yunnan), vol. 3.
            Kunming: Yunnan Renmin Chubanshe.

Liu Baoming
1993   "Lun fazhan minzu jiaoyu yu wanshan minzu quyu zizhi zhidu de
            guanxi" (A discussion of the connection between developing minor-
            ity education and improving the system of minority regional auton-
            omy). *Zhongguo shaoshu minzu* (China's minority *minzu*) 10: 43–50.

Liu Guangzhi
1993   *Yunnan jiaoyu jianshi* (A short history of education in Yunnan).
            Chengdu: Guizhou Renmin Chubanshe.

Liu Yan
1992   "Daizu Fojiaotu de zongjiao shenghuo" (The religious life of the
            Buddhist Tai). *Shijie zongjiao yanjiu* (Studies in world religion)
            1: 101–7.
1993   *Nanzhuan Fojiao yu Daizu wenhua* (Theravada Buddhism and the
            culture of the Tai). Kunming: Yunnan Minzu Chubanshe.

Liu Zhengfeng et al., eds.
1988   *Yunnan minzu jiaoyu yanjiu* (Research on minority education in
            Yunnan). Kunming: Yunnan Minzu Chubanshe.

Lomawaima, K. Tsianina
1994   *They Called It Prairie Light: The Story of Chilocco Indian School.*
            Lincoln: University of Nebraska Press.

Ma Lisan
1985   "Lun Lijiang Diqu minzu jiaoyu de teshuxing ji qi duice" (A dis-
            cussion of the typical features of minority education in Lijiang
            Prefecture and the way to deal with it). *Minzuxue yu xiandaihua*
            (Ethnology and modernization) 2: 34–38.

Ma Xulun
1952   "Guanyu di yi ci Quanguo Minzu Jiaoyu Huiyi de baogao"

(Report on the first National Conference on Minority Education). *Xinhua yuebao,* Feb.: 42–43.

Martin, Dorothea A. L.

1990   *The Making of a Sino-Marxist World View: Perceptions and Interpretations of World History in the People's Republic of China.* Armonk, N.Y./London: M. E. Sharpe, Inc.

McKhann, Charles

1989   "Fleshing Out the Bones: The Cosmic and Social Dimensions of Space in Naxi Architecture." In Chiao Chien and Nicolas Tapp, eds., *Ethnicity and Ethnic Groups in China.* Hong Kong: Chinese University of Hong Kong.

1995   "The Naxi and the Nationalities Question." In Harrell, ed., 1995a.

Megarry, Jacquetta, et al., eds.

1981   *Education of Minorities: World Yearbook of Education.* London: Kogan Page Ltd.

Menghai County Bureau of Education

1989   "Tuoshan chuli xuexiao jiaoyu yu fosi zhijian de guanxi zhenxing Daizu xiangcun de minzu jiaoyu" (Appropriate management of the connection between schools and monasteries vitalizes minority education in Tai villages). *Yunnan minzu yuwen* (Languages of Yunnan's *minzu*) 4: 31–36.

Mi Yunguang

1993   "Yunnan minzu diqu puji jiu nian yiwu jiaoyu mubiao" (The goal of achieving nine years of compulsory education in minority areas in Yunnan). *Minzu gongzuo* (*Minzu* work) 10: 37.

Minzu gongzuo shouci (A handbook on *minzu* work)

1985   Kunming: Yunnan Renmin Chubanshe.

Minzu gongzuo wenxuan (Selected documents concerning *minzu* work)

1986   Nanning: N.p.

Minzu Research Department of China's Academy of Social Sciences et al., eds.

1993   *Zhongguo shaoshu minzu yuyan wenzi shiyong he fazhan wenti* (Problems concerning the use and development of the spoken and written languages of China's minority *minzu*). Beijing: Zhongguo Zhangxue Chubanshe.

Moerman, Michael

1965   "Ethnic Identity in a Complex Civilization: Who Are the Lue?"
        American Anthropologist 67 (5): 1215–30.

1966   "Ban Ping's Temple: The Center of a 'Loosely Structured' Society."
        In Manning Nash et al., eds., *Anthropological Studies in Thera-*
        vada Buddhism. Cultural Report Series, no. 13, Yale University.

1968   "Being Lue: Uses and Abuses of Ethnic Identification." In June
        Helm, ed., *Essays on the Problem of Tribe.* Seattle: University of
        Washington Press.

Morgan, Lewis Henry

1985 [1877]   *Ancient Society.* Tucson: University of Arizona Press.

Mueggler, Erik

1991   "Money, the Mountain and State Power in a Naxi Village." *Mod-*
        ern China 17 (2): 188–226.

Naxizu jian shi (A brief history of the Naxi)

1984   Kunming: Yunnan Renmin Chubanshe.

Naxizu shehui lishi diaocha (Investigation of the social history of the Naxi) 1–3

1986–88   Kunming: Yunnan Renmin Chubanshe.

Ogbu, John U.

1978   *Minority Education and Caste.* New York/San Francisco/London:
        Academic Press.

Ong, Aihwa

1987   *Spirits of Resistance and Capitalist Discipline: Factory Women in*
        Malaysia. Albany: State University of New York Press.

Peng Zhiwei

1991   "Shanqu minzu jiaoyu jie shuoguo" (Education of *minzu* living
        in the mountains shows results). *Minzu gongzuo* (*Minzu* work)
        4: 15–16.

Penth, Hans

1989   "Thai Scripts: An Outline of Their Origin and Development."
        In Princess Galyani Vaddhana, comp., *Yunnan.* Bangkok:
        Watthanaphanit.

Pepper, Suzanne

1996   *Radicalism and Education Reform in Twentieth-Century China.*
        Cambridge, England/New York: Cambridge University Press.

Postiglione, Gerard A.

1992   "The Implications of Modernization for the Education of China's National Minorities." In Ruth Hayhoe, ed., *Education and Modernization*. Oxford: Pergamon Press.

Postiglione, Gerard A., and Regie Stites, eds.

1999   *The Education of China's Minorities*. New York: Garland Press.

Postiglione, Gerard A., Teng Xing, and Ai Ping

1995   "Basic Education and School Discontinuation in National Minority Border Regions in China." In Gerard A. Postiglione and Lee Wing On, eds., *Social Change and Educational Development: Mainland China, Taiwan and Hong Kong*. Hong Kong: University of Hong Kong Press.

Prunner, Gernot

1969   "The Kinship System of the Na-khi (SW-China) as Seen in Their Pictographic Script." *Ethnos* 34: 100–106.

Pu Linlin

1994   "Minzu yuanxiao biyesheng fenpei gongzuo gaige chuyi" (A discussion of the reform of the assignments of graduates from minority schools). *Minzu jiaoyu yanjiu* (Minority education research) 1: 64–67.

Rawski, Evelyn S.

1979   *Education and Popular Literacy in Ch'ing China*. Ann Arbor: University of Michigan Press.

Research Team of the Provincial People's Political Consultative Conference's Commission for Minority Religions

1989   "Xuexiao yu fosi xietiao peihe banhao minzu jiaoyu" (Schools and monasteries cooperate to conduct minority education). *Minzu gongzuo* (*Minzu* work) 11: 9–11.

Rocher, Emile

1879–80   *La Province Chinoise du Yun-nan*. Paris: E. Leroux.

Rock, Joseph F.

1947   *The Ancient Na-khi Kingdom of Southwest China*. Vols. 1–2. Cambridge, Mass.: Harvard University Press.

1963   *The Life and Culture of the Na-khi Tribe of the China-Tibet Borderland*. Wiesbaden: Franz Steiner Verlag.

Rowe, William

1994   "Education and Empire in Southwest China: Ch'en Hung-mou
            in Yunnan, 1733–38." In Alexander Woodside and Benjamin A.
            Elman, eds., *Education and Society in Late Imperial China,*
            1600–1900. Berkeley: University of California Press.

Satyawadhna, Cholthira

1990   "A Comparative Study of Structure and Contradiction in the
            Austro-Asiatic System of the Thai-Yunnan Periphery." In Gehan
            Wijeyewardene, ed., *Ethnic Groups across National Boundaries in*
            Mainland Southeast Asia. Singapore: Institute of Southeast Asian
            Studies.

Schoenhals, Martin

1993   *The Paradox of Power in a People's Republic of China Middle School.*
            Armonk, N.Y./London: M. E. Sharpe, Inc.

Shih Chuankang

1993   "The Yongning Moso: Sexual Union, Household Organization,
            Gender and Ethnicity in a Matrilineal Duolocal Society in South-
            west China." Ph.D. diss., Standford University.

Sipsong Panna Education Research Team, Yunnan Institute of the Nationalities

1983   "Xishuangbanna Zhou minzu jiaoyu diaocha baogao" (Report
            from the investigation of minority education in Sipsong Panna).
            In *Minzu jiaoyu congkan* (A series on minority education) 2.

Sipsong Panna Prefecture Education Commission

1992   *Xishuangbanna Zhou minzu jiaoyu qingkuang* (The educational
            situation of minorities in Sipsong Panna Prefecture). Jinghong,
            unpublished report.

Sipsong Panna Prefecture Normal School, ed.

1994   *Dai yuwen* (Tai language), vols. 1–8. Unpublished teaching mate-
            rial for Tai classes in normal school.

Sixiang pinde (Ideology and morals), vols. 1–10

1993   Compulsory teaching material for primary education. Beijing:
            Renmin Jiaoyu Chubanshe.

Sixiang pinde (Ideology and morals)

1991   Supplementary teaching material for the third year of primary
            school in Yunnan. Kunming: Chenguang Chubanshe.

Sixiang zhengzhi (Ideology and politics)

1993   Compulsory teaching material for the three years of junior and senior secondary education. Guangdong: Gaodeng Jiaoyu Chubanshe.

Skinner, William G., and Thomas Kirsch, eds.

1975   *Change and Persistence in Thai Society*. Ithaca, N.Y.: Cornell University Press.

Skutnabb-Kangas

1981   *Bilingualism or Not: The Education of Minorities*. Cleveland: Multilingual Matters.

Smith, Graham H.

1992   "Kura Kaupapa Maori: Contesting and Reclaiming Education in Aotearoa." In Douglas Ray and Deo H. Poonwassie, eds., *Education and Cultural Differences: New Perspectives*. New York/-London: Garland Publishing, Inc.

Solinger, Dorothy

1977   *Regional Government and Political Integration in Southwest China, 1949–1954*. Berkeley: University of California Press.

Sun Hongkai

1992   "Language Recognition and Nationality." *International Journal of the Sociology of Language* 97: 9–23.

Sun Ruoqiong et al., eds.

1990   *Zhongguo shaoshu minzu jiaoyuxue gailun* (An introduction to the education of China's minorities). Beijing: Zhongguo Laodong Chubanshe.

Sun Yat-sen

1926   *Sanminzhuyi* (The Three Principles of the People). Changsha: Minzhi Shuju.

Sun Yuting

1990   "Xishuangbanna Zhou yiwu jiaoyu kaocha baogao" (A report from an investigation of compulsory education in Sipsong Panna Prefecture). In An Tai, chief ed., *Yunnan minzu jiaoyu gaige shixian yu tansuo* (Exploration and implementation of the reforms of minority education in Yunnan). Kunming: Yunnan Minzu Chubanshe.

Sutton, Silvia B.

1974   *In China's Border Provinces: The Turbulent Career of Joseph Rock, Botanist-Explorer.* New York: Hastings House.

Tanabe, Shigeharu

1988   "Spirits and Ideological Discourse: The Tai Lu Guardian Cults in Yunnan." *Sojourn* 1: 1–25.

Thoegersen, Stig

1994   "Educational Modernization and Social Change in Rural China." Work report, Australian National University, Contemporary China Centre.

1997   "Learning in Lijiazhuang: Education Skills and Careers in 20th-Century Rural China." Paper presented at Education and Society in Twentieth-Century China conference, Toronto, September 26–28.

Unger, Jonathan

1982   *Education under Mao.* New York: Columbia University Press.

Wang Binxiang

1994   "Tigao Yunnan minzu jiaoyu touzi xiaoyi de zhibiao fenxi he duice" (Analysis and suggestions on how to increase the results of the investments in minority education in Yunnan). *Minzu yanjiu* (*Minzu* research) 2: 34–41.

Wang Tianxi

1988   *Minzu fa gailun* (An introduction to the laws concerning *minzu*). Kunming: Yunnan Renmin Chubanshe.

Wang Xihong et al., eds.

1990   *Zhongguo bianjiang minzu jiaoyu* (Education of China's minorities living in border areas). Beijing: Zhongyang Minzu Xueyuan Chubanshe.

Wellens, Koen

1998   "What's in a Name? The Premi in Southwest China and the Consequences of Defining Ethnic Identity." *Nations and Nationalism* 4 (1): 17–34.

Whyte, Geoffrey M., and Chavivun Prachuabmoh

1983   "The Cognitive Organization of Ethnic Images." *Ethos* 11 (1/2): 2–33.

Wiens, Herold

   1967 [1954]   *Han Chinese Expansion in South China.* Hamden, Conn.: Shoestring Press.

Wijeyewardene, Gehan, ed.

   1990   *Ethnic Groups across National Boundaries in Mainland Southeast Asia.* Singapore: Institute of Southeast Asian Studies.

Williams, Brackette

   1989   "A Class Act: Anthropology and the Race to Nation across Ethnic Terrain." *Annual Review of Anthropology* 18: 401–44.

Woodside, Alexander

   1983   "Some Mid-Qing Theorists of Popular Schools." *Modern China* 9 (1): 3–37.

   1992   "Real and Imagined Continuities in the Chinese Struggle for Literacy." In Ruth Hayhoe, ed., *Education and Modernization.* Oxford: Pergamon Press.

——, and Benjamin A. Elman

   1994   "The Expansion of Education in Ch'ing China." In Alexander Woodside and Benjamin A. Elman, eds., *Education and Society in Late Imperial China, 1600–1900.* Berkeley: University of California Press.

Xiao Yunhe

   1993   "Minguo shiqi Cheli Xian de xuexiao jiaoyu" (School education in Cheli County in the Republican period). In Commission for Historical Accounts of the Chinese People's Political Consultative Conference, Jinghong Commission, ed., *Jinghong wenshi ziliao xuanji* (Collection of historical material from Jinghong). Jinghong.

Xie Benshu et al., eds.

   1994   *Minzu diqu aiguozhuyi jiaoyu jianming duben* (An elementary study of patriotic education in minority areas). Kunming: Yunnan Renmin Chubanshe.

Xie Qihuang et al., eds.

   1991   *Zhongguo minzu jiaoyu fazhan zhanlüe jueze* (Choosing a strategy for developing China's minority education). Beijing: Zhongyang Minzuxueyuan Chubanshe.

Xishuangbanna Daizu Zizhi Zhou gaikuang (A survey of Sipsong Panna Tai Autonomous Prefecture)

1986   Kunming: Yunnan Minzu Chubanshe.

Xishuangbanna Daizu Zizhi Zhou tongji nianjian (Statistical yearbook of Sipsong Panna Tai Autonomous County)

1989   Jinghong.

Xishuangbanna dili (Geography of Sipsong Panna)

1991   Teaching material for secondary schools in Sipsong Panna Prefecture. Sipsong Panna Prefecture Normal School.

Yan Ruxian and Song Zhaolin

1983   *Yongning Naxizu de muxi zhi* (The matrilineal system of the Yongning Naxi). Kunming: Yunnan Chubanshe.

Yan Sanlong et al., eds.

1992   *Xishuangbanna minzu jiaoyu* (Minority education in Sipsong Panna). Kunming: Yunnan Minzu Chubanshe.

Yang Chonglong

1995   *Yunnan jiaoyu wenti yanjiu* (Reseach on Yunnan's educational problems). Kunming: Yunnan Jiaoyu Chubanshe.

Yang Qichang

1987   "Naxizu re'ai wenhua jiaoyu de youliang chuantong" (The fine tradition of Naxi affection for education). *Minzuxue yu xiandaihua* (Ethnology and modernization) 1: 29–34.

1992   "Lijiang Naxizu Zizhi Xian lishi renkou" (Population in the history of Lijiang Naxi Autonomous County). In Guo Dalie, ed., *Naxizu yanjiu lunwen ji* (Collected research essays on the Naxi). Kunming: Minzu Chubanshe.

Yang Shangzhi

1988   "Wo de zhongxue shidai" (My time in secondary school). In *Naxizu shehui lishi diaocha*, vol. 3.

Yunnan difang shi (Yunnan local history)

1992   Teaching material for normal schools in Yunnan. Teachers Training Bureau, Yunnan Province Education Commission.

Yunnan jiaoyu sishi nian, 1949–1989 (Forty years of education in Yunnan, 1949–1989)

1990   Yunnan Province Education Commission. Kunming: Yunnan Daxue Chubanshe.

Yunnan lishi (The history of Yunnan)

1991   Teaching material for junior secondary school. Commission for Examining and Revising Teaching Materials for Primary and Secondary Schools in Yunnan Province. Kunming: Yunnan Jiaoyu Chubanshe.

Yunnan minzu gongzu 40 nian (Forty years of *minzu* work in Yunnan)

1994   Kunming: Yunnan Minzu Chubanshe.

Yunnan minzu jiaoyu fazhan gaikuang (An introduction to the development of minority education in Yunnan)

1992   Yunnan Province Education Commission, Office for Educational Gazetteers. Kunming: Yunnan Daxue Chubanshe.

Yunnan Province History Society et al., eds.

1990   *Aiguozhuyi yu lishi jiaoyu* (Patriotism and history education). Kunming: Yunnan Daxue Chubanshe.

Yunnan Sheng Lijiang Naxizu Zizhi Xian di san ci renkou pucha shougong huizong ciliao huibian (A compilation of manually collected material from the third census Lijiang Naxi Autonomous County, Yunnan Province)

1983   Lijiang.

Yunnan Sheng Xishuangbanna Zhou Jinghong Xian di san ci renkou pucha shougong huizong (A manual of the third census in Jinghong County, Sipsong Panna Prefecture, Yunnan Province)

1983   Jinghong.

Yunnan tongji nianjian 1991 (Yunnan statistical yearbook, 1991)

1991   Kunming: Zhongguo Tongji Chubanshe.

Zha Xili et al.

1993   "Meiguo Jidujiao chuanru Cheli" (The spreading of American Christianity in Cheli). In Commission for Historical Accounts of the Chinese People's Political Consultative Conference, Jinghong Commission, ed., *Jinghong wenshi ziliao xuanji* (Collection of historical material from Jinghong). Jinghong.

Zhang Daqun

1988a   "Jian guo yilai Lijiang Naxizu jiaoyu fazhan gaikuang" (A general survey of the development of education among the Naxi in Lijiang since the founding of the nation [the PRC]). In Liu Zhengfang et al., eds., *Yunnan minzu jiaoyu yanjiu.*

1988b   "Lue lun Lijiang Naxizu lishishang de xuexiao jiaoyu" (A brief discussion of school education during the history of the Naxi in Lijiang). In Liu Zhengfang et al., eds., *Yunnan minzu jiaoyu yanjiu.*

1988c   "Shi tan Lijiang Naxizu gu wenhuazhong de jiaoyu yinsu" (Exploring educational elements in the ancient culture of the Naxi in Lijiang). In Liu Zhengfang et al., eds., *Yunnan minzu jiaoyu yanjiu.*

Zhang Shiya

1992   *Jitan yu jiangtan—Xinan minzu zongjiao jiaoyu bijiao yanjiu* (Altar and platform—A comparative study of religious education among the southwestern *minzu*). Kunming: Yunnan Jiaoyu Chubanshe.

Zhang Yuanqing

1991   "Daizu chuantong jiaoyu de zuoyong he yingxiang" (Functions and effects of traditional Tai education). In Chinese Ethnological Society, ed., *Minzuxue yanjiu* (Ethnological research), no. 10. Beijing: Minzu Chubanshe.

Zhao Chunxiao

1953   *Baiyi bian min yanjiu* (Research on the Baiyi border people). Hong Kong: Freedom Press.

Zhao Lu

1988   "Jiyizhong de Li Zhong 'xuesheng yuandi'" (Memories of "the scope of student activities" at Lijiang Secondary School). In *Naxizu shehui lishi diaocha*, vol. 3.

Zheng Xiaoyun and Yu Tao

1995   *Women Bathed in Holy Water: The Dais.* Kunming: Yunnan Jiaoyu Chubanshe.

Zhongguo lishi (The history of China)

1993   Compulsory teaching materials for three years of junior and three years of senior secondary education. Beijing: Renmin Jiaoyu Chubanshe.

Zhongguo minzu tongji (Statistics concerning China's *minzu*)

1992   Beijing: Zhongguo Tongji Chubanshe.

Zhongguo tongji nianjian 1993 (Statistical yearbook of China, 1993)

1993   Beijing: Zhongguo Tongji Chubanshe.

Zhou Houkan

1992   "Jingzhen Bajiaoting Si ban hesheng xuexiao diaocha baogao"
            (Report from research in the novice class of Jingzhen Octagonal
            Monastery). In Yan Sanlong et al., eds., 1992.

Zhou Yaowen

1992   "Bilingualism and Bilingual Education in China." *International
            Journal of the Sociology of Language* 97: 37–47.

Zhou Yu et al., eds.

1991   *Yunnan minzu gongzuo sishi nian yanjiu* (Reseach on forty years
            of *minzu* work in Yunnan). Kunming: Yunnan Renmin Chubanshe.

Zhu Weizheng

1992   "Confucius and Traditional Chinese Education: An Assessment."
            In Ruth Hayhoe, ed., *Education and Modernization: The Chinese
            Experience.* Oxford: Pergamon Press.

Zhuo Huanxiong

1992   "Minzu jiaoyu gaige mubiao moshi de xuanze yu zhiding"
            (Choosing and formulating methods and aims for reforming
            minority education). *Minzu jiaoyu yanjiu* (Minority education
            research) 2: 17–22.

Zou Zhenxie

1992   "Fazhanzhong de Xishuangbanna minzu jiaoyu" (The develop-
            ing minority education of Sipsong Panna). In Yan Sanlong et al.,
            eds., *Xishuangbanna minzu jiaoyu.*

Index

A'chang, 89
agricultural schools, 60, 104; establishment of, 21; during the Great Leap, 56
aiguozhuyi jiaoyu. See patriotic education
Akha (Hani): classification of, xv, 6; relation to Tai, xvi, 89; responses to Chinese education, xvi, 144, 168; script, 6; level of development (of Hani), 13; population (Hani) in Sipsong Panna, 88; autonomous government and, 93; boys in Tai schools, 95; on state farms, 124; script and, 125; primitive society and, 135, 152; Chinese education and, 151–56; relation to Tai, 151, 153; religion, 154
Akhe, 6
attendance, school, 75; methods of increasing, xiii; in Lijiang, 39, 48, 53–54, 58; in Sipsong Panna, 104, 105, 107, 119, 122; of novices, 119
autonomy law of 1984, 19

Bacot, James, 27*n*4
Bai, 23, 45, 62; population in Lijiang, 27
baihua. See vernacular language
Baisha, 49
Ban Ping village, 89, 110
baojia system, in Sipsong Panna, 92
Bernstein, Thomas P., 17
bilingual education, 7, 160; development of, xiii, 5–6; after 1980, 18; among Naxi, 67; in Sipsong Panna, 125–31; among Tai, 156–57; value of, 161

Blang, 88, 114, 152; script and, 125; primitive society and, 135
boarding schools: establishment of, 16; views on, 21–22, 132; in Lijiang since 1981, 61; in Sipsong Panna, 131–34, 149–50; Tai language in, 150; Akha and, 153; Jinuo and, 153. *See also* minority schools
Book of Odes, 30
Buddhist monasteries: Chinese schools and, xv, 165–66; education of novices in, 93, 94, 105–6, 110–16; Tai language in, 100; Great Leap Forward and, 103–4; Cultural Revolution and, 105–8; revival since 1980, 109–16; prevalence in Sipsong Panna, 111; parents view on education in, 112; Chinese schools and, 115, 118; rules concerning education in, 119–22; Tai students' views on, 147–49
Bulang. *See* Blang
Burma, 36, 88, 89, 101, 126, 158, 167; monks from, 111

cadres: views on Tai, 130; views on education, 133–34
campaigns: against "local nationalism," 16, 57; Rectification Campaign, 16, 56; Three Statements" (San Lun), 16; Lei Feng, 71, 71*n*6, 140; "four clean-ups," 103; reidentification of classes, 103; to "politicize the frontiers," 106–7; against "counterrevolutionary rebellion," 139
Canon of History, 30